AFRICAN RELIGION

AFRICAN RELIGION

The Moral Traditions
of Abundant Life

LAURENTI MAGESA

ORBIS BOOKS
Maryknoll, New York 10545

The Catholic Foreign Mission Society of America (Maryknoll) recruits and trains people for overseas missionary service. Through Orbis Books, Maryknoll aims to foster the international dialogue that is essential to mission. The books published, however, reflect the opinions of their authors and are not meant to represent the official position of the society.

Published by Orbis Books, Maryknoll, NY 10545-0308

Manufactured in the United States of America.

Library of Congress Cataloging in Publication Data

Magesa, Laurenti, 1946–
    African religion : the moral traditions of abundant life /
Laurenti Magesa.
        p. cm.
    Includes bibliographical references and index.
    ISBN 1-57075–105–6 (alk. paper)
    1. Africa, Sub-Saharan—Religion.   2. Ethics—Africa. Sub-Saharan.
I. Title.
BL2462.5.M34   1997
299´.6—dc21   97–19051
                                                                    CIP

To the Elders and Ancestors,
especially the following:
Odiria Nyakwesi Chuma
Cornelli Magoti Mujora
Anastazia Nyangeta Magoti
and
John J. Rudin, M.M.

CONTENTS

FOREWORD

It is both a great joy and privilege for me to introduce to the readers Laurenti Magesa's new book. Laurenti Magesa, a priest of Musoma Catholic diocese, Tanzania, holds two doctorates in theological sciences from universities in Canada. He has been professor of moral theology at the Catholic University of Eastern Africa, Nairobi, and a visiting professor at the Maryknoll School of Theology in the United States. During the summer, he teaches master's-level courses in African studies in Nairobi. He has published numerous scholarly articles in academic journals within Eastern Africa and worldwide. He continues to combine academic work with active pastoral ministry within his home diocese.

I first met Magesa at an international conference at Jos University in Nigeria in 1975, which focused on the study of African Christianity. Ever since, I have enjoyed reading and being challenged by his publications. We met again in 1985, this time as members of the same academic faculty at the Catholic University, Nairobi. We became friends and shared many insights. When I left Nairobi for Uganda in 1988 and he later left for Tanzania, our sharing of ideas never stopped. Once a year we meet together with others at Sagana, Kenya to reflect on African realities and the challenges they pose for African theologians.

To his students, academic colleagues, and readers of his published works, Magesa is renowned for his clarity of thought, accurate research, persuasive arguments, and his total commitment to the liberation of Africa and the Africans and to spearheading the powerful movement of inculturation of Christianity in Africa. These are the qualities he brings out forcefully in this new book.

The serious study of African Traditional Religion (ATR) began several decades ago with a marked emphasis on generalized conclusions about Black Africa. This movement was opposed by many African academics who preferred to consider in-depth case studies that would present an accurate picture of ATR within each ethnic entity. For several decades now, numerous case studies on ATR have been presented in universities and theological colleges both within Africa and abroad. The time has come, and indeed is overdue, to draw some fundamental general conclusions on the subject for the entire area of Black Africa.

This is Magesa's unique contribution in this book. He brings into an organic whole the moral tradition of African Religion from a rich variety of case studies from Black Africa. He argues convincingly why we should talk of African Religion in the singular, rather than African Religions in the plural. Black Africa is intimately linked in the ethos of culture, religion, and morality.

By treating African Religion as a world religion, Magesa challenges both African and non-African students of religion to desist from "marginalizing" African Religion. The power of myth and taboos that underlie African Religion is strongly established in the worldview of Black Africans.

The central thesis of the entire book is given in Chapter 3: *The promotion of life is the criterion of African morality.* This is life in its fullness, the mystique of life. Using this theme Magesa analyzes the transmission of life force, the enemies of life, the restoration of the force of life, and the "political" ethics in Africa.

The book presents several main challenges to students of African Religion and morality; to African public and religious leaders, and to Black Africans in general. Our understanding of marriage and procreation should be based on the pro-life criterion. Our understanding of immorality should be based on anti-life forces. All our efforts to restore life and harmony should be guided by the life principle. This pro-life criterion should be used to judge good and bad leaders, parents, and persons. And to judge good and bad systems and structures—be they political, economic, cultural, religious, or environmental—again, the same principle is the only sure guide.

Black Africa has had a terrible experience of the destruction of life and community and cultural values. The "peculiar institution" of the slave trade was an unprecedented enemy of life and community in Africa. Colonialism and racism targeted life, human dignity, and human rights of the Africans. Since the independence of African nations, life has continued to be destroyed, distorted, and harmed in so many cruel ways by our fellow African leaders, often supported by foreign self-seekers. The unjust world economic order continues to be an enemy of life to the majority of Africans.

As we plan for the success of this recent "second liberation" of Africa that has come with the new winds of change, Magesa's book challenges Africans to be totally pro-life, to unite together to promote life in its fullness for all the people in Africa, and to be determined to eliminate all anti-life attitudes and forces, the enemies of life, on the Black continent. To be able to do this properly we need to know and to utilize the moral traditions of African Religion.

On this point Basil Davidson writes: "The problems and solutions of today have to be envisaged within a historical framework, an indigenous historical framework, no matter what contribution an external world may have made."

One of the root causes of the many anti-life forces, systems, and problems in Black Africa has been our failure to embark on the movement of re-awakening our own moral and religious values and to construct the future on them. No sane society chooses to build its future on foreign cultures, values, or systems. Every society is obliged to search deep in its own history, culture, religion, and morality in order to discover the values upon which its development and liberation, its civilization, and its identity should be based. To do otherwise is nothing less than communal suicide. This is the powerful challenge that Magesa's thought-provoking book puts before the readers.

It is my innermost wish that religious, cultural, and political leaders in Africa will read and study this book in order to become more committed to the protection and promotion of life, life in its fullness, in Africa. Scholars and students of religion, morality, and ethics, both within and outside Africa, should use this book to discover the unique riches of African culture and religion; they should become excited to explore areas that can enrich humanity. The friends of Africa abroad and those who make policies at the international level that affect Africa will find powerful lessons in this book. Magesa presents a challenging contribution that I very much hope will touch the mind and heart of every reader.

—*John Mary Waliggo*

PREFACE

A person's religious commitment and identity are certainly indicated by his or her public profession to observe certain laws and perform certain rites and rituals. But they are much more profoundly determined by the motivation or impulse for such observance or performance.

While laws, rites, and rituals may evolve and even change, the motivation for religious behavior, even in such changed circumstances, may hardly have altered. New rituals, for example, might be intended to say one thing, but a convert to a religion might give them quite another meaning. Much more to the point, the convert may publicly claim the new, intended meaning while unconsciously ascribing to them a different one, the one that constitutes his or her motivation.

This book is based on the premise that this is the situation in which most African converts to Christianity (or Islam) find themselves. Certainly, they have been influenced by the latter, whether Christianity or Islam. Certainly, they publicly profess the respective laws, rites, and rituals to be the source of their new spiritual guidance. But what is their inner motivation for religious life? Evidence suggests overwhelmingly that it remains African Religion.

The purpose of this book is to describe in some detail this motivation, this impulse, although I do not deny subsequent cross-fertilization between and among religions and cultures. So if I use a non-historical approach to describe this motivation, it is not to say that change has not taken place in African Religion; instead, it is to show as clearly as possible how the main principles constituting African Religion remain the force behind African religiosity and identity, the source and basis of religious meaning.

Christians in Africa know very well the story of "missionary"

Christianity. It has been told over the years in very clear ways. What I am attempting to make clear in this book is the story of African Religion and its persistent power on Black Africans generally, the other side of the coin of religious influences on Africans. Where we go on from here in terms of "critical correlation" of the two is another book.

And a note to the reader. While I myself heartily resist using exclusive language, I have not adjusted the language in quoted material. Initially, I attempted to indicate such language by the use of [sic]; however, as this seemed to become increasingly distracting, in the end I decided to let the usage stand as it first appeared.

ACKNOWLEDGMENTS

The core of the material in this book was first presented as a course in three institutions: the Maryknoll Institute of African Studies (MIAS) in Nairobi, Kenya, in July 1994; the Maryknoll School of Theology (MST) during the Fall Semester of 1994; and the Maryknoll Mission Institute in New York, in January 1995. I wish to thank the students of those institutions for their positive reception of the thesis I set forth and their critical contribution to it. They have thereby encouraged its publication as a book.

The Director of MIAS, Dr. Michael C. Kirwen, virtually laughed me into putting this material in book form, as he dares all others who teach at his institute. In my case, this is only one of the many examples where an African "joking relationship" has produced positive results. I hope that all those in a position to do so will continue to prod young African scholars into delving more and more deeply and positively into the forgotten or ignored treasures of African Religion and culture and to make them known.

The book took final shape thanks to the excellent library facilities of the MST in New York. The librarians there, Mr. James O'Halloran and Ms. Zay Green, were generous and untiring in their help in locating needed resources. Ms. Green also read some chapters of the book and made useful suggestions concerning content. Brother Joseph Lips, one of my students at MST, read some chapters as well and suggested stylistic adjustments. Another student, Ms. Clara Gloria Garcia, typed the first draft of the manuscript while working at her own thesis! I am grateful to all the above and to any one I cannot now remember who has, directly or indirectly, made it possible for this book to see the light of day.

Finally, I am deeply grateful to Ms. Susan Perry and Mr.

William Burrows, editors at Orbis Books, for encouraging me to write for their publishing house.

My ancestors, I know, have watched the progress of this endeavor constantly from start to finish. May the book be an offering and libation to them. May they see to it that it contributes to the life force and resilience of the African people. May the elders be pleased with the effort.

Chapter 1

DEFINING AFRICAN RELIGION

A people's history must rediscover the past in order to make it reusable . . . Such a history must deal with the past with a view to explaining the present. It must therefore be not only descriptive but also analytical; it must deal not only with objective developments but also bring the discussion to the realm of value judgements.

The past should not be the object of mere contemplation if the present is to be meaningful. For if the past were viewed as a "frozen reality" it would either dominate and immobilize the present or be discarded as irrelevant to today's concerns.

Renato Constantino[1]

Although my goal in this book is to describe the system of moral theology and ethics of African Religion, I am going to begin with some general comments about African Religion itself. I realize that what African Religion is may not be clear to everyone; the path to its understanding is often obscured by a conceptual overgrowth. It seems necessary, therefore, as a first task to clear away some bushes that impair many people's vision of the reality of African Religion.

THE RELATIONSHIP BETWEEN MORALITY/ETHICS AND RELIGION

I use the terms morality and ethics almost interchangeably.

---

[1]Quoted in R. Armes, *Third World Film Making and the West* (Berkeley: University of California Press, 1987), pp. vii and 305.

1

Morality is "a normative ordering, in terms of perceived meanings, values, purposes and goals of human existence, of the lives of persons with regard to the ways in which they can choose to relate themselves to reality."[2]

When we stand back and try to understand this system of ordering of meanings and values, we see the ethics of a people. Ethics then is "the scientific study of such normative order."[3] If this study is done within the context of religious belief, one can be said to be doing religious ethics or moral theology.

Morality or ethics is of the very nature of religion. Clifford Geertz, for example, has described it as intimately connected to religious belief and as the very expression of the religious belief. As he puts it, "Religion is never merely metaphysics." Its very nature leads to concrete action in the form of ritual in which the needs and desires of human life are reflected. In other words, it leads to worship. "For all peoples the forms, vehicles, and objects of worship are suffused with an aura of deep moral seriousness. The holy . . . not only encourages devotion, it demands it; it not only induces intellectual assent, it enforces emotional commitment."[4] Of course, the exact formulation of the holy that demands human emotional commitment will differ from culture to culture and from place to place. This is to be expected, given the culture- and time-conditioned perspectives about the Divine. Yet, as Geertz continues to say,

> Whether it be formulated as *mana,* as *Brahma,* or as the Holy Trinity, that which is set apart as more than mundane is inevitably considered to have far-reaching implications for the direction of human conduct. Never merely metaphysics, religion is never merely ethics either. The source of its moral vitality is conceived to lie in the fidelity with which

---

[2]N. J. Rigali, "The Uniqueness and the Distinctiveness of Christian Morality and Ethics," in C. E. Curran, ed., *Moral Theology: Challenges for the Future* (New York: Paulist Press, 1990), pp. 74-5.
[3]Ibid., p. 75.
[4]C. Geertz, "Ethos, World-View and the Analysis of Sacred Symbols," in A. Dundes, *Every Man His Way: Readings in Cultural Anthropology* (Englewood Cliffs, New Jersey: Prentice Hall, 1968), pp. 302-3.

it expresses the fundamental nature of reality. The power-ful coercive "ought" is felt to grow out of a comprehensive factual "is," and in such a way religion grounds the most specific requirements of human action in the most general contexts of human existence.[5]

The study of morality or ethics, therefore, involves the study of religion. But understanding religion calls for an appreciation of symbols. Religious meanings, Geertz further explains, are contained or "stored" in a certain number of sacred symbols particular to a given culture. For the culture in question, such symbols, most abundantly expressed in rituals and myths, explain the origin, purpose, and meaning of the world and humanity's place in it. They are understood to integrate within them "what is known about the way the world is, the quality of the emotional life it supports, and the way one ought to behave while in it." It is this relationship of symbols to meaning, and particularly human meaning, that makes them such a fundamental aspect of religion. "Sacred symbols thus relate an ontology and a cosmology to an aesthetics and a morality: their peculiar power comes from their presumed ability to identify fact with values at the most fundamental level, to give to what is otherwise merely actual, a comprehensive normative import."[6]

Consequently, understanding the morality of the African people—that is, their perception of the Holy that demands and enforces their emotional and behavioral commitment and so gives direction to their lives—requires us to examine the worldview and ethos[7] contained in their religious symbols. Such an exercise will open the door through which we can enter the mind

---

[5]Ibid., p. 303.

[6]Ibid., p. 303. See also K. Koech, "African Mythology: A Key to Understanding African Religion," in N. S. Booth, ed., *African Religions: A Symposium* (New York: NOK Publishers, 1977), pp. 117-39.

[7]Concerning the sense of these terms, it is worth quoting Geertz at some length. "In recent anthropological discussion [he writes], the moral (and aesthetic) aspects of a given culture, the evaluative elements, have commonly been summed up in the term 'ethos,' while the cognitive, existential aspects have been designated by the term 'world-view.' A people's ethos is the tone, character and quality of their life, its moral and aesthetic style

and heart of Africa and truly appreciate the controlling motivations of her values and her people's attitudes.

PERSISTENCE AND CONTINUITY OF AFRICAN RELIGION

I would hope that the value of this study transcends the present circumstances in Africa. In many religious quarters now and at various levels of the churches, and particularly in the mainline Christian churches, there is an emphasis on interreligious dialogue. The different religions of the world, it is currently argued, must converse as equals about their beliefs if religious belief is to contribute to the peace and survival of our fractured and precarious universe. One strong advocate of this view of religions is theologian Hans Küng. He has ventured the opinion that today there can be no peace without religious dialogue. Besides institutional dialogue among world religious bodies, spiritual dialogue carried on by religious communities, and dialogue among local and regional religious structures, Küng also emphasizes the need for

---

and mood; it is the underlying attitude towards themselves and their world that life reflects. Their world-view is their picture of the way things, in sheer actuality are, their concept of nature, of self, of society. It contains their most comprehensive ideas of order. Religious belief and ritual confront and mutually confirm one another; the ethos is made intellectually reasonable by being shown to represent a way of life implied by the actual state of affairs which the world-view describes, and the world-view is made emotionally acceptable by being presented as an image of an actual state of affairs of which such a way of life is an authentic expression. This demonstration of a meaningful relation between the values a people holds and the general order of existence within which it finds itself is an essential element in all religions, however those values or that order be conceived. Whatever else religion may be, it is in part an attempt (of an implicit and directly felt rather than explicit and consciously thought-about sort) to conserve the fund of general meanings in terms of which each individual interprets his experience and organizes his conduct."

But the world-view and ethos do not exist as totally separate realities. This is important for our discussion of the morality of African Religion. As Geertz attests in the same essay, "The tendency to synthesize . . . [them] at some level, if not logically necessary, is at least empirically coercive; if not philosophically justified, it is at least pragmatically universal" ("Ethos, World-view and the Analysis of Sacred Symbols," p. 303).

the scientific dialogue of religious specialists. "We need," he writes, "a more intensive philosophical and theological dialogue of theologians and specialists in religion which takes religious plurality seriously in theological terms, accepts the challenge of the other religions, and investigates their significance for each person's own religion."[8]

Be that as it may, seldom has there been the kind of dialogue in Africa that Küng and many other voices envisage. Dialogue between Christianity and African Religion has never been a real conversation at any of these levels. On the contrary, contact between Christianity and African Religion has historically been predominantly a monologue, bedeviled by assumptions prejudicial against the latter, with Christianity culturally more vocal and ideologically more aggressive. Therefore, what we have heard until now is largely Christianity speaking about African Religion, not African Religion speaking for itself. This has been the case particularly in the area of moral or ethical thought, an important cornerstone of any religious system.

Christian notions of morality and ethics in academic studies have so overshadowed ethical notions of African Religion that the latter have almost always come to be seen exclusively in the light of the former. The result has been the intellectual suppression of the ethical points of view of African Religion in academic circles and in many geographical areas of the continent where Christianity has succeeded in gaining large numbers of converts. Yet insofar as Africa and Africans themselves are concerned, this suppression has truly been minimal, more apparent than real. Despite the strong influence of Christianity in many areas of African life, the basic attitudes and religious philosophy of many Africans—in fact perhaps more than in theory—have been similar to that expressed many years ago by a Central African Kwena man to David Livingstone: "To be plain with you, . . . we should like you much better if you traded with us and then went away, without forever boring us with preaching that word of God of yours."[9]

---

[8]H. Küng, *Global Responsibility: In Search of a New World Ethic* (New York: Crossroad, 1991), pp. 137-8.

[9]Cited in R. Desai, ed., *Christianity in Africa as Seen by Africans* (Denver: Alan Swallow, 1962), p. 2.

The moral perspectives of African Religion are essentially alive throughout the continent. It is easy to be misled though. By using statistics on conversion to Christianity in his *World Christian Encyclopedia,* for example, David Barrett might give the mistaken impression that African Religion is "moving toward extinction" in Africa. On the other hand, John Mbiti, a non-Western pioneer scholar of African Religion, correctly analyzes such statistics: they do not mean exactly what they appear to say. Mbiti has clearly seen that acceptance of Christianity or Islam in Africa means that Africans "come out of African religion but they don't take off their traditional religiosity. They come as they are. They come as people whose world view is shaped according to African religion."[10] If there are any changes during this process, Mbiti points out quite accurately, they "are generally on the surface, affecting the material side of life, and only beginning to reach the deeper levels of thinking pattern, language content, mental images, emotions, beliefs and response in situations of need. Traditional concepts still form the essential background of many African peoples... "[11]

Indeed, African religious perspectives persist despite the odds against them, and they serve a positive purpose. "Adapted to neocolonial realities and interpreted according to traditional sensibilities," Josiah Young notes, "they are [still] rich in liberating values."[12] They have preserved for the people their identity as Africans through such massive crises as slavery and colonialism. They continue to exert a more important and fundamental influence on African spirituality than many Christian leaders and Western or Westernized academics care or dare to admit.[13] But this remains a reality. One of the common com-

---

[10]Quoted by Burleson, *John Mbiti: The Dialogue of an African Theologian with African Traditional Religion* (Ann Arbor, Michigan: University Microfilms International, 1986), p. 12.

[11]J. S. Mbiti, *African Religions and Philosophy* (New York: Frederick A. Praeger, 1969), p. xi.

[12]J. U. Young, "Out of Africa: African Traditional Religion and African Theology," in D. Cohn-Sherbok, *World Religions and Human Liberation* (Maryknoll, New York: Orbis Books, 1992), p. 96.

[13]See also Aylward Shorter, "African Traditional Religion: Its Relevance in the Contemporary World," *Cross Currents,* XXVIII:4 (Winter 1978-79), pp. 421-31.

plaints of Christian leaders concerns the "duality" of African Christians' way of life, meaning that African Christians do not always adhere to religious and ritual demands that are formulated and expressed by the leaders of their churches. Many times they seek comfort in their own religious symbol systems, even though these may not correspond exactly to those inculcated and expected by their Christian leaders. Indeed, these are often symbols and rituals that church leaders have explicitly condemned. Aylward Shorter has described this situation quite honestly.

> At baptism, the African Christian repudiates remarkably little of his former non-Christian outlook. He may be obliged to turn his back upon certain traditional practices which, rightly or wrongly, have been condemned by the Church, but he is not asked to recant a religious philosophy. Consequently, he returns to the forbidden practices on occasion with remarkable ease. Conversion to Christianity is for him sheer gain, an "extra" for which he has opted. It is an "overlay" on his original religious culture. Apart from the superficial condemnations, Christianity has really had little to say about African Traditional Religion in the way of serious judgements of value. Consequently the African Christian operates with two thought-systems at once, and both of them are closed to each other. Each is only superficially modified by the other.[14]

The Nigerian Chief Obafemi Awolowo, writing in 1960 and using terminology then in vogue to describe African Religion, made substantially the same point with reference to his own country. There was plenty of evidence, he pointed out, that "Christian and Moslem beliefs and practices are, with many a Nigerian, nothing but veneers and social facades: at heart and in the privacy of their lives, most Nigerian Christians and Moslems

---

[14]A. Shorter, "Problems and Possibilities for the Church's Dialogue With African Traditional Religion," in A. Shorter, ed., *Dialogue with the African Traditional Religions* (Kampala: Gaba Publications, 1975), p. 7.

are heathens and animists [sic]."[15] Other scholars may not go so far, but today most would argue that African conceptions of God, the world, and morality continue to penetrate Christianity in Africa.

This is not merely a theoretical assertion; it is an empirically demonstrable fact noted by several scholars. Samuel G. Kibicho, for instance, clearly shows the role that the Gikuyu conception of God (*Ngai*) played in their struggle against colonialism in the 1950s and how it has been an important factor in their response to Christian evangelization from the beginning.[16] Gabriel Setiloane also describes this in a paper entitled "How the Traditional World-view Persists in the Christianity of the Sotho-Tswana." Citing approvingly the document of the World Council of Churches' Yaoundé Faith and Order Commission Report, *Giving Account of the Hope in Us,* he makes no secret of his conviction that "Because of the cultural form in which it is clothed, the Christianity of the missionaries cannot be assimilated, nor can it help (our) people to face up to difficult situations."[17]

It is sometimes contended that the persistence of African Religion is felt only in the independent churches. Yet John Mary Waliggo, another African scholar very much concerned with this issue, demonstrates successfully how African Religion persists, even in the mission churches and specifically in the Catholic church. Waliggo analyzes the causes of this resistance in the Buganda area of Uganda and how it has manifested itself in the recent history of the region. According to Waliggo, Christian evangelizers convinced themselves that the Baganda had been "civilized," that is, completely won over to Christianity. But when Kabaka Mutesa II, their king, was exiled in 1953, many

---

[15]Quoted in V. E. Akubueze Okwuosa, *In the Name of Christianity: The Missionaries in Africa* (Philadelphia and Ardmore: Dorrance & Company, 1977), p. 26.

[16]S. G. Kibicho, "The Continuity of the African Conception of God into and through Christianity: A Kikuyu Case-study," in E. Fashole-Luke et al., eds., *Christianity in Independent Africa* (Bloomington & London: Indiana University Press, 1978), pp. 370-88.

[17]Ibid., pp. 403-12

Baganda Christians identified with traditionalists, rejecting Christian prayers as ineffective in bringing him back. Also in 1961 many Buganda Catholics "turned a deaf ear" to Archbishop Kiwanuka's pastoral letter against the traditionalist-tinted political party Kabaka Yekka and continued to support it. Finally, despite the phenomenal spread of Christianity in Buganda, many expressions of African Religion such as divination and the use of healing practices continue, even though they are expressly forbidden by Christianity.[18]

Much as they might want to deny it at times, this dual thought-system noted by scholars still influences many Western-"educated" Africans, who show their true African religious face particularly in times of crisis. Many African professors, ministers of government, and members of parliament have been known to "revert" in secret to the diviner or medium in order to know what lies ahead, while at the same time vigorously protesting in public that diviners are relics of by-gone "primitive" times and that they possess no mystical powers. There is, however, such a depth of attachment to and inner identification with these realities that to speak of these African men and women "reverting" is perhaps incorrect. The question is whether they or any other African Western-educated person ever completely abandons this religiosity.

Christianity in Africa today may be said to have two different forms of thought-systems and faith expressions—one official and one popular. Official Christianity is the faith expression that is promulgated in the seminaries and other centers of training, as well as in sermons and homilies by various pastoral agents. The vast majority of the Christian faithful, however, appropriate the teaching of the official church according to their own circumstances and needs using the dominant symbol system of African Religion. Indeed, these people struggle to respond to their Chris-

---

[18]J. M. Waliggo, "Ganda Traditional Religion and Catholicism in Buganda, 1948-75," in Fashole-Luke, pp. 413-25. See also F. B. Welbourn, *East African Christian* (London: Oxford University Press, 1965), pp. 34-42 and E. Ikenga Metuh, ed., *The Gods in Retreat: Continuity and Change in African Religions—The Nigerian Experience* (Enugu: Fourth Dimension Publishing Co., 1985).

tian calling, but they are compelled from within to do so without denying their culture, the conception and understanding of life that defines them as Africans. This latter faith expression may be referred to as popular Christianity. In reality it is a form of syncretism between official Christianity and African Religion. But because the specific characteristics of African Religion are officially frowned upon, they are not openly acknowledged. This tension results in what we might call a "crisis" in African Religion.

This crisis—which is in reality a crisis of the African person with regard to Christianity—must be seen in a larger context. It has been preceded by a long history of Christian theology that, early on, became rather abstract and disconnected from the historical core and reality of its religious foundations. One of the most remarkable disjunctions in the history of Christianity is its separation of the Christian Scriptures (the New Testament) from the Hebrew Scriptures (the Old Testament), out of whose very bowels the Christian Scriptures emerged and continue to be a part. In the words of the Dutch Scripture scholar Hans Renckens, both "have much to tell us about God, about being a people, and about the Messiah. They cover so many areas of life, that the epilogue added by the New Testament literally hasn't a leg to stand on without them. It's not more than a single head, without body or limbs."[19] Renckens adds that one error of Christian theology is that it "pays insufficient attention to the *common stream* of living history revealed in the two Scriptures."[20] In reference to this lack of historical consciousness on the part of Christian theology, Renckens continues to argue that even though "Systematic theology is aware that the New Testament refers to old words, . . . [it] is often misled by their antiquity and concreteness to treat the Old Scriptures as if the New revealed meanings and worlds that were not available in the Old." Renckens is quite right that this is not only a mistaken, but a dangerous course of thought that loses much of the richness of the Hebrew Scriptures. The Old Scriptures are seen as having nothing to give to the New.

---

[19]See Renckens, *A Bible of Your Own: Growing with the Scriptures.* Trans. N. Forest-Flier (Maryknoll, New York: Orbis Books, 1995), p. 13.
[20]Ibid., p. 12. Emphasis mine.

Instead they are perceived as ruins: "They are an abandoned building occupied by squatters. The furniture (the language) can be seized by those who care to take it and make themselves comfortable."[21]

Something akin to this has taken place in Africa. On meeting African Religion, missionary Christianity looked upon it as "an abandoned building occupied by squatters." To parallel Renckens's thought, missionary theology and missionary Christianity were misled by the antiquity and concreteness of the forms of belief and practices of African Religion into thinking that Christianity revealed meanings and worlds not available in African Religion. And so they relegated African Religion to a system of "old facts," whose meanings were no longer valid. Misguided, they thus failed to perceive the new in the old and the old in the new. They failed to see authentic inspiration in African Religion and its importance for humanity's search for God.

The mistake of missionary Christianity was to disregard "the common stream of living history" that joins one tradition to other religious traditions of humanity. Its error consisted in actually stressing "aspects of discontinuity between Christianity and African cultures and traditional religion to such an extent that they excluded the aspects of continuity" between them.[22] Father P. Perlo of the Consolata Missionaries to Kenya, to cite but one example, committed this error in decrying the lack of a moral system among the Gikuyu in Kenya. He blindly and chauvinistically wondered, "How . . . morals [could] be found among this people who in their age-long abandonment have become so corrupt as to raise practices openly immoral to be a social institution . . . " His criterion of judgment was, of course, his own Christian "civilization." He argued that "every moral principle in which *our* civilization glories and which *our* religion commands is here, at least in practice, simply reversed in its terms: and that is enough to argue that whatever inference is drawn in this connection it must always confront us with a state of things essentially

---

[21]Ibid., p. 12.
[22]Fashole-Luke, "Introduction," in Fashole-Luke, *Christianity in Independent Africa*, p. 357.

deplorable, barbarous, inhuman."[23] He made no reference whatsoever to the standards, values, and religious thought forms of the Gikuyu people themselves, illustrating the unmitigated ethnocentrism of early white colonizers' and evangelizers' views of African culture.

A certain amount of ethnocentrism is inevitable in comparative studies of cultures and religions, given the limitations imposed on us as human beings by time and space. Yet there is little evidence that Father Perlo and other Christian missionaries tried to curb what Alan Dundes has called the ravages of such bias. Looking upon Africa, they compared the continent's *practices* (its real culture) to the *ideals* of Europe (its ideal culture). The conclusion was, of course, that African culture was inferior. This obvious confusion could have been avoided to some degree. Centuries earlier the much celebrated Jesuit missionaries Matteo Ricci (1552-1610) and Roberto de Nobili (1577-1656) had realized the intrinsic inadequacy of such biased approaches with regard to China and India respectively. This intuition is also unmistakably present in the Christian Scriptures, particularly in the book of Acts (chapter 10, for example). However, "If one does insist on cultural comparisons (and the crucial question here is what and whose value system is to be employed in making evaluative comparisons), one should at least compare the real culture of the people under study with one's own real culture" (or the ideal culture with one's own ideal culture).[24]

Ashley Montagu has accurately diagnosed the cause of this bias to be a Western "ortholinear view of development." In this view, as Montagu sees it, what is earlier is less developed and "primitive," and, in comparison to the later, inferior; what is later is more advanced and superior. But the truth is not so simple: "The truth is that evolutionary processes do not proceed in straight lines but are more accurately observed to assume a retic-

---

[23]Quoted in Kibicho, "The Continuity of the African Conception of God," p. 377. Emphasis mine.

[24]Dundes, introducing K. George's essay, "The Civilized West Looks at Primitive Africa: 1400-1800, A Study in Ethnocentrism," in Dundes, *Every Man His Way*, p. 23.

ulate form. And so it has been in the evolution of man, both physically and culturally."[25]

We cannot afford to sever the link between the old and the
new, between one form of religious system and another. Religious
truth is relational, not exclusive. Just as we cannot, as Renckens
says, "be reminded enough of . . . the 'surplus of meaning'of the
Old Scriptures," so also we must always keep in mind the surplus
of meaning of African Religion. Akubueze Okwuosa, a Nigerian
scholar, is right: "Had missionaries taken time to view the
African form of religion from a much more friendly perspective,
they would have discovered a common ground for cooperation."[26]

For the sake of the religious enrichment and growth of men
and women everywhere, we need to spell out what African Religion has to say about God, humanity, and creation. We need to
establish the foundational religious view of Africa in order to
share it with other religious orientations and faiths. This is long
overdue. Christianity (and the other religions) in Africa needs to
own up to the fact that "A great deal has happened, and too little conversion has taken place—not only conversion of the heart,
but also of the theological head . . . The main point is that we
need to free ourselves from the inherited burden which maintains
a superficial climate . . . "[27]

What does African Religion have to tell us about being children of God? About desiring and living the abundant life that is
the gift of God to humanity? The perspective of African Religion

<hr />

[25]A. Montagu, "The Fallacy of the 'Primitive,' " in A. Montagu, ed., *The
Concept of the Primitive* (New York: The Free Press, 1968). This book
clearly debunks biases by anthropologists against cultures different from
their own. The contributors are anthropologists who have come to realize
the error of their ways, so to speak.

[26]Akubueze Okwuosa, *In the Name of Christianity*, p. 16. The theology
of inculturation is just beginning to try to do that now. See Shorter,
Towards a Theology of Inculturation (Maryknoll, New York: Orbis
Books, 1988); P. Schineller, *A Handbook on Inculturation* (New York:
Paulist Press, 1990); J. M. Waliggo et al., *Inculturation: Its Meaning and
Urgency* (Nairobi: St. Paul Publications, 1986); V. Donovan, *Christianity
Rediscovered* (Maryknoll, New York: Orbis Books, 1985), among others.

[27]Akubueze Okwuosa, *In the Name of Christianity*, p. 8.

on these fundamental issues helps us to understand its interconnectedness with other religious traditions. Even more important, I hope to show that African Religion has a unique moral contribution to offer to the universal human quest for the Truth.

AFRICAN RELIGION OR RELIGIONS?

The first issue, simply put, is this: Is African Religion one or many? Is what is seen as multiplicity to be considered realistically and accurately absolute or merely as various elements and expressions of one reality? Africanist Newell Booth has framed the question a little more graphically:

> A question which may be raised at this point is whether African religion can properly be spoken of in the singular or only in the plural. Our reading and observation turn up a profusion of phenomena to which we may attach such labels as supreme gods, nature spirits, ancestor rituals, initiation practices, divine kings, secret societies, sorcerers, and demons with considerable variety from place to place. Perhaps we will decide that there is no such thing as "African religion" but only "African religions."[28]

This question concerning the homogeneity or multiplicity of indigenous religious belief in Africa is of long-standing duration. Different scholars have applied different approaches to it.[29] Early on, Western anthropologists/ethnologists and missionary scholars almost invariably considered the labels Africans attached to their religious phenomena as evidence of the non-existence of one basic, universal African Religion. If there was such a thing approximating religion at all in Africa, they argued, it was "ani-

---

[28]Booth, "An Approach to African Religion," in Booth, *African Religions,* p. 3.

[29]See A. Shorter, *African Christian Theology—Adaptation or Incarnation?* (Maryknoll, New York: Orbis Books, 1977), pp. 38-60. See also E. Ikenga-Metuh, *Comparative Studies of African Traditional Religions* (Onitsha, Nigeria: IMICO Publishers, 1987), pp. 5-10.

mism" or "fetishism," a multiplicity of ritual actions with natural objects as deities. The logical consequence of this notion, at that time at least, was for the Christian missionary to do everything possible to do away with "the black man's spirits, give him a new sense of sins, do away with the practice of religion as a base superstition and win him over to a new superior white God."[30]

Trained by Western anthropologists and missionaries, African scholars of African Religion in the 1960s and 1970s exhibited a similar mind-set. For example, the work of John Mbiti explores the oneness or the plurality of African Religion. A strong advocate of the authenticity of African Religion, Mbiti argues nevertheless in his influential book *African Religions and Philosophy*, published in 1969, that the phenomenon of religion in Africa has to be considered multiple. He cites the fact that there are numerous different peoples in Africa, each having a very different religious system of beliefs, ceremonies, rituals, and its own religious leaders. Consequently, according to Mbiti, one has to speak about African *religions* in the plural. African philosophy, he continues, is another matter. For while the religious expressions in Africa are concrete and observable, one cannot claim the same thing about the thinking behind them. The latter has to be concluded from observation of the practices. The philosophy underlying the religious expression of the African people, Mbiti argues, is a philosophy in the singular.[31]

Mbiti's method leads inevitably to his conclusion. Yet, by positing a philosophy (not *philosophies*) underlying all African religious expressions, he indirectly admits what he perhaps would like to explain away. In the words of the Vatican Secretariat for Non-Christians, "Ritual manifestations apparently different are based on the same religious beliefs and proceed from a common mental structure," the structure of complementarity, symmetry and integration.[32] Again, this had been recognized much earlier. Already in the 1920s a study conference of mis-

---

[30]L. Van Der Post, quoted in R. Desai, "Christianity in Danger," in Desai, *Christianity in Africa*, p. 14.

[31]Mbiti, *African Religions and Philosophy*, pp. 1-2. Also E. Ikenga-Metuh, *Comparative Studies of African Traditional Religions*, pp. 5-10.

[32]See Secretariatus Pro Non-Christianis, *Meeting the African Religions* (Rome: Libreria Editrice Ancora, 1968), p. 7.

sionaries held at Le Zoute, Belgium, had realized this. Having noted the diversities that mark Africa geographically, linguistically, and even in the physical appearance of its various peoples, the Le Zoute conference nevertheless acknowledged the African people's essential unity: "Underlying all the divergence that marks the pagan [sic] Negro tribes, there is a fundamental unity of belief and outlook upon the world . . . Africa is a unity—a unity in diversity. Nothing is lost, and much is gained, by trying to look at the New Africa as a whole."[33] Two decades later, E. W. Smith wrote in the same vein: "In spite of . . . cultural diversities there is, I believe, an underlying identity in religion. I do not deny or minimize the differences you may find between the highly organized Yoruba or Baganda, with their hierarchy of gods, on the one hand, and the more simple peoples, on the other hand. But the difference is one of emphasis and development, not of essence. There is sufficient identity to warrant our speaking of African religion."[34]

In recent times, most African scholars, including Mbiti, studying African Religion from the "inside" agree. They now see African Religion as one in its essence. Although its varieties cannot be denied, there is a "basic world-view," as John V. Taylor asserts in a work published before Mbiti's, "which fundamentally is everywhere the same."[35] The varieties are more those of

---

[33]E. W. Smith, *The Christian Mission in Africa* (London: The International Missionary Council, 1926), p. 7. The Le Zoute conference was ready to include in this unity African peoples further north in the continent: "This Negro culture has permeated the Libyan peoples of the north, so that whether in physical structure or in mentality, it is impossible to say where Negro begins and Libyan ends" (p. 7). The conference has historically not been alone in asserting this. The Roman Secretariatus Pro Non-Christianis affirmed the same thing as recently as 1968: "Between the African societies, in addition to apparent diversity, there are bonds of symmetry, of contrast and of complement, the root cause of which is very probably the unity of character among the Negro-Africans and even among the Negro-Berbers" (*Meeting the African Religions*, p. 7).

[34]Quoted by G. Parrinder, *West African Psychology: A Comparative Study of Psychological and Religious Thought* (London: Lutterworth Press, 1951), p. 4.

[35]J. V. Taylor, *The Primal Vision: Christian Presence amid African Religion* (London: SCM Press, 1963), p. 19.

expression than basic belief. They are much like the varieties of expression we find in any major religion, such as Christianity (in the form of denominations) or Islam, for instance. They may be referred to by different names, such as Roman Catholic, Lutheran, Anglican, Presbyterian, or Baptist in Christianity, or Shia, Suni, or Sufi in Islam. Nonetheless, they remain Christian or Muslim.

Similarly, varieties in African Religion must not be taken to mean a diversity of fundamental belief. In the words of Jacques Maquet, who emphasized the unity of African culture (and religion) south of the Sahara, "Africanity, like every broad cultural synthesis, . . . is based on a similar experience of the world shared by various societies and on the dissemination of several culture traits among these societies." This is made possible by "the development of similar ways of adapting to the natural environment and the diffusion of culture traits. These two mechanisms, each reinforcing the other, combine to create a common culture [and a common religion]."[36]

Much has been made of the differences within African Religion based on the distinctive lifestyles of the peoples of Africa. It is not possible to deny that these lifestyles affect the religious symbols of the people. Yet to conclude that there is therefore no internal, essential unity in the various expressions of African Religion is to exaggerate. Robert Moore shows clearly in his study of the Nandi of Kenya that pastoral and agricultural lifestyles as unbridgeable cultural elements never existed in Africa in the past, nor do they now. They can only be accepted as "stereotypes," as approximations in the sense of "more or less." As far as can be ascertained, Moore indicates, the African "agriculturalist differs from the pastoralist, not so much in lacking cattle (frequently he has them), but in the way he structures his society: it is crop-oriented rather than cattle-oriented. However, the African is used to adjusting, and needs no more than a generation or two to restructure his society according to

---

[36]J. Maquet, *Africanity: The Cultural Unity of Black Africa*. Trans. J. R. Rayfield (New York: Oxford University Press, 1972), p. 16.

necessity. There is no reason to believe that this adaptability is recently acquired."[37]

If we study African Religion in a specific place among a specific ethnic group, as many scholars have done and still do—and, indeed, as it is necessary to continue to do—it is for the sake of depth and should not be used to support the argument that African Religion is not a generic whole. Obviously the actual implementation of African religious ideals differs from place to place. This is illustrated most clearly by those religious expressions of African origin in the diaspora, in Brazil, Surinam, and the Caribbean, for instance. In spite of the fact that these peoples trace their ancestry to Africa through many generations, the African kernel of their religious thought-systems and expressions is unmistakable. Their religion has developed distinctive practices, and even borrowed from the Catholicism predominant in some of those regions. But they are still a form of African Religion, as Mircea Eliade and Ioan Couliano attest.[38]

IS AFRICAN RELIGION A WORLD RELIGION?

A second issue in the study of African Religion has to do with its status as a world religion. Even though the study of African

---

[37]R. O. Moore, *Nandi Origins: The Evidence from Language* (Ann Arbor, Michigan: University Microfilms, 1974), p. 10. See as well the essay of D. Forde, "The Cultural Map of West Africa: Successive Adaptations to Tropical Forests and Grasslands," in S. and P. Ottenberg, *Cultures and Societies of Africa* (New York: Random House, 1960), pp. 116-38. Also D. J. Stenning, "Transhumance, Migratory Drift, Migration: Patterns of Pastoral Fulani Nomadism," ibid., pp. 139-58.

In M. Douglas and P. M. Kaberry, eds., *Man in Africa* (London: Tavistock Publications, 1969), see the essays by R. Horton, "From Fishing Village to City-State: A Social History of New Calabar," pp. 37-58; I. M. Lewis, "From Nomadism to Cultivation: The Expansion of Political Solidarity in Southern Somalia," pp. 59-77; and P. Morton-Williams, "The Influence of Habitat and Trade on the Polities of Oyo and Ashanti," pp. 79-98.

[38]M. Eliade and I. P. Couliano, *The Eliade Guide to World Religions* (San Francisco: HarperSanFrancisco, 1991), pp. 19-20. Other useful sources to consult in this connection include R. Bastide, *The African Religions of*

Religion engages the interest of many scholars today, its status as a world religion has not yet been comfortably accepted in some quarters of the academic and Christian religious world. The tendency of some philosophers, theologians, and students of comparative religion is still to regard African Religion as a "primal" or "ethnic" religion, thus robbing it of its universal character. (In some people's minds, it is still identified pejoratively with "tribal" practices of fetishism and magic.) This attitude also reduces the capacity of African Religion to interact with other religions and to influence and change the world and minimizes its role in conversation with other religions. It becomes a subordinate partner rather than an equal. The study of African Religion, from this perspective, then becomes merely a description of appearances instead of a portrayal of a phenomenon with moral power that shapes and directs the lives of millions of people in their relationship with other human beings, the created order, and the Divine.

This attitude has developed for several reasons. First, it is obviously a prejudice of nineteenth-century scholarship, tainted by Darwinism, slave trading, and a colonial mentality. It is exemplified, among many others, by Henry Morton Stanley's description of the African person as a barbarous, materialist, childish, and inarticulate creature, "almost stupefied with brutish ignorance, with the instincts of man in him, but yet living the life of a

---

Brazil: Toward a Sociology of the Interpretation of Civilizations. Trans. by H. Sebba (Baltimore/London: The John Hopkins University Press, 1978); E. E. Simpson, *Black Religions in the New World* (New York: Columbia University Press, 1978); S. and L. Leacock, *Spirits of the Deep: A Study of an Afro-Brazilian Cult* (Garden City, New York: Anchor Books, 1975); A. Metraux, *Voodoo in Haiti.* Trans. by H. Charteris (New York: Oxford University Press, 1959); M. Rigaud, *Secrets of Voodoo.* Trans. by R. B. Cross (New York: Arco Publishing Company, 1969); K. Kristos, *Voodoo* (Philadelphia/New York: J. B. Lippincott Company, 1976); J. Haskins, *Voodoo & Hoodoo: Their Tradition and Craft as Revealed by Actual Practitioners* (New York: Stein and Day, 1978); and M. L. Kilson and R. I. Rotberg, *The African Diaspora: Interpretive Essays* (Cambridge, Massachusetts, 1976), pp. 342-65. Various parts of chapters 10 and 11 of this book are also worth reading with regard to this issue. See also R. D. Abrahams, ed., *Afro-American Folktales: Stories from Black Traditions in the New World* (New York: Pantheon Books, 1985).

beast."[39] This kind of prejudiced scholarship led the African scholar Okot p'Bitek to respond in 1970 that Western scholars studied the institutions of non-Western and, in this case, African societies, not in their own right, but so as to compare them with their own in order to demonstrate to themselves the superiority of the latter. More important, p'Bitek saw the study of social anthropology in Africa by Western scholars as "not only the handmaiden of colonialism in that it analyzed and provided important information about the social institution of colonized peoples to ensure efficient and effective control and exploitation, it has also furnished and elaborated the myth of the 'primitive' which justified the colonial enterprise." P'Bitek affirmed (correctly in my view) that "The study of African religions was part and parcel of this exercise,"[40] and he protested vigorously against it.

The same protest has since been made by many others, including Cameroonian theologians F. Eboussi Boulaga and Jean-Marc Ela.[41] Eboussi Boulaga's book *Christianity Without Fetishes* is written to show, among other things, "how a Christianity of the empire imposes itself only by tearing up its converts by the roots, out of where-they-live, out of their being-in-the-world, presenting them with the Faith only at the price of depriving them of their capacity to generate the material and spiritual conditions of their existence." Having been uprooted and destroyed in this

---

[39]Desai, "Christianity in Danger," p. 14. See, for example, Darwin's description of the people of Tierra del Fuego, "The Tierra del Fuegians," in Dundes, *Every Man His Way*, pp. 36-47. For Africa see also A. Schweitzer, *On the Edge of the Primeval Forest: Experiences and Observations of a Doctor in Equatorial Africa*. Trans. by C. T. Campion (New York: The Macmillan Company, 1931); and for all non-European cultures, E. B. Tylor, *Religion in Primitive Culture* (New York: Harper Torchbooks, 1958).

[40]O. p'Bitek, *African Religions in Western Scholarship* (Kampala: East African Literature Bureau, 1970), pp. 1-2.

[41]See F. Eboussi Boulaga, *Christianity Without Fetishes: An African Critique and Recapture of Christianity*. Trans. by R. R. Barr (Maryknoll, New York: Orbis Books, 1984); J-M. Ela, *African Cry*, (Maryknoll, New York: Orbis Books, 1986) and *My Faith as an African*. Trans. by J. P. Brown and S. Perry (Maryknoll, New York: Orbis Books, 1988).

way, Boulaga explains, "these dominated persons will be able to find their truth only outside themselves, as the utterly-other-from-themselves-and-their-universe. The missionary discourse has a habit of propounding God, or the content of the faith, as the irruption into one's world of the purest Strangeness, and conversion as the snatching of the candidate for Christianity from the jaws of perdition, which is confused with one's traditional mode of living and being human."[42]

Such missionary discourse has caused enormous problems for both Christianity and African Religion. "How is one to think and to live the necessity, supremacy, and universality of Christianity," Boulaga asks rhetorically, "when the latter is imposed as the dominant religion, or the religion of the dominant? How are the truths, commandments, and rites to be inscribed in one's flesh, when they are received from below, in a state of social, political, economic, and cultural subordination and minority of age?"[43]

This critique of Christianity has also characterized other forms of African thought and literature since the 1960s, specifically the African novel and political speeches.[44] As Newell Booth puts it, it has provided a beginning of a "new phase in the study of African religion . . . made possible by the appearance of African students of African religion. They are able to work at least partially from 'within' the tradition they are studying, even when they are themselves Christian or Muslim."[45] It has also generated in many Africans a healthy attitude in the face of the general disparagement of their own cultural heritage engendered by early missionary activity and colonialism. They have come to realize that interpretations of African culture by Western scholarship

---

[42]Eboussi Boulaga, *Christianity Without Fetishes*, p. 17.

[43]Ibid., p. 2.

[44]For an overview of African novelists' feelings about Christianity and alienation in Africa, see H. Dinwiddy, "Missions and Missionaries as Portrayed by English-speaking Writers of Contemporary African Literature," in Fashole-Luke, *Christianity in Independent Africa*, pp. 426-42. For the politicians and nationalists, see G-C. M. Mutiso and S. W. Rohio, eds., *Readings in African Political Thought* (London: Heinemann, 1975) and M. Minogue and J. Molloy, eds., *African Aims & Attitudes: Selected Documents* (London: Cambridge University Press, 1974).

[45]Booth, "An Approach to African Religion," p. 5.

were sometimes contrived and inaccurate. They recognize the truth of the words of Janheinz Jahn that "those who expect to see in their fellow men fools, blockheads or devils, will find evidence to confirm their prejudices." This is what was done in Africa. "If we are convinced that the other fellow cannot sing," Jahn elaborates, "we have only to call his song 'a hellish row' in order to justify our claim. Simply by applying a certain vocabulary one can easily turn Gods into idols, faces into grimaces, votive images into fetishes, discussions into palavers and distort real objects and matters of fact through bigotry and prejudice."[46]

There are certain objections, however, to characterizing African Religion as a world religion that we need to investigate more carefully. First, because African Religion has no written scriptures even some liberal Western scholars of religion have been reluctant to consider it as any more than a "tribal" religion. "World" religions such as Judaism, Islam, or Hinduism all have their own written sources. Western scholars thus could neither conceive nor allow that a religion dependent on oral traditions, such as African Religion is, could be regarded as an equal. This argument, though, is based on a refusal to look carefully at history. These scholars failed to consider that Judaism, for example, was an orally-based religion for many centuries before its oral story was codified in writing. The same was true for Christianity and Islam, although for a shorter period of time. Other things being equal, orality alone cannot disqualify a religious system from qualitative greatness. In fact, the existence of written scriptures must be seen as only one criterion among many.

This argument must also apply to a second characteristic of religion, that it be "revealed." It is interesting to note that many African (independent) churches that are emerging on the continent in contemporary times do not claim scriptures as the central element of their religious system nor do they see possession of "a sacred book" as a *sine qua non* of the authenticity of their faith. But they do see their faith as "revealed." They place greater emphasis on revelation by means of dreams, by ecstasy or trance or possession, by prophets and divination, or through reincarna-

---

[46]J. Jahn, *Muntu: An Outline of the New African Culture*. Trans. by M. Grene (New York, Grove Press, 1961), p. 20.

tion or events such as calamities than they do on scripture.[47] They also stress the manner of religious living. For them revelation is a continuing and ever-present aspect of religious living. In that sense their religion is much more morally/ethically-based than doctrinally-based.

A third characteristic often raised up to disqualify African Religion from any status as a world religion is its lack of interest in aggressive proselytizing. Christianity and Islam are, of course, aggressive proselytizers. Historically these two religions have sought converts even by means of cunning and deceit, not to mention violence and outright war. However, this argument does not take into account that neither do other major religions, such as Hinduism and Confucianism, for example, actively proselytize. Hinduism and Confucianism are "tribal" in the sense

---

[47]Even though stress is laid upon the Bible and its interpretation in some Independent Churches in Africa, where revelation is concerned the accent is put on these modes of revelation as being of paramount importance. It is mostly through them that the will of God is made known.

There is a host of literature on these churches and their theology. I mention here a few of the more significant studies: D. B. Barrett, *Schism and Renewal in Africa: An Analysis of Six Thousand Contemporary Religious Movements* (Nairobi: Oxford University Press, 1968); D. B. Barrett, ed., *African Initiatives in Religion* (Nairobi: East African Publishing House, 1971); N. I. Ndiokwere, *Prophecy and Revolution: The Role of Prophets in Independent African Churches and in Biblical Tradition* (London: SPCK, 1981); J. D. Y. Peel, *Aladura: A Religious Movement Among the Yoruba* (London: Oxford University Press, 1968); W. M. J. van Binsbergen, *Religious Change in Zambia: Exploratory Studies* (London/Boston, Kegan Paul International, 1981); W. MacGaffrey, *Modern Kongo Prophets: Religion in a Plural Society* (Bloomington: Indiana University Press, 1983); H. W. Turner, *Religious Innovation in Africa: Collected Essays on New Religious Movements* (Boston, Mass.: G. K. Hall & Co., 1979); B. Jules- Rossette, ed., *The New Religions of Africa* (Norwood, New Jersey: Ablex Publishing Corporation, 1979); W. De Craemer, *The Jamaa and the Church: A Bantu Catholic Movement in Zaire* (Oxford: Clarendon Press, 1977); M-L. Martin, *Kimbangu: An African Prophet and His Church*. Trans. by D. M. Moore (Grand Rapids, Michigan: William B. Eerdmans Publishing Company, 1976).

See also W. C. Willoughby, *The Soul of the Bantu: A Sympathetic Study of the Magico-Religious Practices and Beliefs of the Bantu Tribes of Africa* (Garden City, New York: Doubleday, Doran & Company, 1928), pp. 90-177.

that they do not as a rule engage in activities designed to convert people of other religious orientations to their religious view of life.

Balanced studies of African Religion, however, show that using even more significant criteria, it must be counted among the major world religions. The most important criterion is, of course, the understanding of the meaning of religion itself. Hans Küng provides one of the most comprehensive descriptions: religion is "*a believing view of life, approach to life, way of life,* and therefore a *fundamental pattern* embracing the individual and society, man and the world, through which a person (though only partially conscious of this) sees and experiences, thinks and feels, acts and suffers, everything. It is a transcendentally grounded and immanently operative *system of coordinates* by which man orients himself intellectually, emotionally, and existentially."[48]

As will be seen throughout this book, African Religion fulfills all of these requirements. Recognition of its status as a world religion should not be considered a concession, therefore, but rather a reversal of long-standing prejudice. If "the presence and

---

[48]H. Küng et al., *Christianity and World Religions: Paths of Dialogue with Islam, Hinduism and Buddhism.* Trans. by P. Heinegg (Maryknoll, New York: Orbis Books, 1993), p. xvii. Emphasis in original. I have already cited Geertz's scholarship on religion. Another of his well-known definitions of religion is similar to Küng's. In his *The Interpretation of Cultures* (New York: Basic Books, 1973) he defines religion as "a system of symbols which acts to establish powerful, pervasive, and long-lasting moods and motivations . . . by formulating conceptions of a general order of existence and clothing these in such an aura of factuality that moods and motivations seem uniquely realistic" (p. 90).

C. H. Kraft takes over Kroeber and Kluckholm's conception of culture, which is also similar to Küng's and Geertz's, as consisting "of patterns, explicit and implicit, of and for behavior acquired and transmitted by symbols, constituting the distinctive achievement of human groups, including their embodiments in artifacts; the essential core of culture consists of traditional (i.e., historically derived and selected) ideas and especially their attached values; culture systems may, on the one hand, be considered as products of action, on the other as conditioning elements of further action" (*Christianity in Culture: A Study in Dynamic Biblical Theologizing in Cross-Cultural Perspective* [Maryknoll, New York: Orbis Books, 1979], p. 46).

activity of God ... used to be claimed only for the great historic religions," Stephen Kneel explains, "we now see that even the ... religions of Africa ... are intricately woven textures, covering every aspect of the life of a people, and giving assurance of the presence and activity of God in every part of that life."[49]

Writing about three decades ago decrying the arrogant attitude of the so-called "revealed" religion against the so-called "natural" religion, E. E. Evans-Pritchard describes a revealing insight. He correctly sees the contrast between the two notions as neither very insightful nor helpful:

> For nothing could have been revealed about anything if men had not already had an idea about that thing. Or rather, perhaps we should say, the dichotomy between natural and revealed religion is false and makes for obscurity, for there is a good sense in which it may be said that all religions are religions of revelation: the world around them and their reason have everywhere revealed to men something of the divine and of their own nature and destiny.

Evans-Pritchard points out that some had seen this already in the fifth century, referring to Augustine. "We might ponder the words of St. Augustine: 'What is now called the Christian religion, has existed among the ancients, and was not absent from the beginning of the human race, until Christ came in the flesh: from which time the true religion, which existed already, began to be called Christian.' "[50]

For Africans, religion is far more than "a believing way of life" or "an approach to life" directed by a book. It is a "way of life" or life itself, where a distinction or separation is not made between religion and other areas of human existence. If one is to speak of "revelation" or "inspiration," it is not to be found in a book, not even primarily in the people's oral tradition, but in their lives. Herein lies the "notoriety" or "incurability" of

---

[49]S. Kneel, *Salvation Tomorrow: The Originality of Jesus Christ and the World's Religions* (Nashville: Abingdon, 1976), pp. 28-9.
[50]E. E. Evans-Pritchard, *Theories of Primitive Religion* (Oxford: The Clarendon Press, 1965), pp. 2-3.

African religiosity noted by Mbiti and others.[51] For Africans religion is quite literally life and life is religion. Thus, one must wonder what criteria—other than ignorance or prejudice—were used by a certain early Portuguese traveler to the southern coast of Africa, who avowed that the people there "have no religion."[52]

Archaeology continues steadily to unearth more and more evidence by the day that Africa may be the original home of all humankind and the cradle of civilization, or at least one of them. Paleontologists such as Dr. Louis S. B. Leakey have made important discoveries in this respect along the Rift Valley of East Africa.[53] And Cheikh Anta Diop, the Senegalese philosopher, physicist, and historian, argues with an abundance of evidence how European and Semitic civilizations and religions derive from Egypt, and how "Ancient Egypt was a Negro civilization." If, as Diop establishes, "The ancient Egyptians were Negroes," then

> The moral fruit of their civilization is to be counted among the assets of the Black world. Instead of presenting itself to history as an insolvent debtor, that Black world is the very initiator of the "western" civilization flaunted before our eyes today. Pythagorean mathematics, the theory of the four elements of Thales of Miletus, Epicurean materialism, Platonic idealism, Judaism, Islam, and modern science are rooted in Egyptian cosmogony and science. One needs only

---

[51]See Mbiti, *African Religions and Philosophy*, p. 1, and *Introduction to African Religion* (London: Heinemann, 1975), p. 12. Also B. W. Burleson, *John Mbiti*, pp. 59-61.

[52]See Booth, "An Approach to African Religion," p. 1.

[53]See C. A. Diop, *The African Origin of Civilization: Myth or Reality*. Ed. and trans. by M. Cook (New York: Lawrence Hill & Company, 1974), pp. 260-75. Dr. Leakey's writings on his discoveries include *The Stone Age Races of Kenya* (Oxford: University Press, 1935) and *The Progress and Evolution of Man in Africa* (Oxford: University Press, 1961). Of interest also are A. T. Browder, *Nile Valley Contributions to Civilization* (Washington, D.C.: The Institute of Karmic Guidance, 1992); F. C. Howell et al., *Early Man* (New York: Time-Life Books, 1965), passim; F. C. Howell and F. Bourliere, eds., *African Ecology and Human Evolution* (Chicago: Aldine Publishing Company, 1963), passim; and W. W. Bishop and J. D. Clark, eds., *Background to Evolution in Africa* (Chicago: The University of Chicago Press, 1967), passim.

to meditate on Osiris, the redeemer-god, who sacrifices himself, dies, and is resurrected to save mankind, a figure essentially identifiable with Christ.

A visitor to Thebes in the Valley of the Kings can view the Moslem inferno in detail (in the tomb of Seti I, of the Nineteenth Dynasty), 1700 years before the Koran. Osiris at the tribunal of the dead is indeed the "lord" of revealed religions, sitting enthroned on Judgement Day, and we know that certain Biblical passages are practically copies of Egyptian moral texts . . .

Anthropologically and culturally speaking, the Semitic world was born during protohistoric times from the mixture of white-skinned and black-skinned people in western Asia. That is why an understanding of the Mesopotamian Semitic world, Judaic or Arabic, requires constant reference to the underlying Black reality. If certain Biblical passages, especially in the Old Testament, seem absurd, this is because specialists, puffed up with prejudices, are unable to accept documentary evidence . . .

The triumph of the monogenetic thesis of humanity (Leakey), even at the stage of "Homo sapiens-sapiens," compels one to admit that all races descended from the Black race, according to a filiation process that science will one day explain.[54]

Indeed, the contributions of Africa to world civilization cannot be limited to antiquity. There is also recorded evidence of

---

[54]Diop, *The African Origin of Civilization*, pp. xiv-xv. Diop advises his African readers to be aware of the historical reality of their place in human civilization: "Far be it from me to confuse this brief reminder with a demonstration," he writes. "It is simply a matter of providing a few landmarks to persuade the incredulous Black African reader to bring himself to verify this. To his great surprise and satisfaction, he will discover that most of the ideas used today to domesticate, atrophy, dissolve, or steal his 'soul,' were conceived by his own ancestors. To become conscious of that fact is perhaps the first step toward a genuine retrieval of himself; without it, intellectual sterility is the general rule, or else the creations bear I know not what imprint of the subhuman.

"In a word, we must restore the historical consciousness of the African peoples and reconquer a Promethean consciousness" (p. xv).

more recent contributions. The Sudanese scholar Ahmed Baba may be cited as one example. Before the city of Timbuktu was conquered and pillaged by the Moroccans in the sixteenth century, it boasted of the famous university of Saknore, which had been in existence for five hundred years. Ahmed Baba, a professor there, is described as "a scholar of great depth and inspiration . . . [and] the author of more than forty books on such diverse themes as theology, astronomy, ethnography, and biography." He had a library of more than sixteen hundred volumes.[55]

We must consider what consequences all of this has in terms of the relationships among the humanity's religions. If human culture and civilization have Africa as their "mother," the religions of humanity cannot but have an African element in them. Thus Paul Cardinal Marella can assert that African Religion belongs to humanity, that it is "a very clear manifestation of an inherent religious endowment within human nature." The cardinal does not entertain the slightest doubt that every person's religious character can be found "in the many religious expressions of Africa . . . "[56]

The geographic and demographic spread of African Religion also testifies to its universal character. Even though it does not, and never did, engage in proselytism, African Religion spread to all parts of the world through the circumstances of history. The slave trade, in particular, hastened its spread to the "New World," even though in the United States it has almost completely lost its more conspicuous traits.[57] We might add that today it is observable also among the considerable black populations in the larger cities of Europe and Canada.

---

[55]Quoted by Akubueze Okwuosa, *In the Name of Christianity*, p. 6. See also J. Maquet, *Civilizations of Black Africa*. Trans. by J. Rayfield (New York: Oxford University Press, 1972), passim, and N. Q. King, *African Cosmos: An Introduction to Religion in Africa* (Belmont, California: Wadsworth Publishing Company, 1986), p. 1.

[56]P. Card. Marella, "Preface," in Secretariatus Pro Non-Christianis, *Meeting the African Religions*, p. 5.

[57]But see Jahn, *Muntu*, pp. 217-39.

BETWEEN CULTURAL ANTHROPOLOGY AND ETHICS

One additional question must be addressed at this point. How does one distinguish a moral/ethical system in a religious tradition that is exclusively oral, as African Religion has been up to the present? If the method used is anthropological in nature, isn't there a danger of turning anthropology into theology? Does ethics, then, become merely applied anthropology?

"Anthropology," in the words of Aylward Shorter, "is the study of man—not man as an isolated individual, but man in his own community, man as the product of his society."[58] Shorter continues to explain that pastoral anthropology differs from philosophy or theology but that "it can and should provide material for philosophical and theological anthropology."[59] Ethics, on the other hand, attempts to evaluate these ideas and behavior in terms of standards of right and wrong. The issue is the difference between describing how people live (the function of social or cultural anthropology) and how they *should or ought to* live. The proper field and function of ethics is evaluating a way of life in terms of what is good or bad on the basis of certain principles.

The distinction between the two fields of study, though real, can be exaggerated. While admitting that there can be a conflict between custom and morality, Godfrey Wilson nevertheless insists that they should not be arbitrarily disjointed: "Good manners are usually good morals, good law, and good policy too."[60] He distinguishes four elements as criteria for morality in African societies.

(i) Manners—sanctioned by public approval and disapproval. (ii) Morality—sanctioned by religion.[61] (iii) Com-

---

[58]A. Shorter, *African Culture and the Christian Church: An Introduction to Social and Pastoral Anthropology* (Maryknoll, New York: Orbis Books, 1973), p. 1.

[59]Ibid., p. 3.

[60]G. Wilson, "An African Morality," in Ottenberg and Ottenberg, *Cultures and Societies of Africa*, p. 346.

[61]Wilson's view of "religion" here is rather restricted. Surely it would be reductionist to say that the African's (Wilson investigates only the Nyakyusa of Tanzania which at his time of writing was called Tanganyika)

mon Policy—sanctioned by the rewards and punishments which inhere in any reciprocal relationship between individuals or groups and which make "honesty (i.e., conformity with traditional right behavior) the best policy." The working of all social institutions involves such reciprocal relationships. (iv) Law—sanctioned by institutionalized inquiry, followed by compulsion or punishment.[62]

The connection between the study of theology and anthropology, as indeed between theology and other social sciences, is critically important. The majority of Christian theologians recognize that human beings cannot describe the reality of the Numinous except by imaginatively using the symbols, images, and signs of their own existence and experience, and stretching them to the limit. There is no other way. Consequently, to understand a people's God-talk, one has to be familiar with the symbols and entire system of language they employ for this purpose; thus the necessity of studying the people and their culture, the necessity of knowing their philosophy, psychology, and so on. This is true for all religions and religious groups, large and small, old and new. This is also how we come to understand the principles people use to determine what is right and wrong and how their societies deal with such situations.

Swailem Sidhom contends that a proper understanding of theology in context requires a proper appreciation of the self-understanding of a particular people, because

> There is no doubt that the pattern of life within any given society is an expression of a particular view of man held by that society. The shape of political life, for instance, rests on a particular view of man. The practices of religion are as much the outcome of its doctrine of God as of its estimate of man. There is a sense in which the doctrine of

understanding of religion refers only to "i. the cult of the dead relatives (ancestor-cult); ii. the belief in witchcraft; iii. the use of 'medicines' (magic)." See ibid., p. 347. Obviously, I do not subscribe to such a restricted definition of religion in the African sense.

[62]Ibid., p. 346.

God can be viewed as an expression of a certain view of man. Evidently, wherever we may turn, the question of who man is cannot be avoided.[63]

The anthropological/ethnological (and other social-scientific) study of African Religion has investigated and documented the horizon toward which African religionists aim; it has also attempted to clarify the methods they have established to construct in a more or less accurate way the moral/ethical system of African Religion. I say "more or less" because as a symbolic language the meaning of religious discourse and the significance of systems of belief to a people cannot be fully exhausted.

For any religious orientation, but here specifically for African Religion, the most important principles that determine the system of ethics revolve around the purpose or goal of human life. Within this horizon African communities shape and direct their manner of living in terms of what is or is not acceptable to them. Human experience and responsibility are judged in light of this goal, which does not change. From the dialectic between the established goal and human responsibility to realize it existentially and experientially arise values and norms of behavior, what Africans would generally call "customs," in the most morally-laden sense of the word. These customs help the community and individuals within it to keep the goal of life in sight, to strive toward it, and to have a basis with which to deal with their shortcomings in this endeavor. For African Religion, all principles of

---

[63]S. Sidhom, "The Theological Estimate of Man," in K. A. Dickson and P. Ellingworth, eds., *Biblical Revelation and African Beliefs* (Maryknoll, New York: Orbis Books, 1969), p. 113.

Due to the inseparability of the religious and secular models of African existence, the link between anthropology and theology is especially important. As the Secretariatus Pro Non-Christianis puts it, "Religion has been the nurse of African civilizations, and even now we cannot understand them, particularly in the domain of the arts, unless we feel the religious breath that has inspired them." Likewise, we cannot understand African religion unless we are helped by social scientific analysis. *Meeting the African Religions*, p. 25. See also E. A. Nida, *Customs and Cultures* (New York: Harper & Brothers, 1954), and I. C. Brown, *Understanding Other Cultures* (Englewood Cliffs, N.J.: Prentice Hall, 1963).

morality and ethics are to be sought within the context of preserving human life and its "power" or "force."

PERSPECTIVE OF STUDY

The discussion in this book is intended solely to reflect on
the ethical perspective of African Religion. My primary purpose
is not to "prove" anything, least of all to argue that African
morality is just as rich as Christian or any other religious morality, as many other authors have endeavored to do. I am not
engaging in an intellectual argument with any of the many ide-
ological views of African Religion. To my mind, that kind of
discussion is no longer very useful; it promotes neither mature
ecumenical discussion nor authentic inculturation. In other
words, this is not a study in "aggressive" comparative ethics. I
intend simply to indicate the fundamental elements of ethics
that the religious experience of the African peoples has determined throughout the ages to be proper for themselves.[64]
    Generally I have employed a synthetic and expository
approach. To a large extent, I have also been non-historical. This
stance may need some justification. Quite consciously and deliberately I have decided to keep a certain distance from some of the
changes that appear to have influenced African Religion. This is
because I see them as rather superficial. It is the fundamental persistence and continuity of African Religion that I am concerned
with: how a people's view of themselves—in this case, the foundational ethical values of past generations—intrudes upon them
and directs the foundations of their life-orientation despite the
passage of time and the reality of much apparent change. In this
sense this book is not a nostalgic exercise in resuscitating
"archaeological behavior," but a study of a people's dominant
moral conscience.
    Use of the English language is somewhat of a drawback, as it
gives some concepts a slightly different connotation than that
contained in African Religion, but this is a risk I must take. The

---

[64]See Jahn, *Muntu*, p. 25.

use of language translates ideas from one world-view to another. Nevertheless, I attempt seriously to use concepts and explicate categories of thought to accurately convey the African reality and its conceptualizations.[65] My conviction is that only if and when African Religion's moral stance is clarified can real conversation between it and other religious systems genuinely begin.

I need to mention, as will readily be seen, that this book is not a result of my own scholarship alone, nor of any one particular scholar, for that matter. I regret that I have not had the time or finances to conduct extensive personal field work on the issues. But then, it is not always necessary to reinvent the wheel. Satisfactory groundwork in unearthing the orientations of African Religion's moral theology has been done by many and various scholars: anthropologists, ethnologists, students of comparative religion, African and Africanist theologians, and even historians and politicians. I have drawn liberally and extensively from the findings and insights of these scholars. I hope I have clearly, accurately, and sufficiently acknowledged my indebtedness to all my sources. For that reason, many will find some aspects of this work, and particularly the African conceptualization of the world, to be familiar.

But I have not used my sources blindly. I have been very selective. I have been very conscious of the pejorative attitudes and language of many of them concerning Africa and the Africans, and I have rejected these attitudes. Thus, I have used certain aspects of written sources to corroborate the results of my own observation as an African and a Christian student of African culture. I hope it will be clear throughout that the conclusions I have drawn are a result of my own perceptions of the moral underpinnings and the ethical orientation of African Religion. Nevertheless, I have made every effort to be faithful to genuine data provided by scholarship, regardless of its source, and I trust

---

[65]Foreign languages are always a serious drawback in the discussion of African Religion and other African realities. African theologians are realizing that efforts must be made to study Africa's realities in the indigenous languages of the continent to evoke more genuinely and more accurately their content.

that I have succeeded in that task.[66] Still, I cannot entertain the illusion that this book will measure up to everyone's expectations of theological argument because, in a sense, it is a new approach, being particularly inductive, that views morality as a result of the collective religiosity of a given society. I hope that it will be seen and judged in the context of the thesis it wishes to expose—that for the sake of the dignity and survival of the Africans themselves as a distinctive and psycho-religiously healthy people, African Religion cannot and must not be disregarded by them today.

---

[66]See T. Ranger, "The Invention of Tradition in Colonial Africa," in E. Hobsbawm and T. Ranger, eds., *The Invention of Tradition* (Cambridge: Cambridge University Press, 1983), pp. 211-62, for a discussion of how colonial rule in Africa (in this case, British rule), attempted and to an extent succeeded in introducing a new tradition to make government easier. He also discusses the African reaction to this. The essay makes very interesting and informative reading. However, I do not subscribe to his summary rejection of the studies and records of colonial officials and even anthropologists as offering no sort of guide to Africa's past. Despite the bias that almost all of these records and studies exhibit, particularly in their use of condescending and even insulting language, I believe that the record of the main facts of African Religion were quite accurate. I have no hesitation at all in using them as sources for this study.

Chapter 2

THE MORAL UNIVERSE

How does African Religion view the world and humanity's place and role within it? What elements make up the universe and how do they influence human life? What is the purpose of human existence, and what implications does this have for the practical order of things? In African Religion, the answers to these questions delineate the conception of morality in the universe: the understanding of the good that sustains life and the bad that destroys it. They establish both the context and the content of African morality and ethics.

African Religion's conception of morality is steeped in tradition; it comes from and flows from God into the ancestors of the people. God is seen as the Great Ancestor, the first Founder and Progenitor, the Giver of Life, the Power behind everything that is. God is the first Initiator of a people's way of life, its tradition.[1] However, the ancestors, the revered dead human progenitors of the clan or tribe, both remote and recent, are the custodians of this tradition. They are its immediate reason for existence and they are its ultimate purpose. The ancestors, who are in constant contact with both God and humanity, often "intrude" into the life of humanity with specific intentions. They do so on their own or through the agency of the spirits. The spirits are active beings who are either disincarnate human persons or powers residing in nat-

---

[1]See J. S. Mbiti, *Concepts of God in Africa* (New York: Praeger Publishers, 1970); E. W. Smith, ed., *African Ideas of God* (London: Edinburgh House Press, 1950); A. Shorter, *African Culture and the Christian God: An Introduction to Social and Pastoral Anthropology* (Maryknoll, New York: Orbis Books, 1974), pp. 53-56.

ural phenomena such as trees, rocks, rivers, or lakes. Like God and the ancestors, but of lesser power, the spirits also play a part in the moral behavior of human beings. God, the ancestors, and the spirits are all powers or forces that impinge on human life in one way or another. In that sense they are all moral agents. The way they act has been determined by the ancestors and is "stored" in the tradition of the people. Tradition, therefore, supplies the moral code and indicates what the people must do to live ethically.

The African moral code has its own particular emphases and orientation because the ancestors, from whom it immediately derives and claims legitimation, "had a certain self understanding, a view of their world and their place within it, a life style that was their own making and in which they felt at home, a religious attitude that responded to their experience of the transcendent in the immanent, . . . a self-contained and independently developed cultural integrity that was sufficient for coping with the realities of their world of experience."[2] One important vehicle to insure that this particular understanding of life—that which constitutes tradition—is preserved and handed over from generation to generation is myth.

MYTH AND THE MORAL TRADITION

For Africans, as with many other peoples of the world, myth, together with ritual, constitutes what students of language, such as Paul Ricoeur, have called "primary language." It is a form of symbolic language that expresses the truths of human existence in a way that rational language cannot. But mythical language is not an "irrational" form of expression, as was long thought. On the contrary, as John Middleton has argued, myth constitutes a deliberate and conscious statement by a given people: "A myth is a statement about society and man's place in it and in the surrounding universe. Such a statement is, in general, a symbolic one, so that an important anthropological [and theological]

---

[2] L. Mbefo, quoted in E. Martey, *African Theology: Inculturation and Liberation* (Maryknoll, New York: Orbis Books, 1993), p. 73.

problem becomes one of understanding the reality that the statement is used to symbolize."[3] We face this same problem of interpretation with African myths, which contain elements with the greatest religious significance for people.

A category of myth of great importance among many African societies relates to cosmology. More than all other myths, cosmogonic myths contain the primordial and pristine moral tradition of any given people. There are, quite naturally, numerous such myths among the various peoples of the continent; it is neither possible nor necessary to refer to all of them since their basic tenets of moral vision are similar. It will suffice, for the time being, to recall the extremely sophisticated and complex cosmogonic myth of the Dogon people of Mali.

To recount it in a very abbreviated form, the Dogon see the present order of the universe as a magnified projection of the original order of creation. The creative process began with a primordial egg of the universe, divided into two placenta by its own internal vibration. Each placenta contained a pair of male and female twins (*Nommo*), each of which was equipped with two spiritual principles of the Supreme God (*Amma*).

> The male *Nommo* in one placenta emerged before the time appointed by *Amma* and flew down with a torn part of its placenta intending therewith to create a world of its own. This being, *Yurugu* (or *Ogo*), and his earth were from the beginning solitary and impure. *Yurugu* therefore returned to heaven to recover the female *Nommo*, but *Amma* had already given her away to the other pair. *Yurugu* returned to the dry world and began to procreate incomplete beings, offspring of incest, for he created from his own placenta.[4]

---

[3]J. Middleton, "Introduction," in J. Middleton, ed., *Myth and Cosmos: Readings in Mythology and Symbolism* (Garden City, New York: The Natural History Press, 1967), p. x.

[4]E. Ikenga Metuh, *Comparative Studies of African Traditional Religions* (Onitsha, Nigeria: IMICO Publishers, 1987), p. 32. This passage has been slightly modified in punctuation and italicization. For a very brief but good synopsis of this myth, see also M. Ani, *Yurugu: An African-Centered Critique of European Cultural Thought and Behavior* (Trenton, New Jersey: Africa World Press, 1994), p. xi.

The world was thus in chaos, but *Amma* regained control of it by killing *Yurugu's* female principle and sprinkling her blood all over the earth to restore thereby the primordial order of twinness or pairing.[5]

Like these primordial beings, man possesses two souls of opposite sexes, one of which inhabits his body while the other dwells in the sky or in the water and links it to him. The vital force (*nyama*), which flows in his veins with his blood, is associated with the eight seeds which are distributed equally between his two clavicles. These seeds, united in pairs, are the basis of various notions concerning human personality and the changes it undergoes and they recall the original groups of four pairs of twins . . . Since the condition of a person mirrors the condition of the universe, everything which affects the one has repercussions on the other; that is to say, in some way all a man's actions and all his circumstances must be conceived as closely connected with the functioning of things in general.

The seeds symbolize the food of mankind; they are the pivot on which turns the life of the cultivator, which depends as much on the seasonal renewal of vegetation as on the daily intake of food. They recall also the renewal of human life itself, which vanishes momentarily from its possessor only to be reborn in his descendants. Finally, the regular and appointed series attributed to the seeds is the sign of the universal order established on earth since the descent of *Nommo*.

Disorder among the seeds, which for an individual results especially from the breaking of the rules of life, prefigures the universal disorder which spreads by stages from the individual to his close kinsmen, his family, his clan, his

---

[5]Ibid., p. 32. See also G. Dieterlen, "The Mande Creation Myth," in E. P. Skinner, ed., *Peoples and Cultures of Africa: An Anthropological Reader* (Garden City, New York: The Doubleday/Natural History Press, 1973), pp. 634-53.

people. But the disorder may be arrested and removed at any stage by appropriate rituals. Exact and complicated, they make it possible both for the individual to be restored and the general order to be preserved. Thus the individual, through his family and the society in which he lives, is linked in his structure and in his evolution with the universe; and this connexion operates in both directions.[6]

This myth contains a synopsis of the forces comprising the African moral conception of the universe. The task is to clarify the intricacies of the elements of tradition it contains, their interaction among themselves, and their relationship to human values and norms.

FOUNDATIONS OF VALUES AND NORMS

In the conception of African Religion, the universe is a composite of divine, spirit, human, animate and inanimate elements, hierarchically perceived, but directly related, and always interacting with each other. Some of these elements are visible, others invisible. They correspond to the visible and invisible spheres of the universe: the visible world being composed of creation, including humanity, plants, animals and inanimate beings, and the invisible world being the sphere of God, the ancestors, and the spirits. Placide Tempels referred to all these as "forces of life" or "vital forces."[7] At the top of the hierarchy of the universe is the Divine Force, which is both the primary and the ultimate life-giving Power, God the Creator and Sustainer, the Holy.

Geertz's understanding of ethics indicates that morality derives from people's understanding of the Holy. The Holy does not only encourage commitment, Geertz points out, it demands

---

[6]M. Griaule and G. Dieterlen, "The Dogon," in D. Forde, ed., *African Worlds: Studies in the Cosmological Ideas and Social Values of African Peoples* (London: Oxford University Press, 1954), p. 88.

[7]Placide Tempels, *Bantu Philosophy.* Trans. by C. King, mimeo, n.d., pp. 17ff.

it. Ethical commitment is ultimately anchored in the people's conception of God who is the Holy, and in their interpretation of what God demands of them in real life. Invariably, this interpretation flows from their image of God and their perception of their relationship with God. In all religions, but much more obviously in African Religion, the most general moral argument seems to be: "As God is and does, so human beings must be and do." Admittedly, the similarity can only be approximate and not complete; however, the understanding of God remains the standard against which the moral standards of human beings are measured. It is imperative, therefore, to understand the moral qualities attributed to God by African Religion in order to get an accurate understanding of the African ethical system itself.

The supremacy of God above all created order is the starting point. African Religion never questions nor debates God's ultimate importance. It is a given. It is because of the place God occupies in the universal order of things that human beings can even speak of their own existence, let alone their tradition. God is known and honored as the Great Ancestor, the *Unkulunkulu* (Zulu), *Omukama* (Ganda), *Nyame* (Akan), *Olodumare* (Yoruba), *Leve* (Mende), and so on.[8] As Primal Ancestor and ultimate source and sanctioner of the tradition that sustains and nourishes the people, God possesses certain moral qualities that human creatures must emulate. This is also a given.

All of these qualities or attributes of God are derived from human experience of what is good and noble. They are metaphors or, in one word, anthropomorphic attributes, maximized to fit divine status. Among the most important of these attributes mentioned by Mbiti is the love of God, the kindness and the justice of God.[9] God is also conceived of as Father or Mother, accentuating the positive qualities of fatherhood or

---

[8]For concepts of God in Africa, see the extensive and very rich published surveys, including E. W. Smith, ed., *African Ideas of God: A Symposium* (London: Edinburgh Press, 1950); John S. Mbiti, *Concepts of God in Africa* (New York/Washington, Praeger Publishers, 1970); H. Sawyerr, *God: Ancestor or Creator? Aspects of Traditional Belief in Ghana, Nigeria and Sierra Leone* (London: Longman, 1970).

[9]Mbiti, *Concepts of God in Africa*, pp. 31-42.

motherhood. It is important to remember that these are not abstract qualities within African Religion. They are qualities "in relationship." God is in relationship, or even better, in communion, with humanity and the entire world. Gabriel Setiloane speaks of the Sotho-Tswana's interpretation of the thunderbolt that "pierces" the earth as God (*Modimo*) returning to God's own, in the same way one would return home after a trip or as "an animal returns to its lair."[10]

A Yoruba myth of the origin of *Olodumare*, God, illustrates this essential communion between God and the universe. As Bolaji Idowu recounts it, the primordial being was a large boa. From it was born *Olodumare,* whose original name was *Olodu.* He was extremely strong and good, so strong and good that the earth was not able to bear these qualities. Therefore *Olodu* withdrew to heaven where these qualities continued to develop. But before he withdrew, *Olodu* made a covenant with the boa, his parent, that they would not forget each other, and that they would be in touch from time to time. "The rainbow which occurs in the sky is the sign of that age-long covenant and communion between Olodu and the boa, a sign that the covenant remains forever."[11]

The relationship between God and creation—specifically, humanity—is one of solicitude on the part of God. To associate God with anything that is not good, pure, just and honorable is ridiculous. The expression "It is God's will," uttered when Africans experience difficulties from which they cannot escape, delineates this belief. People know that misfortune can and does happen, but they believe that it is always with the knowledge or the permission of God. Yet, as we shall see, God is never blamed for this; instead the ultimate source of misfortune and suffering is to be found in the created order.[12] God "is constant and does not change from good to bad and vice versa according to the sit-

[10]Gabriel M. Setiloane, *The Image of God Among the Sotho-Tswana* (Rotterdam: A. A. Balkema, 1976), p. 82.

[11]E. Bolaji Idowu, *Olodumare: God in Yoruba Belief* (New York: Frederick Praeger, 1963), p. 35.

[12]See E. Ikenga Metuh, *God and Man in African Religion: A Case Study of the Igbo of Nigeria* (London: Geoffrey Chapman, 1981), p. 43.

uation. The fact that he is above the petty influences of man and does only what he himself wants . . . make[s] his character primarily good."[13]

God's protection for humanity is comprehensive. According to Harry Sawyerr, it "extends over all kinds of action."[14] People acknowledge that the power of God makes success possible; in failure or adversity, on the other hand, the usual interpretation is that God has withdrawn protective power from the afflicted person. Sawyerr illustrates this with an expression from the Mende of Sierra Leone: "God is at his back," which acknowledges that the person is protected by God, and when one exclaims "May God come away from his back," one is praying that God should cease guarding the person in question. This notion of God is operative throughout Africa, even if the precise metaphors will differ. For the Mende, the metaphor is in keeping with their social custom whereby "protection is thought of as coming from behind the protected person, the stronger man as it were backing the weaker." Along a narrow path, women and children go ahead of the men. The latter, carrying protective weapons, bring up the rear.[15]

Humanity, however, is prone to strain its relationship with God. Besides the Dogon myth above, an ancient Dinka myth makes this clear. In Godfrey Lienhardt's brief rendering of the myth,

> God created in the beginning a man and a woman, and the earth was so near to the sky that men on earth could easily reach God in the sky by a rope which stretched between them. Sickness and death were unknown, and a single grain of millet was sufficient for a day's food. God forbade them to pound more than this single grain; but the woman wanted more food, and began to pound more grain with the

[13]R. E. S. Tanner, *Transition in African Beliefs: Traditional Religion and Christian Change—A Study in Sukumaland, Tanzania, East Africa* (Maryknoll, New York: Maryknoll Publications, 1967), p. 7.

[14]H. Sawyerr, *Creative Evangelism: Towards a New Christian Encounter With Africa* (London: Lutterworth Press, 1968), p. 15.

[15]Ibid., p. 15.

long-handled pestle the Dinka use. In doing so she struck God, who withdrew above and sent a finch to sever the rope which once had allowed man easy access to him. Therefore man has since had to work hard to get his food, and death and sickness, unknown when God and man were near together, are his lot.[16]

Myths like this in various African societies are designed to explain the separation of God from the world and the implications of this separation: that is, the source of suffering, the nature of the relationship between the sexes and so on.[17] A long analysis of these implications is not necessary at this point, but I do wish to indicate the moral or ethical role of God indicated by these myths. They clearly identify the rebelliousness of humanity against God as the reason for God's consequent withdrawal from humanity. Yet, they also stress the point that if God is not now immediately and directly involved with human ethical life, human beings are still ultimately accountable to the Divine in all aspects. Since the original fault of humanity, God requires and deserves respectful distance, but does not seek total non-involvement in the ethical life of humanity.

Michael Kirwen cites another myth that deals with the existence of "original fault," the separation between the abode of God and that of humanity. In the myth, this time a man, in the heat of an argument with another man, shot an arrow into the heavens. He drew blood and the heavens moved farther away from the earth. As a consequence of this action, "the rains began to fail, starvation entered, and death became the lot of

---

[16]G. Lienhardt, "Morality and Happiness Among the Dinka," in G. Outka and J. P. Reeder, *Religion and Morality: A Collection of Essays* (Garden City, New York: Anchor Press/Doubleday, 1973), p. 109. For a more extended discussion of the myth, Professor Lienhardt refers the reader to his previous study, *Divinity and Experience: The Religion of the Dinka* (Oxford: Clarendon Press, 1961).

[17]For a similar myth from West Africa, see J. Bailey et al., *Gods & Men: Myths and Legends from the World's Religions* (Oxford: Oxford University Press, 1981), pp. 16-19. See also Ikenga Metuh, *God and Man*, pp. 1-18.

humankind."[18] In African Religion, drought, starvation and death are supremely moral situations because they have to do with life and life's force. But they are ultimately under God's power. The point of the myth is once again that it is because of human fault that God is now far removed from the earth, and that human beings experience pain and want.

In African Religion, one of the incontestable attributes of God is the power to punish.[19] But, as Lienhardt points out, the Dinka are agreed that God's punishment is really a consequence of human behavior. "Although it would be held in general that it is God who punishes . . . offenses," Lienhardt writes, "Dinka [as is generally the case with all other ethnic groups] also recognize that the misery of guilt and anxiety is intrinsic to them."[20] However, God's mercy toward humanity endures and cannot be faulted in spite of human fallibility. If approached, God always shows the eternal goodness that is the mark of divinity. In spite of everything, people can expect that God will provide them with the power to overcome adverse situations. Through methods established by tradition, they can always turn to God to implore God for rain or good health with confidence that they will be helped. God can never be accused of lack of mercy and care for humanity and the world.[21]

God's care and concern for humanity are demonstrated particularly when humanity faces such "limit" experiences as drought, lack of food, illness, premature death and other calamities. Even though human beings and spirits may be the immediate causes of these disasters, God has the final say in what does or does not happen because God stands as Creator, Molder, Begetter, Bearer of the World, Potter, Fashioner, Builder, and Originator of All. But God is also Helper in Trouble, Healer,

---

[18]See Michael C. Kirwen, *The Missionary and the Diviner: Contending Theologies of Christian and African Religions* (Maryknoll, New York: Orbis Books, 1987), p. 4.

[19]Sawyerr, *Creative Evangelism*, p. 15.

[20]Lienhardt, "Morality and Happiness," p. 115.

[21]See R. J. Gehman, *African Traditional Religion in Biblical Perspective* (Kijabe: Kesho Publications, 1989), p. 191.

Guardian along the Path, Ruler, Water Giver, Distributor of Goodness, Sustainer of All. In Nigeria, for example, characteristic names of the Divine are The One Who Is Most Merciful (*Onye kasi ebele* in Yoruba) or The One Who Bestows Gifts (*Onibuore* in Igbo).[22] Other African peoples employ names with similar implications for the Divine.[23] The complete goodness or impeccability of the Divine is also seen in names given to various individuals. Among the many theophoric names bestowed on children, the Igala people of West Africa use such names as The Mercies of God or I Lean on God.[24] The positive connotations implied in human attributes ascribed to God, such as Father, Mother, Grandparent, Elder or Great Ancestor, serve to emphasize not only the moral power, but also the moral goodness of God toward fallible humanity.

An important feature of African Religion's moral vision with reference to God is its refusal to speculate on the reasons why the Divinity does what it does. God is God. For African Religion, it is enough to know and trust that God is "The Wings of the People." God is always there for humanity to snatch people out of danger when need be, to place them out of reach of any agent bent on destroying the fullness of life. When God refuses to do these things, it is always temporary and indicates that it is time for humanity to examine itself to see what it has done wrong, and then to correct its behavior and repair the damage.

Because God is so solicitous of humanity, every individual and every community should observe proprieties of behavior. One ought not to behave improperly before one's elders, as will be shown. This is particularly true in matters that touch the Great Elder, God. In behaving disrespectfully before one's elders, one

---

[22]See Mercy Amba Oduyoye, "Names and Attributes of God," in E. A. Ade Adegbola, ed., *Traditional Religion in West Africa* (Nairobi/Kampala: Uzima/CPH, 1983), pp. 356-7.

[23]See Mbiti's survey, *Concepts of God in Africa.* Also E. B. Idowu, *Olodumare: God in Yoruba Belief* (London: Longmans, 1962).

[24]See J. Onuche, "Theophoric Igala Names," in Adegbola, ed., *Traditional Religion,* pp. 347-8.

risks incurring "shame."[25] An individual or group who behaves disrespectfully in serious matters that touch on tradition risks even greater shame and mortal danger for the individual and entire community. In the moral vision of African Religion, God stands as the ultimate guardian of the moral order of the universe for the sole, ultimate purpose of benefitting humanity. Humanity, being central in the universal order, is morally bound to sustain the work of God by which humanity itself is, in turn, sustained. Humanity is the primary and most important beneficiary of God's action.

ANCESTRAL, SPIRIT, HUMAN, AND MATERIAL POWERS

Every creature has been endowed by God with its own force of life, its own power to sustain life.[26] Because of the common divine origin of this power, however, all creatures are connected with each other in the sense that each one influences the other for good or for bad. "Nothing moves in this universe of forces without influencing other forces by its movement. The world of forces is held like a spider's web of which no single thread can be caused to vibrate without shaking the whole network."[27] This relationship between and among created vital forces— just as that existing between God and creation—is therefore essential as well. It is also causal. Causation flows all directions to maintain life in the universe, but the seriousness and depth of its effects normally depend on the quality of having life and primogeniture. The force

---

[25]I am aware that the notion of "shame" as used in depth psychology in the West today has a different connotation. But I use it throughout this book to denote the African feeling of personal unworthiness when a wrong a person has committed has been discovered and has been made public. This is an important element in African moral thought, and we shall discuss it at greater length in another chapter.

[26]See also P. Baudin, *Fetichism and Fetich Worshippers*. Trans. by M. McMahon (New York: Benziger Brothers, 1885) for an interesting description of the relationship of God and the spirits among the peoples of West Africa. Because of the early date of its publication, however, it is linguistically condescending and even offensive.

[27]Ibid., p. 24.

of the older and animate creatures is always perceived to be the stronger, and is understood to claim allegiance of the younger and the inanimate. As Tempels notes with relation to human beings, "The child, even the adult, remains always...a force ...in causal dependence and ontological subordination to the forces which are his father and mother. The older force ever dominates the younger. It continues to exercise its living influence over it."[28] Consequently, subordination is owed to God by all creation on account of the rank God holds as the first of all existence, as Ancestor *par excellence*. All life, and the power that is life or existence, flows from God. It follows that by right of their primogeniture and proximity to God by death, God has granted the ancestors a qualitatively more powerful life force over their descendants. It has to be kept in mind that the ancestors consist of the founders of the clan. These are the pristine men and women who originated the lineage, clan or ethnic group and who provide the people with their name(s). But ancestors also include "the dead of the tribe, following the order of primogeniture. They form a chain through the links of which the forces of the elders [now with the community] exercise their vitalizing influence on the living generation."[29]

Similarly, Geoffrey Parrinder notes that it is impossible to grasp the meaning of the religious foundations of Africa without going through the "thought-area" occupied by the ancestors.[30] If we compare the interaction of vital forces in the universe to a spider's web, then in day to day life the ancestors form the principal strand without which the fabric collapses. Thus, "it is the superhuman quality of their power, not its omnipotence, that makes it

---

[28]Tempels, *La Philosophie Bantoue*. Trans. A. Rubbens (Paris: Présence Africaine, 1948), p. 41.

[29]Ibid., p. 42. As Tempels explains, "The spirits of the first ancestor[s], highly exalted in the superhuman world, possess extraordinary force in as much as they are the founders of the human race and propagators of the divine inheritance of vital human strength. The other dead are esteemed only to the extent to which they have increased and perpetuated [sic] their vital force in their progeny" (p. 31).

[30]See G. Parrinder, *African Traditional Religion* (London: Hutchinson's University Library, 1954), p. 57.

so valuable, and sometimes, so dreadful, to their descendants in any extremity."[31] More than any other force, the ancestors are the protectors of the society as well as its most feared direct critic and source of punishment.[32] Above all, they are the direct watchdogs of the moral behavior of the individual, the family, the clan and the entire society with which they are associated. No serious misbehavior or anti-life attitude among their descendants, in thought, word and deed, escapes their gaze. The ancestors are in a real sense "authority figures, who maintain the norms of social action and cause trouble when these are not obeyed."[33]

However else ancestors may be conceived (such as metaphysically as ontological spirits), ancestorship primarily implies moral activity. These *badugu, bakurugenji, batale* (Sukuma, Tanzania), *badimo* (Sotho-Tswana, Botswana), and *kpime* (Dagaare, Ghana) are not separate from the family, lineage or clan from which they come. On the contrary, they remain part and parcel of it and in the same relationship, that is, father as father, mother as mother, sister as sister, and so on. Expectations of these ancestors likewise remain similar to those that govern the social order among the living. The operating principle is that of presence. The ancestors, though dead, are present and continue to influence life in their erstwhile communities on earth; indeed, they are expected to do so. The presence of the dead is assumed and invoked when the life of the tribe is threatened with disaster. Thus, for example, the Temne of Sierra Leone invoke the aid of their renowned ancestors when the catch of fish falls below a certain expected minimum or when there is a plague of mosquitoes. The same principle holds firm for the well-being of the family and the individuals within it. It is through reality of their presence that the ancestral spirits come to be the co-guardians of the *mores* of the family, the clan and the tribe. So, for instance, two related

---

[31]W. C. Willoughby, *The Soul of the Bantu: A Sympathetic Study of the Magico-Religious Practices and Beliefs of the Bantu Tribes of Africa* (Garden City, New York: Doubleday, Doran & Company, 1928), p. 80.

[32]See C. Nyamiti, *Christ as Our Ancestor: Christology from an African Perspective* (Gweru: Mambo Press, 1984), pp. 15-17.

[33]E. Kuukure, *The Destiny of Man: Dagaare Beliefs in Dialogue with Christian Eschatology* (Frankfurt am Main: Peter Lang, 1985), p. 67.

Yoruba men who have a dispute readily go to the grave of an ancestor and take oaths of innocence, each invoking his death, if he makes a false oath.[34]

On account of the relationship that exists between ancestors and descendants, any capriciousness of the ancestors is not taken kindly by the living, just as it would not be acceptable from any elder in society. It is expected that "just as in real life a father would take action against his son with extreme reluctance, so in the life of the ancestor spirit, he would be similarly reluctant to be angry, except under what he considers to be extreme provocation."[35] Wherever there is evidence of injustice, jealousy or any unjustified behavior from the ancestors (who in invocations are sometimes referred to as "gods" because of the strength of their vital force, but never as "God"), the living do expostulate with or even reprimand them. They can be scolded, much as an individual would do, "if meeting his respected kinsman in the flesh at a family council, he had strongly disapproved of his line of conduct."[36] Whenever the living feel that the ancestors are acting irrationally or unjustly, the usual questions put to the ancestors as part of a ritual would be: "Why are you doing this to us? What have we done? What have we not given you that was our duty to give?" One such scolding remonstration was recorded among the Thonga of South Africa. The scenario is that of a sick child. The elders of the family are offering a sacrifice to the ancestors for the child's recovery, during which they address the ancestors in the following normal way: "You, our gods, you—so and so . . . here is our offering. Bless this child and make him live and grow. Make him rich, so that when we visit him, he may be able to kill an ox for us." But soon follows the scolding, as if to shame the ancestors for being negligent in their responsibilities: "You are useless, you gods! You only give us trouble! For although we give you offerings you do not listen to us! We are deprived of everything! You, so and so (naming the god . . .) you are full of

---

[34]Sawyerr, *Creative Evangelism*, p. 26. See also M. Potts, *Ancestors in Christ* (Kampala: Gaba Publications, No. 17, 1970), pp. 1-2, 9-13.

[35]Tanner, *Transition in African Beliefs*, p. 26.

[36]Willoughby, *The Soul of the Bantu*, p. 85.

hatred! You do not enrich us! All who succeed do so by the help of their gods." Finally, there is a petition in the hope that the ancestors will rectify the situation: "Now we have made you this gift. Call your ancestors—so and so; call also the gods of the sick boy's father, because his father's people did not steal his mother. These people, of such and such a clan, came in the daylight . . . So come . . . Eat and distribute among yourselves our ox . . . according to your wisdom."[37]

When there is evidence of jealousy among the ancestors as the reason for an affliction, one may address the ancestors, in sacrifice, using words that remind them of the destructiveness of this emotion, and remonstrating that they ought to "eat" together so as to bring healing among themselves and in the world.

> There is your food. All ye spirits of our tribe, summon one another. I am not going to say, "So-and-so, there is your food," for you are jealous. But thou So-and-so, who art making the man ill, call all the spirits; come all of you to eat the food. If it is you, I shall see by the recovery of this man whom it is said that you have made ill . . . Let the man get well. Come together, all of you of such-and-such people, who did so-and-so.[38]

The patience of the ancestors in view of the mistakes and wrongdoing of the living is a point of crucial importance in the moral view of African Religion. Just as God does, the ancestors will refrain from bringing misfortune onto their descendants unless it is extremely necessary to remind them of the demands of the order of the universe—for their own good. This justifies the punitive actions of God and the ancestors against humanity while, at the same time, it absolves them of any moral culpability. People may complain to God and the ancestors, but they will never accuse them of any *moral* wrongdoing. Moral culpability is always on the shoulders of humanity.

Let me make explicit what we have touched on in passing: the

---

[37]See ibid., p. 85.
[38]Ibid., pp. 82-3.

same norm of primogeniture that orders the invisible part of the universe applies as well in the visible world. Animate beings constitute a hierarchy of rank and strength of vital force over inanimate beings. Over all visible beings, in terms of intensity of vital force, stands humanity. But persons also constitute a hierarchy among themselves according to their age or function in society. As a rule, the older the individuals, the more powerful their vital force; the greater the responsibility they hold in society, the more intense their mystical powers. It is in order, therefore, that serious religious/social functions are usually associated with maturity of age, that is with a stronger, more experienced life force.

In African Religion, the centrality of the human person in the universal order is indicated by the religious practice it fosters. Charles Nyamiti explains how "African religious behavior is centered mainly on man's life in this world, with the consequence that religion is chiefly *functional,* or a means to serve people to acquire earthly goods (life, health, fecundity, wealth, power and the like) and to maintain social cohesion and order."[39] This is why all life forces, that is, all creation, are intended to serve and enhance the life force of the human person and society. The belief of African Religion is that this is part of the Divine plan. Universal order can be maintained only if this plan of the interaction of vital forces for the sake of the enhancement of the vital force of humanity is adhered to and observed. African moral values and ethical behavior are therefore vitalistic, existential (dynamic), holistic, relational, anthropocentric and mystical. They cannot be understood apart from these factors. Life implies the existence and interaction of mystical powers in the universe. Conversely, the continuous blending of mystical powers in the universe makes life possible. Thus, "reality is seen and judged especially from its dynamic aspects closely related to life. The farther a being is from these elements, the more unreal and valueless it is conceived to be."[40] This life, this power, is as a rule concentrated in certain

---

[39]C. Nyamiti, *African Tradition and the Christian God* (Eldoret: Gaba Publications, Spearhead, No. 49, n.d.), p. 11.

[40]C. Nyamiti, *The Scope of African Theology* (Kampala: Gaba Publications, 1973), p. 20.

beings or certain parts of the body. But it is also diminished or fortified in certain situations of existence. Illness is obviously a diminishment of vital power, and so is fatigue, worry, lack of certain material resources, and so on. Parched land indicates a loss of vital force, as do floods that result in the destruction of plants and animals. Plenty of food and livestock in the village, on the other hand, is evidence of the presence of a strong force of life. The sole purpose of existence, however, is to seek life, to see to it that human life continues and grows to its full capacity.

But one cannot ensure the full enhancement of life by oneself. One's life force depends on the life forces of other persons and other beings, including those of the ancestors and, ultimately, God. Once again, this is a matter of communion and communication: "The present world is closely connected with the world after death, and one lives in close contact with one's ancestors and other spirits."[41] Human participation and solidarity, not only with God, the ancestors and other spirits, but also with other elements of creation, are essential aspects of the enhancement of life. As Nyamiti has explained, "Man is regarded as intimately related to other fellow-men and beings; and the universe is conceived as a sort of organic whole composed of supra-sensible or mystical correlations or participations." These participations, he writes, these relationships, intricately woven throughout creation, are what give meaning to life. "One form of existence, when considered isolatedly without relation to other forms or beings, is seen to be incomplete and unauthentic. Things are conceived as symbols of each other. Symbols, on their part, not only unify the objects they symbolize, but are also believed to participate somehow in the reality which they express."[42]

This African view of the universe contains the following major themes: the sacrality of life;[43] respect for the spiritual and mystical nature of creation, and, especially, of the human person; the sense of the family, community, solidarity and participation; and

---

[41]Ibid., p. 21.
[42]Ibid., p. 22.
[43]The secular outlook is not totally absent from African culture, but it is not predominant and is in every serious case overshadowed by the sacral, religious view of life.

an emphasis on fecundity and sharing in life, friendship, healing and hospitality.[44] Created order other than humanity must be approached with care and awe as well, not only because of its communion with God, but also because of its own vital forces and its mystical connection with the ancestors and other spirits.

Besides the ancestors, there are two other types of pervasive spiritual elements in the invisible world that influence human life and with which humanity has constantly to deal. The first group consists of human spirits or ghosts. These are spirits of the dead who have passed out of the memory of the living. They are spirits of children who passed away without proper initiation or without children of their own, or spirits of people who, upon death, did not receive a proper burial. The second group is the non-human spirits whose existence has never been anything but spirit. Both types of spirits occupy either of two abodes, the earth or the air. The Nuer people, for example, refer to the spirits who dwell in the air as "spirits of the above," and the spirits who dwell on earth are referred to as "spirits of the below."[45] The spirits of the above are usually associated with such phenomena as the sun, rain, lightning, thunder, and so on. Although they usually dwell in the air, as their collective name implies, in practice they are often associated with earthly phenomena and events. Some of these spirits may be identified with rivers, streams, lakes, trees, or spears. Cattle or other forms of property may be named after them. Sometimes sacrifices and offerings *must* be made to placate them. Just as the spirits of the below, they can also possess people, either permanently or temporarily. In these cases, the possessed may have special powers, particularly "priestly" powers to sacrifice, to divine, or to prophesy.

Spirits of the earth or of the below inhabit natural objects and are exclusively associated with them. Thus, people will speak of spirits of the water, the river, or the lake. They will refer to tree spirits, rock spirits, mountain spirits, snake spirits, and so on, as powers more or less identical to these realities.[46] The mightier the

---

[44]See Nyamiti, *The Scope of African Theology*, pp. 9-11.
[45]See E. E. Evans-Pritchard, *Nuer Religion* (Oxford: The Clarendon Press, 1956), pp. 28-105.
[46]See Parrinder, *African Traditional Religion*, pp. 43-54.

force, the greater the awe paid to it by human beings. But spirits of the below are generally considered weaker than spirits of the above. The most important aspect of the spirits of the earth is that they are sometimes identified with the clan as "collateral lineages with the same ancestor." They thus render the reality in which they are believed to dwell worthy of great respect by the clan and not to be harmed by it in any way. This is the totemic system, a significant aspect of African Religion to which we will later return.

Because of their influence on humanity, spirits may also be referred to as "gods." This is the case, as among many West African societies, where the earth, water, or a devastating disease such as smallpox is concerned.[47] In East Africa, great mountains, such as Kilimanjaro (Tanzania), *Kere-Nyaga/Kenya* (Kenya), and Rwenzori (Uganda), are all named with reference to the gods. But just as in the case of the ancestors, the ascription "god" in reference to these spirits is derivative and is never taken to supplant the power of the Creator God. This is a very intricate relationship. Evans-Pritchard attempts to explain it in relation to the Nuer by saying that spirits, *qua* spirits, are also God. "God," he writes, "is manifested in, and in a sense is, each of them." When the people communicate with spirits, they are communicating with God. "They are . . . addressing God in a particular spiritual figure or manifestation," Pritchard notes.

> They speak to God directly or they speak to God in, for example, the figure of *deng* [spirit], whichever mode is most appropriate in the circumstances. They do not see a contradiction here, and there is no reason why they should see one. God is not a particular air-spirit but the spirit is a figure of God . . . The spirits are not each other but they are all God in different figures.[48]

[47]See G. Parrinder, *West African Religion: A Study of the Beliefs and Practices of Akan, Ewe, Yoruba, Ibo, and Kindred Peoples* (London: Epworth Press, 1961), pp. 37-49.
[48]Evans-Pritchard, *Nuer Religion,* pp. 51-2.

In African Religion, spirits are omnipresent. E. Bolaji Idowu explains that in this perception they "are ubiquitous; there is no area of the earth, no object or creature, which has not a spirit of its own or which cannot be inhabited by a spirit."[49] As to the nature of spirits, Idowu writes that they can be conceived in terms of human physical characteristics, "but they are more often than not thought of as powers which are almost abstract, as shades or vapors which take on human shape; they are immaterial and incorporeal beings." They have the ability to change their appearance and form at will and they do so whenever they wish to manifest themselves to human beings: "they can be either abnormally small, fat or thin. It is believed that especially when they appear beside the natural object which is their residence, they may appear in the form or shape or dimensions of the object."[50] Some of the more significant spirits—or *chi* (Ibo), *orisha* (Yoruba), *obosom* or *abosom* (Ashanti), *balubaale* (Ganda), *vudu* or *vodu* (Ewe-Fon), *kuth* (Nuer)[51]—have definite names and are understood to perform distinct functions in society. Some of the spirit names are Orisha-Nla, Orunmila, Oduduwa, Ogun, Eshu[52] (West Africa), Kyobe Kibuuka, Kungu, or Ssezibwa (Uganda). However, our main interest here is to understand what these spirits do and what role they play in the ethical perspective of the African people.

Many of the spirits are feared, because they are often thought to be malevolent. This applies mainly to human spirits, both of the air and the earth. The reasons are understandable. For one thing, all such spirits have left the normal memory of the living. In ordinary circumstances they receive no recognition through

---

[49]E. B. Idowu, *African Traditional Religion* (Maryknoll, New York: Orbis Books, 1975), p. 174.

[50]Ibid., pp. 173-4.

[51]See N. Q. King, *Religions of Africa: A Pilgrimage into Traditional Religions* (New York: Harper & Row, 1970), passim; Ikenga-Metuh, *God and Man*, pp. 60-84; Parrinder, *West African Religion*, pp. 26-59.

[52]Eshu is the important "trickster spirit" of great social, religious and theological significance throughout West Africa. See the interesting study by R. D. Pelton, *The Trickster in West Africa: A Study of Mythic Irony and Sacred Delight* (Berkeley: University of California Press, 1980).

prayers or sacrifices because they are not ancestors in the usual sense of the word. What better way to attract attention to themselves, then, than by causing trouble for people? Moreover, many such spirits lived badly on earth, and so they are just doing what they used to do on earth. The spirits who did not receive a proper burial, those who died without fulfilling life's expectations of acquiring wealth and children, those who died as young children, and so on, can only be characterized as angry and vengeful. Unless frequently and quickly placated by offerings and sacrifices, they can easily cause grave harm to the community by destroying life through disease, starvation, or death. As totems, spirits of the earth are not feared as much; in general, they are perceived to be more benevolently disposed toward the clans with which they are identified. But some spirits of the below may also cause harm, such as when a river overflows or dries up, fire burns property, lions or leopards maul people or livestock, or there is a small catch of fish from the lake.

Ethically, the significance of spirits in African religion is that of all other vital forces. Their presence and relationship to humanity means that they are part of humanity by the interconnection of vital powers and thus cannot be ignored. One characteristic peculiar to them gives them even more profound significance in the religion's ethical consciousness: their powers for good or for bad cannot be easily distinguishable in human affairs until they effect damage. And so, as we have mentioned above, they must be placated almost daily. Thus, shrines for some of them (for example, those of Eshu in West Africa) are to be found in the courtyards of many homes. This is why, as David Kyeyune has noted, before one does anything of importance, drinking water or beer or eating food, one offers a little bit to the spirits.[53] In this way one is sure that all the spirits are content and will not cause harm.

Spirits can also be used as protection by harnessing their power to take revenge on one's enemies or to prevent them from

---

[53]See D. Kyeyune, "Dialogue Between Christianity and African Religion in Uganda. The Relation Between the Spirits and the Living Relatives," in *Dialogue with the African Traditional Religions* (Kampala: Gaba Publications, No. 37, 1975), p. 41.

harming oneself. We refer again to the spirit Eshu to illustrate this. "By feeding him with his favorite dish of palm oil, and then offering him his great taboo of palm-kernel oil in the name of an enemy, it is expected that Eshu will fly off and avenge himself on this insulting enemy."[54] Spirits thus become an important factor in the practice of harmful or good medicine and healing. They are also a factor when one acquires through possession supra-human powers for the benefit of life or, as in the case of witches, for its destruction.

ETHICAL CONSCIOUSNESS

At the risk of seeming to repeat myself, I want to address more specifically the question of the general moral/ethical conscious- ness that the African view of the world engenders and enforces, for it is this consciousness that informs the whole of African moral life. If, as I have spelled out above, African perceptions of the universe consist of the interaction of various (ultimately divine) vital forces, then the African ethical consciousness cannot but be a religious one. The world as a sacred abode of the life forces of God, the ancestors, and diverse spirits is what gives human action its necessarily sacred character. Consequently, African ethical consciousness must, and does, answer to religious demands. What are these demands? We cannot do justice to that question before briefly considering some fundamental character- istics of African Religion. The immediate question here is, how does African Religion understand itself? Or rather, what do Africans consider their religion to be?

John Mbiti has characterized this as "a big question."[55] Indeed it is, because African Religion, including the worldview it gives rise to and incorporates, is entirely a lived religion, not a doctrinal one. It requires no formal induction. One is born into it and one learns it from childhood throughout one's life through

---

[54]Parrinder, *West African Religion*, p. 57.

[55]J. S. Mbiti, *Introduction to African Religion* (London: Heinemann, 1975), p. 10.

normal socialization. It is a religion that is taken for granted within the community and generally needs neither proselytizers nor converts. Even people brought into a different ethnic group, as for example, through capture, were not required to abandon their own spirits and ancestors. Instead, these were usually accepted as a cherished addition to the spirits and ancestors of the dominant group. Since it involves the whole of life, whatever one thinks, says, or does is religious or, at least, can have religious implications. At all times in a person's life, a religious consciousness is always explicitly or implicitly present. In no way is anything understood apart from the context of God, the ancestors, and the spirits; in no way is any thought, word or act understood except in terms of good and bad, in the sense that such an attitude or behavior either enhances or diminishes life.

Such comprehensiveness does not make African Religion easily amenable to analysis. Yet we must attempt an analysis for the sake of clarity and understanding, even if by doing so we risk distinguishing what, in African Religion, should not be separated from the whole. We must always keep in mind, though, that, just as with regard to its view of the universe, African Religion forms the African people's ethical consciousness as a whole united system wherein each factor influences the other. In this system, "being" is the same thing as "doing," and *vice versa*. Thus, "Not until one has understood that for the African 'the ontologically good is the ethically good' can one appreciate and understand the moral sense of the African and the direction of ethical pursuit."[56]

The agents for moral action in African Religion are the vital forces of the entire created universe, both the visible and invisible worlds. But it must be pointed out that even though, "The visible world is one with the invisible; [and] there is no break within the two, still less between their inhabitants, since the family, the clan, the tribe and the nation . . . extend beyond death, and thus form the invisible and most important element in the commu-

---

[56]Adegbola, "The Theological Basis of Ethics," in K. A. Dickson and P. Ellingworth, eds., *Biblical Revelation and African Beliefs* (Maryknoll, New York: Orbis Books, 1969), p. 118.

nity,"[57] it is more particularly and directly the visible world, the cosmos, where contending forces act themselves out. The world of humanity is the stage for morality. African Religion arises "structured by the quest to bring opposite forces into equilibrium and symmetry," as Josiah Young notes. "Opposite forces, signified by the leitmotifs, the visible and the invisible, are integrated in myth and ritual in order to valorize their proportion in relation to one another." At the center of this cosmological "matrix" that constitutes African Religion, "are human beings whom . . . [forces from the invisible world] possess in order to enforce morality and prescribe remedies for healing and wholeness."[58]

Yet, religious reverence must be accorded to the world and what is in it and around it. This is a moral requirement because the world is the manifestation of God, God's power, and benevolence. Accordingly, the big rock where people go to sacrifice is not just a big rock, but it incorporates, shows, and for that reason is, in fact, some supernatural quality of the Divine. The same can be said in different African societies of practically anything that inspires awe: mountains, trees, snakes, certain animals, and so on. While African Religion understands very well that these elements are by no means God but creatures, as we have emphasized, it also recognizes that they have divinity in them because they exist by the will and through the power of the Divinity. In a sense, therefore, they "represent" the Divinity and surely demonstrate God's will and power to humanity. The sun, for example, is such a potent representation of God that among many peoples God is simply named after it or in reference to it (*Rua, Ijua, Izuva, Yuva, Ilyuva, Lyoba, Zyoba,* in East African Bantu languages, and *Nyame,* in West Africa among the Akan, Ashanti and Fanti).[59] Nyamiti speaks of such objects similarly as "hieropha-

---

[57]V. Mulago, "Vital Participation," in Dickson and Ellingworth, *Biblical Revelation and African Beliefs,* p. 149.

[58]See J. S. Young, "Out of Africa: African Traditional Religion and African Theology," in D. Cohn-Sherbok, ed., *World Religions and Human Liberation* (Maryknoll, New York: Orbis Books, 1992), p. 107.

[59]See Shorter, *African Culture,* p. 54. See also his *African Christian Theology—Adaptation or Incarnation?* (Maryknoll, New York: Orbis Books, 1977), pp. 61-78.

nies," or manifestations of the holy. "Everything unusual becomes a hierophany. There is always a correspondence between the mode of being of an object and the modality of the sacred it reveals: a particular aspect of the sacred is revealed through the object's specific mode of existence."[60] Thus, no one may treat creatures, particularly animate ones, callously or with impunity. Again, in the words of Josiah Young, "the ancestors teach us that . . . we must listen to this earth, feel its pulse, if we are to recognize our connection to the sacred."[61]

The world becomes even more important in African ethical thought because it is recognized that human life directly depends upon it and its vital forces. African Religion underlines the fact that "the earth is our home, and the prolongation of humankind is ultimately bound to the earth's fecundity. The sky, the earth, and all the living and breathing things that give life and balance to the cosmos are essential to the quest for . . . humanity, [for life in its fullness]."[62] So, even though the first and most important participation of the human person is in and through one's community, the community cannot be sustained without another kind of participation, namely, "the link which binds one to the earth, the economic 'substratum' or heritage," as Vincent Mulago has shown. "Community based on common means of existence is thus included in the community based on sharing in a common life."[63] Quoting Levy-Bruhl, Mulago underlines how in African ethical thought, "The group, like the individual, is not made up only of flesh and blood; it is a complete and self-sufficient whole, animated by a diffused life." In a way, the group, like the individual, is the microcosm of the universe. The whole universe subsists, so to speak, in it.

> The beings of which it is composed are not all visible; around animals and men there move the geniuses of the ground, the forces of vegetation, the spirits of the dead. The bond between them is that of participation. The special

---

[60]Nyamiti, *African Tradition*, p. 66.
[61]Young, "Out of Africa," p. 107.
[62]Ibid., p. 107.
[63]Mulago, "Vital Participation," p. 144.

function of religion is to recognize, classify and propitiate them. This progress of ideas consists in differentiating them and placing them in a hierarchical order.[64]

Thus, once again, to callously disturb created order by abusing it disrespectfully means nothing else, ultimately, than to tamper dangerously with human life. This is very serious. The implications of such a course of action often go even further than this. If the world is disturbed, God, the spirits and the ancestors—or, in other words, their powerful, invisible, but diffused life forces throughout the universe—are likewise unsettled. There is no telling what calamity might befall a community as a result of such behavior. For God and the ancestors desire peace and order above all.

In African religious ethical understanding, the earth is given to humanity as a gratuitous gift and all human beings possess an equal claim to it and the resources it offers. This is especially true of the essentials of life such as land, air, water, fire, and so on. These cannot be alienated from the clan and ethnic group. What this means is that an individual person can only hold land in trust for oneself and one's descendants on behalf of the clan or ethnic group. Water sources, mineral resources, forests, and so on, are in principle public property and have to be cared for and used as such. In the strict sense, African morality does not and cannot sanction private ownership of land, and the natural resources under the ground. In the final analysis, God's representative on earth, in the form of the chief or another recognized leader, has the responsibility of overseeing their use. In fact, if they are misused by an individual or the community, that is, if their vital force is uselessly disturbed and disaster befalls the community, the ruler is ultimately responsible.

Later, I shall discuss the understanding and practice of the ownership of goods in African communities. But let me simply note here that these arise out of the ethical interpretation of the dual participation of human beings in the human and ancestral community, on the one hand, and in the sacred forces of the uni-

---

[64]See ibid., p. 144.

verse, on the other. Furthermore, the world represents in various ways the being and personality of the Divine Giver who always has the final claim on it. As all human beings are children of God, no one can claim to have a monopoly of ownership over those aspects of creation that are deemed to have been placed by God's will in public trust for the public good. Perhaps a good way to describe this understanding is to see goods and resources in terms of the image of the lender, the borrower, and the article lent or borrowed. In African ethical thought, the universe has been lent by God to humanity through the ancestors and the living leaders to use on the condition that it must be kept in good order and used by all for the promotion of life, good relationships, and peace, at least within the clan or ethnic group. If those conditions are broken, humanity forfeits the right to it and often deserves chastisement if reparations in the form of sacrifice or offering are not offered.

What constitutes misuse of the universe? This question can be answered in one word: greed. In the African moral outlook, greed is the antonym of hospitality and sociability or, in a word, good company. It goes beyond simply describing unsocial behavior in the sense of being outwardly rude or unwelcoming, or unapproachable and unhelpful. It means that, but it means much more than that. Greed constitutes the most grievous wrong. Indeed, if there is one word that describes the demands of the ethics of African Religion, sociability in the sense of hospitality, openhearted sharing, is that word. Hospitality negates greed. It means the readiness and availability to form community. It means that one remembers and honors God and the ancestors and is ready to share with them through sharing the gift and power of life with other members of the family, lineage, or clan. The purpose of hospitality is to enhance life in all its dimensions. Its foundation is in the very structure of existence itself. For, as Mulago has argued, "The fact of having been born in a particular family, clan or tribe plunges us into a specific vital current, 'incorporates' us into it, fashions us according to this community, 'ontically' modifies our whole being, and turns it in the direction of the community's way of life and behavior." Thus, he says, every individual person is an intimate part of a larger entity that must be preserved:

the family, clan or tribe is a whole, of which each member is only a part. The same blood, the same life which is shared by all, which all receive from the first ancestor, the founder of the clan, runs through the veins of all. Every effort must be directed to the preservation, maintenance, growth and perpetuation of this common treasure. The pitiless elimination of everything which hinders this end, and the encouragement at all costs of everything which furthers it: this is the last word in [African] Bantu customs and institutions, wisdom and philosophy.[65]

Perhaps the significance of hospitality and sharing might be elucidated by recalling what Nyakyusa parents expect of their children. A Nyakyusa father is gratified and feels very proud if his son brings many of his friends home to eat. A father will come home only to learn that much of the food prepared for that day by his wives has been eaten by his son and his friends. The more companions his son has, the prouder the father will be. Monica Wilson learned that among the Nyakyusa, "If a young man came home often alone to eat, his father would beat him, or even take a spear and wound him, and when people asked why he would say: 'This great fool comes *alone* to my place again and again.'"[66] The implication is that such a character isolates a person, that is, it makes one inhospitable or greedy.

Reluctance or utter refusal to share with God, one's ancestors, other persons in the community, and the community itself—in a word, greed—destroys the "communitarian" purpose of the universe and is immoral. It is imperative, therefore, for example, that one share life by begetting children. The presence of children assures that the life of the individual, the clan, and the lineage continues as the children bear the names of their ancestors. If the lineage of a given family in the clan has to cease, to *die*, because of lack of offspring to carry it on by name, part of the life of the

---

[65]Mulago, "Vital Participation," pp. 139-40.
[66]M. Wilson, *Good Company: A Study of Nyakyusa Age-Villages* (London: Oxford University Press, 1951), p. 67.

clan radically ceases as well. It *dies*. For a person to cause this to happen knowingly and intentionally constitutes one of the worst crimes or moral wrongs against oneself, the community, and society generally. For what is demanded as the ultimate good is that life be preserved and perpetuated in every way possible, in its past, present, and future forms. This is taken so seriously in Africa that for a person to so much as wish otherwise, even without verbally articulating such a wish, is seen as evil. Even such a wish represents an internal personal trait of seeking to destroy life that must be struggled against, for it can externalize itself in various sinister ways, including the practice of witchcraft. Because this valuing of life is so crucial to the system of African ethical thought, we shall study it at greater length in a discussion of the agents of diminution or destruction of life.

THE RELATIONSHIP IMPERATIVE

The realization of sociability or relationships in daily living by the individual and the community is the central moral and ethical imperative of African Religion. Relationships receive the most attention in the adjudication of what is good and bad, what is desirable and undesirable in life. Not only is the view of the universe at the service, so to speak, of the formation and execution of good relationships, but relationships make possible the continuing existence of the universe. Harvey Sindima has noted that where African religion is concerned, "We cannot understand persons, indeed we cannot have personal identity without reference to other persons...The notion of being-together is intended to emphasize that life is the actuality of living in the present together with people, other creatures, and the earth."[67] And in the words of Mulago, "The life of the individual...[can only be] grasped as it is shared. The member of the tribe, the clan, the family,

---

[67]H. Sindima, "Community of Life: Ecological Theology in African Perspective," in C. Birch et al., eds., *Liberating Life: Contemporary Approaches to Ecological Theology* (Maryknoll, New York: Orbis Books, 1990), pp. 144, 146.

knows that he does not live to himself, but within the community. He knows that apart from the community he would no longer have the means of existence."[68]

Bondedness is the key to the understanding that "What falls on one, falls on all. In such a relationship, the issue is the re-establishment of community, the re-establishment of the circulation of life, so that life can go on transcending itself, go on bursting the barriers, or the intervals, the nothingness, go on being superabundant."[69] The ethical consequence is that "We must repair every breach of harmony, every wound and lesion. We must demand reparation for ourselves because we are not merely ourselves, and for others because they are also ourselves, the what-and-who of our pre-existence and survival, the what or who of some manner of our 'presupposing' ourselves."[70] In a single phrase made famous by John Mbiti, the guiding principle of African people's ethical behavior may be summed up in the consciousness that "I am, because we are; and since we are, therefore I am."[71] Or as K. A. Opoku expresses proverbially, "Life is when you are together, alone you are an animal."[72]

The moral thought of African Religion becomes clear through the understanding of relationships. The refusal to share is wrong. It is, in fact, an act of destruction because it does not serve to cement the bonding that is required to form community. Quite the contrary, it is perceived as an element that seeks to weaken and break such bonds. Nothing that weakens community bonds, or in any way helps to abet such weakening, can be morally wholesome. The unity of the community—equally the living, the living-dead (or the remembered-dead) and the yet-to-be-born—a unity that is the community's life in its fullest sense, is the paramount good. The opposite constitutes the paramount destructiveness.

---

[68]Mulago, "Vital Participation," p. 139.
[69]Sindima, "Community of Life," p. 145.
[70]Ibid., p. 146.
[71]J. S. Mbiti, *African Religions and Philosophy* (New York: Frederick A. Praeger, 1969), pp. 108-9.
[72]Quoted by P. Bock, "Exploring African Morality," in *Cross Currents,* XXVIII:4 (Winter 1978-9), p. 483.

The remembered-dead or ancestors, as well as those to be born, all have a part to play in African religious consciousness. They all form elements of the African community. The ancestors, in particular, are very much active in the universe under various forms, effecting good or bad experiences that are dependent on the behavior of the living. But the principal moral actors are the living; by their behavior they determine what is to befall them and the universe. The yet-to-be-born are not yet directly involved in the sphere of morality. Still, they are members of a given community, albeit *in potency,* and care must be taken that they are not wronged by the living in any way. The most serious wrong against the latter would be for the living to deprive them of the chance to be born and to participate in the life of the family and the clan in this world. Such an action would deprive them of a most fundamental right.

Participation-sharing is thus a central principle or imperative for human existence in African Religion, the "quintessence of authentic humanity [*Obuntu*]," as Emmanuel Twesigye has described it.[73] This is something I shall refer to again and again throughout this book. For the moment, however, we should look at how—by what means and agents—balance in life, the most important ethical need and the greatest good, is preserved.

Theo Witvliet, citing Engelbert Mveng, has noted how, "for African people the determinative feature of humanity lies in its involvement in the dramatic conflict between life and death, which becomes meaningful in the ultimate victory of life over death." Witvliet points out that for the African people, "Human life is the battlefield for the struggle between life and death, and human beings are combatants who opt for or against life."[74] In this struggle it is the people's rulers, who are also their religious leaders, who are structurally entrusted with the promotion of life. It is easy to identify who the people's rulers/leaders are.[75] In gen-

---

[73]See E. K. Twesigye, *Common Ground: Christianity, African Religion and Philosophy* (New York: Peter Lang, 1987), p. 109.

[74]T. Witvliet, *A Place in the Sun: An Introduction to Liberation Theology in the Third World.* Trans. J. Bowden (Maryknoll, New York: Orbis Books, 1985), p. 92.

[75]See, for example, J. S. Mbiti, *Introduction to African Religion* (London: Heinemann, 1975), pp. 150-63.

eral, they are referred to as "the elders," but they can be distinguished by the specific functions they perform in and for the community. Among the elders there are, for example, herbalists, rainmakers (or more correctly, rain-askers), diviners, mediums, prayer leaders, and prophets. These are the ethical experts of and for the people. They are teachers, counselors, and moral guides. They are expected to lead a visibly ethical life themselves so their leadership will be both credible and acceptable to the people. In the final analysis, people turn to them to learn what is wrong with a suffering individual or society, and what ought to be done in the given circumstances to set things right with the vital forces.

The most important obligation of every leader is to do whatever is in his or her power to protect and prolong the life of the family and the community, following the order of the universe established by the ancestors and transmitted by tradition. Neglect of this duty has consequences to the authority the leader wields. A leader must be a person with "a cool heart," as the Dinka say, and not "a hot-head."[76] Leadership requires maturity, thoughtfulness, patience, understanding, and wisdom. An irascible, abusive, or irresponsible leader cannot be tolerated for long because such an attitude indicates irresponsibility, and it jeopardizes the harmony of ancestral life that the leader is there to uphold. It also puts the community's life at risk. This is true among the Nuer as well as throughout the African religious vision. Authority does not mean that the "leader could order people around," as M. F. C. Bourdillon has written, "but it did mean that in appropriate situations there was a person who could be approached and who could for the moment take on a leadership role."[77] Authority does mean the ability to persuade and settle differences before they result in fiery conflict and destruction of life. Character in leadership is not merely a bonus; it is a moral requirement.

Francis Mading Deng perhaps describes best this nature of "authority-for-life" in the person of the status and function of a

---

[76]See F. M. Deng, *The Dinka of the Sudan* (New York: Holt, Rinehart and Winston, 1972), p. 113.

[77]M. F. C. Bourdillon, *Religion and Society: A Text for Africa* (Gweru: Mambo Press, 1990), p. 68.

Dinka chief. "The spiritual power of the Chief," explains Deng, "can be awesome, but the Dinka know that the Chief should not err and invoke divine power unjustifiably. Abused power is ineffective. The fear of the Chief's religious sanction is therefore not so awesome as it may seem. Persuasion is his primary tool."[78] Deng describes the office of the Dinka chief as being "particularly opposed to physical coercion." In ideal circumstances he should not even see blood, for to spill human blood is abominable. Even in case of war, the Dinka chief blesses his warriors and prays for them far away from the scene of battle. Indeed, the duty of the chief is to do all he can to prevent hostilities that might lead to the shedding of blood. For example, "In a war between his own sub-tribes, he may draw a symbolic line, place his sacred spear on it, and pray that heavy casualties be inflicted on any group crossing the symbolic line in disobedience to his orders against fighting."[79]

It can be said that the most important service of religious personalities in day-to-day life is to counteract witchcraft (*uchawi*).[80] As we shall see, witchcraft is perceived by African Religion to be the greatest wrong or destructiveness on earth, of which all other wrongs are but variations, emanations, or manifestations. Most of the time suffering, sickness, and death have their origin in witchcraft. If religious leaders have any influence on the people, then, it consists in counteracting acts, or even intentions, of witchcraft, for witchcraft constitutes the perversion of everything that is good and desired in human beings; it is the personification or incarnation of all that is anti-life, and therefore the ultimate enemy of life on earth.

---

[78]Deng, *The Dinka,* p. 114.

[79]Ibid., p. 114.

[80]As C. Haule argues, the English word "witchcraft" does not express accurately the inner meaning of this concept within the African reality. He prefers the African concept of *uchawi* (Swahili). As the inner meaning of the African understanding of *uchawi* makes clear later in our discussion, I will use the English expression witchcraft throughout this book to refer to that African reality. See C. Haule, *Bantu "Witchcraft" and Christian Morality: The Encounter of Bantu Uchawi with Christian Morality—An Anthropological and Theological Study* (Schoneck-Beckenried: Nouvelle Revue de Science Missionaire, 1969), pp. xiii-xiv.

Religious leaders also advise and give direction to people in questions of worship and veneration: how to relate to God, the spirits, and the ancestors. Reverencing God, honoring the ancestors, and fearing the spirits are directly relevant to human life. They occur within the context of human needs and wants or, on the other hand, human anxieties and dislikes. If living men and women of the community or the group are the axis or the center around which these activities revolve, the primary purpose of acts of worship and reverence is neither God nor the ancestors, but the well-being of the person or community concerned. African Religion is human-centered, even overtly utilitarian in the communal rather than the individualistic sense, and its officials are charged with the responsibility to see to it that this well-being endures.

It is the responsibility of the religious leaders of the society, as well as the elders in the household, to pass on orally and be examples of all the moral codes of the clan and ethnic group from generation to generation. Only by properly living life in this world, as indicated by tradition, are the individual and the community guaranteed life beyond. Leaders have a unique responsibility to pass on tradition because, by virtue of their being leaders, they are ontologically in closer union and communication with God and the ancestors than the rest of the population. The ancestors possess power over humanity and creation in that they have been endowed with a stronger vital force than the living. They (as well as the spirits) can use this power to effect either harmony or chaos in the world. And this depends entirely on how they are treated by their living descendants. Once again, however, the ancestors themselves, like God, are always beyond moral culpability. If their influence in the world results in goodness and harmony for the community, it is because the community has behaved honorably or morally and has done nothing to upset the ancestors. On the contrary, such harmony is a sign that community members have fulfilled all their obligations to the ancestors, as is required of descendants. If, on the other hand, the ancestors' power is perceived in terms of pain, suffering or the destruction of life in the community, the reason does not lie outside the community but rather within it. It must be searched for and as soon as it is recognized, it has to be rectified so that the ancestors are appeased and may rest in peace. The elders of the community bear the responsibility in this process of appeasement.

The elders must be in constant touch with the ancestors, who are actual members of the human community, together with the yet-to-be-born, and enjoy practically the same rights and responsibilities as the living. Perhaps the ancestors have even slightly more rights and responsibilities on account of the vital power they possess. As elder members of the community, and because of their proximity in existence to the Divine, it is morally imperative that the ancestors be honored. Strengthening the bonds of kinship among the living here on earth is required to strengthen the bonds with the ancestors. The link between the living and their departed ancestors is essential, and it is the living (the junior members in the "partnership") who invariably suffer the consequences for any breakdown of this kinship tie, whether intentional or inadvertent. Again, elders in the community have the responsibility of guarding against this eventuality.

The role of elders in the African religious structure becomes much more evident when we consider the characteristics of African Religion itself.

1. Because African Religion *embraces the whole life* of the people, there is no distinction between religious or secular leaders. The responsibility of any leader encompasses both aspects of life. Their purpose is always to enhance life. The leader is judged on that single criterion. Leadership is good and acceptable if it enhances life; it is bad and ought to be changed if it results in the diminution or destruction of life.

2. Because African Religion is *communal* (everyone belongs to it by birth), religious leaders are responsible to the entire community and are accountable to it. This applies to the entire social hierarchy, from the father of the family, the head of the lineage or clan, to the tribal chief, as well as all the various experts in between. The responsibility and accountability of each leader is seen within the context of that hierarchy.

3. Religious leaders have the responsibility to ensure that *the bond between the living and the ancestors remains intact* and that the community enjoys the wherewithal for the *preservation and*

continuation of life. Leaders are enjoined to see to it that the community enjoys plenty of food, good health, firm security, and numerous offspring. Again, the "religious" and "civil" aspects are two sides of the same reality.

4. Religious leaders, therefore, are charged with the *responsibility to see to it that things are right between the visible and the invisible world and in the visible world* itself. They have to restore by prayers, sacrifices, and offerings, right relationships, good company, or harmony whenever these are threatened or severed.[81]

ETHICAL PRESUPPOSITIONS OF THE AFRICAN WORLDVIEW

This overview of African Religion shows that its main ethical presuppositions have to do, in the final analysis, with the interaction between God, humanity, and the rest of creation on the one hand, and the interpretation of good and bad, or right and wrong, on the other. Even though the practical implications of these presuppositions become clear as individuals and societies experience the ups and downs, the joys and sorrows of life, the existence of African Religion's moral framework is already evident in its view of the universe. To recapitulate, the two spheres of the universe—the invisible world and the visible—are both closely interconnected; each influences the other to create the religion's system of morality or ethics.[82] The all-encompassing principle to be kept in mind throughout is that all morality is life-centered. "For the African, life is the primary category for self-understanding and provides the basic framework for any interpretation of the world, persons, nature, or divinity."[83]

The invisible world—the abode of the Deity, non-human or non-ancestral (created) spirits, spirits of the restless dead, nature

---

[81]See J. Ferguson, "The Nature of Tribal Religion," in Adegbola, ed., *Traditional Religion in West Africa*, pp. 242-3.

[82]See also Mbiti, *Introduction to African Religion,* p. 32.

[83]Sindima, "Community of Life," p. 142.

spirits, and the ancestors—is really an amoral or non-moral world in the sense that ethical judgements cannot be attributed to the actions of its inhabitants. The theater of morality and ethical responsibility is the visible world of the earth where humanity lives. Human beings are the agents of the morally good or bad, or the ethically right or wrong, because only human beings carry the responsibility of maintaining the bond between the two spheres of the universe.

The interaction between the visible and invisible spheres of the universe and human responsibility for them is not simply random. It is controlled by a moral order instituted and sanctioned by God and channeled through the ancestors of any given community. This order is preserved by tradition and, if followed, has the power or force to sustain the existence and operation of the universe, ensuring a bountiful life for humanity. Since the universal order exists for the sake of human life, humanity is its most important element or aspect, its center, as John Mbiti puts it.[84]

The centrality of human beings in the order of the universe by no means implies human license. It does not mean that humanity is allowed to treat the non-visible sphere or other creatures in the visible sphere of the universe without reverence and respect. In fact, reverence for all creation is an essential part of the moral order of the universe and determines everything that happens to or befalls humanity. "Destiny," or what may be called the finality of the human person has its origin in the person's or community's attitudes and behavior with regard to beings in both spheres of the universe, including both the non-human and the human. Once again, sociability with all people and harmony with the universe is the guiding ethical principle. "Man is not the master of the universe; he is only the center, the friend, the beneficiary, the user. For that reason he has to live in harmony with the universe, obeying the laws of natural, moral and mystical order. If these are unduly disturbed, it is man who suffers most."[85]

It bears emphasizing that human beings must be in harmony not only with animate beings but with the entire inanimate cre-

---

[84]Mbiti, *Introduction to African Religion*, pp. 37-9.
[85]Ibid., p. 39.

ation. Inanimate beings, far from being insignificant in the order of creation as African Religion understands it, incarnate within themselves "vital energies" necessary for humanity. These energies, "alive" in their spirits, require linkage with the entire system of the universe. They are not mere symbols of the Divine. Because of the power of the Creator within them and since they are the manifestations of the Creator and the abode of other spirits, they consist of the Divine within them. Human love and fertility, for example, are not simply symbolized by the fertility of the earth; instead, they are deeply imbedded in the earth as it receives the rain and the seed and produces vegetation and crops for human consumption. Thus, they offer up their vital power for the life and fertility of human beings. It follows, then, that in a real and immediate sense the sterility or fertility of the earth affects the fertility of the human community. So also, water and air are not only symbolic of, but *are,* in fact, the purity of the Divine. Polluting water or air in any manner is tampering with God's power and vital force.

Sustaining the universe by maintaining harmony or balance between its two spheres and among all beings is the most important ethical responsibility for humanity and it forms the basis of any individual's moral character. Even more significantly, however, it determines the quality of life of the human community in the universe and the quality of the universe itself. It requires commitment in upholding the sanctity of creation in everyday life, because, as Sindima has emphasized, "All life—that of people, plants and animals, and the earth—originates and therefore shares an intimate relationship of bondedness with divine life; all life is divine life."[86] This means nothing else but that "nature and persons are one, woven by creation into one texture or fabric of life, a fabric or web characterized by an interdependence between all creatures. This living fabric of nature—including people and other creatures—is sacred. Its sanctity does not mean that nature should be worshipped, but does mean that it ought to be treated with respect."[87]

---

[86]Sindima, "Community of Life," p. 144.
[87]Ibid., p. 143.

The sanctity of creation has to be maintained by the human community. Vincent Mulago points out that individually and collectively human beings draw their existence from one and the same "source of power" as the rest of nature. Humanity "turns towards [this] power, is seized by it and seizes it."[88] The universe "is a religious universe. Nature . . . is filled with religious significance . . . The physical and spiritual are but two dimensions of one and the same universe. These dimensions dovetail into each other to the extent that at times and in places one is apparently more real than, but not exclusive of the other."[89] In the final analysis, however, God, acting through the ancestors, but never completely absent from the scene, is the ultimate point of departure and arrival in human ethical life.

"African peoples," Mbiti notes, "have come to these conclusions through long experience, observation and reflection."[90] For them, harmony as the principle for moral order does not mean that people and other members of creation lose their freedom. Harmony is *the* agent of freedom and is meant to enhance it. But what does "freedom" mean? Does it imply license or liberty to do whatever one wants? Such is not the case. In African Religion, freedom is what enables a person to be fully who he or she is. This applies equally to all beings: harmony (or freedom) enables a tree to be fully tree, a stone fully stone, and a person fully human. Without harmony, greed, selfishness, and exploitation—in a word, chaos—set in and triumph over universal moral order. Chaos does not imply simple disorder; it risks putting relationships between the two spheres of the universe on a collision course, inviting great suffering for the human community.

To emphasize the connectedness between humanity and creation and to ward off the chaos that might ensue if this bond is not respected—since for various reasons human beings tend to overlook things—African Religion erects a system of totems and taboos. Although we shall consider the question of taboos in depth later, it is important at this point to introduce the essential elements of the system.

---

[88]Mulago, quoted by Sindima, p. 144.
[89]Mbiti, quoted by Sindima, p. 143.
[90]Mbiti, *Introduction to African Religion*, p. 39.

What Sigmund Freud wrote many years ago about the Australian native people in *Totem and Taboo* is applicable to the religious conception of totem in Africa. Using the language of Freud, we can describe a totem as any species of animal, or less often a plant or species of it, or even in some cases a force of nature, such as rain, water, or lightning, which is perceived to have a special relationship with a given clan. The totem is seen to incorporate or be an expression or representation of an ancestor of the entire clan. It is exclusive to it, for it is not possible that two different clans of the same tribe have the same totem. The totem is understood as having the responsibility of protecting the clan. It cannot harm any of its members. But the obligation is mutual: if the totem cannot harm its tutelaries, the members of the clan of that totem must also not kill or harm it in any way. For example, they must not eat the meat of their totemic animal. "Any violation of these prohibitions is automatically punished."[91] This prohibition is what constitutes a taboo. According to Hutton Webster, taboos may be described, then, as systems of prohibitions with regard to certain persons, things, acts, or situations. The objects considered as taboo are perceived to contain within them a certain assumed danger that always has repercussions against anyone who transgresses them. The danger need not be explained and in many cases it is not; neither is it perceptible to the senses, but it is there, and sooner or later the consequences of transgression invariably boomerang upon the transgressor.[92] It is for this reason that

---

[91]S. Freud, *Totem and Taboo: Resemblances Between the Psychic Lives of Savages and Neurotics.* Trans. by A. A. Brill (New York: Vintage Books, 1946), p. 5. As the subtitle shows, Freud engages in an extremely prejudiced and pejorative discussion of this phenomenon among the Australian native peoples. Despite his brilliance as a psychologist, his lack of understanding of the religious function of the system of totems seems evident. Other early writers, using otherwise very accurate analyses, also demonstrate the same ignorance or prejudice of interpretation. I refer to Emile Durkheim, for example, in his *The Elementary Forms of Religious Life.* Trans. by J. W. Swain (New York: The Free Press, 1965), especially pp. 121-93.

[92]H. Webster, *Taboo: A Sociological Study* (New York: Octagon Books, 1973), p. 13. This is a helpful sociological study of this subject, but like Freud's aforementioned work, its language and attitude are so Eurocentric that the author completely fails to see the moral/ethical significance of the

taboos have great moral authority. Webster considers their authority "unmatched by that of any other prohibition." He explains that this authority is constituted by the fact that "A taboo amounts simply to an imperative thou-shalt-not in the presence of the danger apprehended. That any breach of the prohibition was unintentional or well-intentioned matters nothing; no allowance is made for either the ignorance or the praiseworthy purpose of the taboo-breaker."[93]

Northcote Thomas, speaking about the Polynesians, confirms this. As he sees it, taboo applies to three categories of situations: "(a) the sacred (or unclean) character of persons or things, (b) the kind of prohibition which results from this character, and (c) the sanctity (or uncleanliness) which results from a violation of the prohibition."[94] The connection between totems and taboos in African ethics consists in their convergence to constitute a moral ambiance or to erect moral codes that are intended to serve harmony and the order of the existence of the universe. They are experienced in day-to-day life and are passed from one generation to another to be safeguarded by society, to direct its behavior and that of its individual members. Their origin may be obscure or unknown, but that is not important. What is of consequence is, once again, their purpose: to preserve harmony and to keep chaos at bay. It follows, then, that moral interest in totems and taboos does not usually go beyond their aim. What is important is that the general consequence of diminishment of life results from harming totems or transgressing taboos. Taboos are in a sense their own explanation: breaking them causes otherwise inexplicable calamity, and calamity happens if they are (whether knowingly or unknowingly) transgressed. Taboos exist to make sure that the moral structure of the universe remains undisturbed for the good of humanity.[95]

---

taboos. Throughout the book he tends to dismiss them as fabrications of "primitive man" due to ignorance and fear.

[93]Ibid., p. 17.

[94]Cited in Freud, *Totem and Taboo*, p. 27.

[95]See Parrinder, *West African Religion*, pp. 172-5. For a synthesis of totemism and taboo, see also A. R. Radcliffe-Brown, *Structure and Function in Primitive Society: Essays and Addresses* (New York: The Free Press, 1965), pp. 117-52.

Chapter 3

THE MYSTIQUE OF LIFE

As we have seen, the foundation and purpose of the ethical perspective of African Religion is life, life in its fullness. Everything is perceived with reference to this. It is no wonder, then, Africans quickly draw ethical conclusions about thoughts, words, and actions of human beings, or even of "natural" cosmological events, by asking questions such as: Does the particular happening promote life? If so, it is good, just, ethical, desirable, divine. Or, does it diminish life in any way? Then it is wrong, bad, unethical, unjust, detestable. This most basic understanding of morality in African Religion is incorporated systematically in the people's way of life. It is expressed in their traditions, ceremonies, and rituals. It constitutes what Africans perceive as the mystique of life.

ABUNDANT LIFE REALIZED IN ANCESTRAL COMMUNION

The imperative of community and harmony that determines the ethical agenda of life in African Religion deeply concerns the ancestors. By their character and attributes, they link the individuals in a clan and the visible and invisible worlds. To be a human being, to be a *moral, ethical* person—*Mtu* (in Kiswahili) and *Muntu* (in nearly all other Bantu languages with slight phonetic variations), it is not possible to live in isolation.[1] This was

[1]See N. S. Booth, "The View from Kasongo Niembo," in N. S. Booth, ed., *African Religions: A Symposium* (New York: NOK Publishers, 1977), p. 37. See also J. Mawinza, *The Human Soul: Life and Soul-concept in an East African Mentality Based on Luguru.* Ph.D. Dissertation (Rome: Pontifical Urbanian University, 1963).

discussed at length in the preceding chapter. One can only become truly human in community, in the context of other human beings in the world, and in some sort of relationship to the dead. Kinship is what in large measure constitutes life itself and its mystique. And kinship is most intensely and most meaningfully realized and expressed in and by the ancestor relationship.

Ancestorship is an act of communion in remembrance that is also actualization or resurrection. It constitutes making present among us here and now those who are remembered. Ancestors and their descendants on earth are in continuity. In a sense, as Igor Kopytoff has noted, ancestors are perceived in the same way as the living elders of the society as far as the experience of kinship and communion is concerned.[2] Ignatius Pambe asserts that among the Sukuma-Nyamwezi of Tanzania, "They [the ancestors] remain in talking, and almost tangible, terms with their descendants."[3] In no way does the state of ancestorship weaken the bonds of communion. Far from it, it strengthens them. The state of ancestorship can be characterized in African religion in terms of action. The ancestors and their descendants are in a constant state of exchanging gifts and favors. This is what communion requires; it is what remembrance means. This dialectic strengthens the life force of the world for the sake of living humanity.

While the living are obliged to seek ancestral communion for the sake of their own well-being, the ancestors are not passive in this exchange. They also desire to be in communion with their living kin, to be remembered and honored. They manifest this desire in several ways, such as by using certain other beings of creation as mediums to "visit" the living. Thus, the sight of a particular snake, caterpillar or hyena might indicate an ancestral

---

[2]See I. Kopytoff, "Ancestors as Elders in Africa," in P. B. Hammond, ed., *Cultural and Social Anthropology: Introductory Readings in Ethnology* (New York/London: Macmillan, 1975), pp. 282-91.
[3]I. M. Pambe, *Symbols and Change in African Beliefs: Religious Symbols and the Leader-Specialist Among the Sukuma-Nyamwezi of Tanzania—An Anthropologico-Phenomenological Approach.* Ph.D. Dissertation (Rome: Gregorian University, 1978), p. 119.

visit, and the appropriate consequences would be drawn from it. The ancestors may also come directly into their descendants and possess them. Not an uncommon occurrence in African societies, such possession is widely recognized in African Religion. The ancestors may also appear through dreams and divination. Finally, and most drastically, the ancestors make their will known by visiting calamities on their descendants, catching their attention, and forcing them to make an appropriate reply.[4] The reply is usually made through prayers and rituals meant to restore human and cosmic solidarity.

Aylward Shorter has described religious ritual as an appeal to spiritual beings who have the power to influence events, undertaken with the intention that they do so.[5] He categorizes them into three groups: rituals of redress, rituals of life-crisis or initiation, and rituals of liminality. We shall discuss all of these categories of ritual eventually. Ancestral rituals, however, pertain to the category of redress, but they really go much further than that. They act not only to "repair" wrongs that have been committed and that call down calamities and afflictions; they also go beyond the needs of the living to restore the *status quo ante*.[6] More often, they are used as preventives, as means to maintain the existing, good *status quo* that society or an individual may be enjoying. Both types of rituals of redress are important in that they are both intended to maintain the bonds of communion between the living and their ancestors and the balance of the universe. With reference to the Amba people of Uganda, Edward Winter explains how, besides the routine offerings, "sacrifices are made to the ancestors when it is believed that they have brought about some misfortune, such as sickness." Calamities that befall human beings may be a warning that something is not right in their relationships with their ancestors. "When misfortune befalls an individual it may mean that an ancestor has become annoyed. Thus,

[4]See C. Nyamiti, "African Ancestral Veneration and Its Relevance to the African Churches," in *C.U.E.A. African Christian Studies*, 9:3 (1993), p. 16.
[5]A. Shorter, *African Culture and the Christian Church: An Introduction to Social and Pastoral Anthropology* (Maryknoll, New York: Orbis Books, 1974), p. 126.
[6]See ibid., p. 123.

in addition to a feeling of filial piety, all sacrifices are made in order to prevent the ancestors from causing trouble, or if they have already done so, in order that they may cease their attacks."[7] Keeping the ancestors in good humor is an essential task of the living.

When the ancestors are unhappy about the attitude of their descendants, they make this known and often employing painful means against those who misbehave. Henri Junod gives several examples of the manifestation of ancestral dissatisfaction among the Thonga people of South Africa. To cite only two: The first refers to a woman who was going through a forest, saw an edible fruit called *sala*, plucked it from the tree and ate it. Nothing happened, and she went about her business unharmed. When she did the same thing another time, she found numerous small vipers in the fruit, instead of a stone or pit. She was astonished when the vipers scolded her: "Go on! Eat away! Haven't we seen you every day picking *sala*? And these *sala* are ours, and not yours. What shall we gods have to eat? Have we not made this tree to grow?" Because this was a curse from the gods for her disrespect, the woman went home and died.[8] A second instance concerns a man who, against the rules, went to collect firewood from a forest reserved for the gods. As he was doing so, he was pelted from behind with fruit. He realized that it was the gods doing this and tried to run away, but he could not find the way out of the forest. He then let go of the pieces of wood he had collected as firewood. Only then did the gods allow him to find his way out. In the open, "he perceived that he was carrying nothing, even his axe had been taken from him."[9]

As in the first case above, it might seem that the ancestors intervene directly to cause death to human beings. But, as previously mentioned, this is not usually the case. Ancestors are there to guard life. When they intervene, it is usually to warn human beings. As the most important guides to true morality, they take

---

[7]E. H. Winter, "Amba Religion," in J. Middleton, ed., *Gods and Rituals: Readings in Religious Beliefs and Practices* (Garden City, New York: Natural History Press, 1967), p. 33.

[8]H. A. Junod, *The Life of a South African Tribe: II. Mental Life* (New Hyde Park, New York: University Books, 1962), p. 378.

[9]Ibid., p. 379.

that responsibility seriously. Calamities are meted out for the sole purpose of reminding the living always to remember to keep their ancestral relationships alive and harmonious, for to strain these relationships is to threaten life at its very core. Thus, when the ancestors react as they do in cases of a breach of moral etiquette, it is to benefit the living, to preserve the universal order of love, piety, and respect. What is expected of ancestors is faithfulness to their kin as long as prayers and offerings are made to them. Various means may be used to ensure their faithfulness, including promises or threats.[10] In this drama for universal harmony, God, who is referred to as The Great Ancestor (*Unkulunkulu,* in some parts of the continent), the ultimate foundation of the vital force, solidarity, and harmony, is always assumed to be present. If the ancestors refuse to listen and the desired effects of prayers and offerings are not forthcoming, the living normally turn to God as the last resort. However, it has always to be kept in mind that in the final analysis the culpability of human beings, rather than the responsibility of the ancestors, is the cause of any moral disorder.

From the perspective of African Religion, then, illness, poverty and other calamities point to a moral disorder in relationships, from the most elementary in the family to the most complex in the society. If the family, lineage, and clan enjoy good health and relative prosperity, particularly when the birth rate is good and the children survive to adulthood, it is believed that there is a good rapport in the network of relationships. The ancestors are happy, the vital force is strong, and there is harmony in the land and in creation. Such abundance of life is a clear indication that the population is upright with regard to the ancestors. Abundance of life indicates in clear terms that the norms essential for its preservation have not been disregarded or broken. These norms, often characterized as taboos or tabus (*misiro, miiko* in East Africa), were received from the founding ancestors of the clan, lineage, or ethnic group and are handed down from generation to generation. The ancestors observed them and so assured life for their descendants. It is because they observed them that the ancestors also attained their present exalted status. They

---

[10]See E. Ikenga Metuh, *God & Man in African Religion: A Case Study of the Igbo of Nigeria* (London: Geoffrey Chapman, 1981), p. 94.

stand as "models" or "exemplars" of ethical living, as no one can attain ancestral status without having led a morally good life.

The expectations of the ancestors and the demands of tradition are satisfied most markedly in the rhythm of human life. Certain events in human life carry special significance in the movement to preserve life, and these moments of crisis are used to augment the vital power of the person. They relate primarily to what A. Van Gennep calls "rites of passage," that is, birth, puberty, marriage, and death.[11]

CONCEPTION, BIRTH, AND NAMING

To begin with, it is important to note one significant aspect of the African view of the universe as it relates to the life of a person. For Africans, conception and birth in the human species correspond very closely to the same activities in the plant and animal species. They correspond also to human contact with the soil and its fertility, that is, cultivation, planting and harvesting. Similarly, they are related to the cosmological realities of the seasons, in Africa the rainy and dry seasons. If we keep in mind the relationship of human life to nature, to creation, we can more fully appreciate why in African Religion the beginnings of human life make demands on creation, and how, conversely, "natural" events have immediate religious implications for human life. As Harvey Sindima explains, the reason is that Africans do not conceive of personal identity apart from life in its totality; that is, where they come from, what they do, whom they associate with, their relations, their gods, and so on. These things define their "humanity," so to speak. But this self-understanding becomes complete only when they situate themselves in a very profound way in the "natural" world, in the life of nature. Africans see that human life and activity in constant contact with the life and activity of other people and with nature makes life and living life fully possible. "As nature opens itself to people, it presents possibilities for experiencing the fullness of life, possibilities for discovering how insep-

---

[11]See A. Van Gennep, *The Rites of Passage*. Trans. by M. Vizedom (Chicago: The University of Chicago Press, 1960), p. 5.

arably bonded people are to each other and to all of creation."[12]

The moment of conception is therefore a time of great joy for husband and wife, but also for the whole clan. Conception indicates and assures that the universe is in good order and that the ancestors are happy. It is a very significant step not only for the validity of the marriage contract, but also for its consolidation. Finally, and most important, it is the beginning of the assurance for the parents of their own possibility of living after death, that is, of becoming ancestors themselves. Thus, a failure to conceive can have disastrous consequences both to society and to the world environment in which the society lives.

Conception is not seen as merely a result of man and woman coming together in the act of sexual intercourse. It is most basically understood as the result of a blessing from God and the ancestors. Without divine and ancestral blessing, conception may well not be possible. God, ancestors, mother, and father must all cooperate for conception to take place. Mother and father "copulate to 'beget' jointly and 'give birth,' while God intercedes [intervenes?] to 'create' and the ancestors assist in protecting the creation from the malevolent powers of destruction. Every individual is therefore the outcome of a human act, God's creation, and ancestral blessing."[13] In the act of conception, vast "kinship" relationships are beginning to form between the visible and invis-

---

[12]H. Sindima, "Community of Life: Ecological Theology in African Perspective," in C. Birch et al., eds., *Liberating Life: Contemporary Approaches to Ecological Theology* (Maryknoll, New York: Orbis Books, 1990), pp. 144-5.

[13]F. M. Deng, *The Dinka of the Sudan* (New York: Holt, Rinehart and Winston, 1972), p. 30. G. Wagner in his *The Bantu of Western Kenya: With Special Reference to the Vugusu and Logoli, Vol. I* (London: Oxford University Press, 1949), p. 207, presents a different argument. He says that "the Kavirondo realize that the child is the joint product of both husband and wife. Although . . . conception can . . . be prevented by the interference of spirits and other mystical agents, these agents can never positively become the cause of pregnancy, nor is it thought that the child's mental or physical characteristics are in any way subject to the influence of mystical agents. It is thus realized that conception can only be caused by the sexual union of man and woman."

In excluding the agency of the invisible world in the act of conception, I think that Wagner overstates his case. At any rate, Deng is closer to the general perception of African religion with regard to this matter.

ible worlds. More accurately phrased, they already have formed. As Francis Deng explains, ancestors, in this act of conception, are fathers and mothers and grandfathers and grandmothers. In addition to the immediate biological parents, all of them make the child possible and assist in bringing it into the world. All have power and authority over it, and at any stage of its life, even as an adult or old person, it owes them respect. To the new person coming into the visible world, all of the ancestors are almost like "gods" requiring his or her allegiance. According to this kind of perception, "Even God is referred to in such personal terms as 'Grandfather' or 'Father' and His paramountcy implies His transcendent fatherhood over every person and over humanity at large."[14]

If conception is an occasion of joy, a good, uncomplicated birth of a healthy child is much more so as it validates the relationships discussed above. It is a sign of tranquility in the universe, the pleasure of the ancestors, the good moral standing of the parents, and a sign of the defeat of bad people or malevolent spirits by the protection of the ancestors. A newborn baby, notes Geoffrey Parrinder, is scrutinized for any similarities it might have to any of the dead or living older relatives. For "A newborn child is often thought to be the reincarnation of some ancestor who is seeking to return to this life, or at least part of his spiritual influence returns."[15]

As we have mentioned, the parents must be in good moral standing if the birth is to take place smoothly. A difficult or delayed birth indicates that a sexual taboo has been broken. It is important for the husband and the expectant wife to avoid sexual intercourse for a specified time before the birth. It is also important that they avoid sexual intercourse during menstruation. Most important, however, is that both be faithful to each other during the entire pregnancy. Unfaithfulness of one or the

---

[14]Ibid., p. 31.

[15]G. Parrinder, *West African Religion: A Study of the Beliefs and Practices of Akan, Ewe, Yoruba, Ibo, and Kindred Peoples* (London: The Epworth Press, 1961), p. 95. See also his *West African Psychology: A Comparative Study of Psychological and Religious Thought* (London: Lutterworth Press, 1951), pp. 57- 68 and 115-31.

other spouse, or an incestuous relationship, is sure to result in a difficult delivery, stillbirth, birth of an abnormal child, or death of the child before it has been "taken out" and formally named. With reference to the people of western Kenya, Gunter Wagner explains that "A miscarriage which occurs suddenly and without causing much pain to the woman is regarded as the consequence of an act of adultery committed by the wife during her pregnancy... Suspicions of adultery are also raised if parturition occurs too soon (after seven or eight months) or if the child is stillborn."[16]

Protracted birth and illegitimacy are closely connected. Henri Junod noticed among the Thonga that a woman who knows that she is bearing the child of her lover and not her husband will, in strict privacy, confess to one of the midwives she trusts "to spare herself the pains of a difficult birth."[17] The midwife is honor-bound not to reveal this secret. Failing this, however, in a difficult birth doubt begins to arise as to the true genitor of the child: is it the woman's husband or a lover? A rite must be performed to try to ascertain this so as to save the lives of both the mother and the child. There are various kinds of rituals in such an eventuality. Among the Thonga, a ritual takes the form of the husband taking a little of his semen and mixing it in water in a fruit shell for his wife to drink. If the child is truly his, it will "feel his father," and the woman will deliver promptly. Should the birth continue to be difficult, it will be seen as "proof that the child is really illegitimate and the midwife will force the woman to confess her guilt and name her lover. Should she have had many and hide the names of some of them 'the womb will refuse'... and the birth will be possible only when the confession is complete."[18]

Identification of the true father of the child is crucial to maintain the relationships. That is why all this is done. Otherwise,

---

[16]G. Wagner, *The Bantu of Western Kenya: With Special Reference to the Vugusu and Logoli. Vol. I* (London: Oxford University Press, 1949), p. 297.
[17]H. A. Junod, *The Life of a South African Tribe, I. Social Life* (New Hyde Park, New York: University Books, 1962), p. 40.
[18]Ibid., pp. 40-1.

how can the child properly belong to the family and lineage? Not that the child will be rejected if it is initially "illegitimate." But that is precisely the point: it must be "taken possession of" and inserted into the family and lineage through the proper rites so that it is properly recognized.

Incest may also result in births of abnormal children or still-births. "If it is beyond doubt that the marital relationship between husband and wife does not infringe the laws of exogamy [as far as these are determined by society], the birth of an abnormal child is quite logically attributed to incestuous adultery on the part of the wife."[19] There are different punishments for this, as well as ritual purifications to restore the order of the universe. But, for whatever reason, if stillbirths continue, this may be cause for divorce, because they are indicative of an unidentified moral problem. Sexual immorality is, however, not the only cause of difficult births; other moral shortcomings may also be factors in such circumstances. "Contravening the rights of deities and ancestors," says Deng, "concealing a crime or some moral wrong, and leaving crimes against fellowmen uncorrected are the common causes. Appropriate rites of atonement are recommended to be combined with expert physical assistance."[20]

In this discussion of the beginning of life, it might seem odd to refer to a ritual among the Bahema of Zaire that apparently deals with the end of life. Even though it appears to be a ritual of death, it is most concerned with the handing over of life. In this sense, it is fundamentally also a ritual of life's beginning, a ritual of conception and birth that illustrates the link between the visible and invisible vital forces. As described by Bénézet Bujo, the ritual is simple enough. At the death of the father of the household, each of his sons licks some grains of millet from his hand four times. Each one then jumps over the dead man's corpse an equal number of times. The ethical significance of the ritual is once again what concerns us here. In the words of Bujo, it signifies the "culmination of life's power."[21]

---

[19]Wagner, *The Bantu of Western Kenya,* p. 297.

[20]Deng, *The Dinka of the Sudan,* p. 35.

[21]B. Bujo, *African Christian Morality at the Age of Inculturation* (Nairobi: St. Paul Publications, 1990), p. 78.

At least four ethical demands are indicated by this ritual. First, from now on the sons have the responsibility of bringing forth offspring of their own to prolong their father's lineage. In being remembered by his descendants and having grandchildren named after him, he is assured a place with the ancestors and will become one himself. Second, the sons, on behalf of all the members of the family (in the spirit of corporate personality), undertake to do all that they can to stay healthy and to see that the whole family stays healthy. This obligation is aimed, again, at the continuation of the life of the lineage. Third, the sons, on behalf of everyone else, implore the father to be considerate and not to take with him the means to sustain the family. As head of the family, the material and spiritual goods for the family resided with and in him to dispense for its good. Now the sons ask that he grant this wherewithal to them in even more abundance to continue the vital force of the family. And, finally, the sons ask the father to always give them whatever is required for them not to let down the family, and by extension, the clan and the entire community, in any way.[22]

The idea of conception and birth (or bringing forth new life) is thus an integral part of the way African Religion treats "normal" death, that is, death in mature old age. This kind of death, like conception and birth, is a life-giving reality, and is seen and experienced as such. As Bujo explains, "the deceased who has become an ancestor would now wish to communicate to his family his own gentleness, peace, fertility, good health, success in life, prosperity in cattle and fields, etc."[23] However, this cannot remain a passive desire on the part of the ancestor alone; it must be actively effected by the living. As we shall see below, the initiation process is meant to underline this responsibility.

The beginning of life already contains the end, and the end is in normal circumstances a splendid beginning. For this reason, an

---

[22]See ibid., p. 79.
[23]Ibid., p. 79. It is necessary to mention here a major difference in religious orientation and practice in this matter between some of the predominantly pastoral Nilo-Hamitic and the predominantly agricultural Bantu. The former do not have as elaborate ceremonies for their dead as the latter, and do not see the influence of the dead on their morality in exactly the same way.

expectant woman must be treated with extreme care and solicitude. Everyone directly involved with her, particularly the husband, must be extremely careful not to infringe on any ethical codes during the entire duration of the pregnancy. Almost the same respect is given to a pregnant woman as that shown toward a corpse. Both are "sacred" in terms of their status and the life they carry. Just as the corpse of a person who died "normally" (preferably in old age) is secluded and given a proper burial so the departed person will join in the life of the ancestors, so also is a woman carrying the fullness of life usually secluded to remove her from harm's way. She must be fed with the choicest foods to make sure the life she now carries matures. To neglect to do so constitutes a great wrong that may anger the ancestors, resulting in the loss of the child by miscarriage and the diminution of the family's and the clan's life. Thus in African Religion, both life and death converge toward the desire for a full life. And the same is true of other related activities that signify living and dying, such as cultivation, planting, harvesting, hunting, fishing, marriage, sexual relations, eating, dancing, mourning, and so on. They are realities that attest to the presence of vital power communicated to the living from God through the ancestors.

In certain expressions of African religiosity, as among the Maasai of Kenya and Tanzania, God is directly called upon to enhance the fertility of the people. Eugene Hillman describes one such rite where God is asked to guarantee the continuation of life. The rite is performed under an ancient tree "which, when struck with a stick, yields a sweet tasting milky liquid." The tree and its sweet liquid symbolize, of course, a life of plenty and happiness. Characteristically, the prayer chant of these women goes, "God, I beg motherhood."[24] The rite is not an expression of doubt in God's benevolence, as Hillman notes. The people, "Far from having any doubts about the Originator's positive response, are confident that many children will soon be born into their families. A deep sense of trust and hope become palpable through this ritual enactment."[25]

---

[24]E. Hillman, "Maasai Religion and the Christian Mission," in *CHIEA African Christian Studies*, 7:2 (1991), p. 8.
[25]Ibid., p. 9.

What justifies the desire for children among the Maasai, as everywhere else in the continent, is the need to preserve the life force so that the life of the family, community, and clan may continue without end. This purpose supersedes all others (such as the parents' personal economic or social standing through offspring), and is made clear in the naming practices of African Religion. Here is where the convergence between life and life-giving death, and the responsibilities implied in it, can be seen quite clearly. More than merely symbolic or for purposes of identification, real re-presentation (making present again) takes place in the act of naming. Naming involves the incarnation or actualization of a person (an ancestor), a certain desired moral quality or value, a physical trait or power, or an occasion or event. "To confer a name is therefore to confer personality, status, destiny, or express a wish or circumstances in which the bearer of the name was born."[26]

The way in which names are given indicates a specific understanding of "reincarnation" throughout the continent. The Agni people of Côte d'Ivoire are a typical example. In this society, people "give a first-born son the name of his paternal grandfather; a first-born girl takes that of her maternal grandmother. Other children have the names of brothers of the paternal grandfather, and girls those of the sisters of the grandfather or of the sisters of the child's father. There is matrilineal inheritance, but names come through the father. If a child's father dies while his wife is pregnant, the baby when born will take its father's name."[27] Reincarnation here is real, but in the sense that the life force of the deceased comes to inhabit, protect, and shape the character of the child. The ancestor does not thereby cease to exist: he or she continues to live in the beyond and may give his or her vital force to innumerable other descendants. In fact, the more this is done, the better it is for the particular ancestor's vital force and for the family, lineage, or clan concerned. In this sense, the name is a verb, an act of resurrection that raises the person whose name is con-

---

[26]C. Nyamiti, "The Naming Ceremony in the Trinity: An African Onomastic Approach to the Trinity," in *CHIEA African Christian Studies*, 4:1 (1988), p. 42.
[27]Parrinder, *West African Psychology*, pp. 118-9.

ferred from the dead to become present, as it were. It also necessitates that the person named live and act according to the name. The naming rite signifies that the transmission of life is completed. It is a matter of grave concern if a baby dies without having been ritually named. Such babies are said to be taken by spirits and they themselves usually become malevolent spirits bent on destroying life.

A person usually enjoys more than one name, even though one of them will be more widely used than the others. As both Geoffrey Parrinder and Henri Junod have observed,[28] names are conferred according to circumstances of birth, likeness to ancestors or elders, or by choice of an ancestor or divinity through some sort of oracle or revelation. Thus, a person may be named *Tabu, Mashaka* (Kiswahili, East Africa), or *Mashiku, Makoye* (Kisukuma, Tanzania). These are personal names generally denoting hard times. Such names are often used for historical reasons, bringing to mind the difficult times that existed at the time the person was born. In this sense, they are negative re-presentations: they make present to the person, the family, and the clan those difficult historical circumstances. The real significance of these names, however, lies in their active, ethical demands of all concerned. Naming implies much more than memory: Memory for what? Why recall these particular circumstances?

The ethical significance is that the historical situation is recalled so that the person and the community will do all they can to prevent the same situation from occurring again. Recalling actualizes in the present the responsibility to create a new social, political, or economic order in which everyone can enjoy a full life. The logic is the same with names expressing desirable occasions, events, and physical or moral qualities. In naming a child Hope (*Tumaini* in Kiswahili), Love or Charity (*Pendo*), Good Luck (*Bahati*), Income (*Faida*) and so on, it is expected the child will be a living expression of these qualities and a reminder to others of their importance, again for the sake of preserving the vital force of the clan. All this is done in the name and power of God and the ancestors.

---

[28]See G. Parrinder, *Religion in Africa* (Baltimore, Maryland: Penguin Books, 1969), p. 80, and Junod, *The Life of a South African Tribe, Vol. I,* pp. 38-9.

To the same extent as the living members of the family, if not more so, the ancestors are directly interested in and concerned about the birth of a new baby into *their* community, *their* clan. It is important to note that in birth, in most cases, it is an ancestor's vital force that returns to earth in the person named. "The children's children, after they have matured, take over the roles of their mother's parents" among the Zaramo of Tanzania indicating their presence again in the visible world. "A mother's mother can be heard to rejoice at the maturing feast of her daughter's son because it is her 'wedding.' "[29] An informant in western Kenya told Gideon Were that "if a child cried persistently the people just knew that the dead ones had come back so that they might be named after. For example, if I begot a baby and he cried endlessly I would know that my late father Wambati is the one disturbing him. He would ask me to name the child after him. When we name the child Wambati (after my father) my late father will be pleased saying: 'My son has given my name [i.e., my identity] to his child.' "[30]

It is not surprising, then, that the child is often perceived to take on the physical and (later, as it matures) the moral characteristics of the ancestor after whom it is named. It is expected to live these characteristics, to lead a virtuous and exemplary life in whatever sphere of life the ancestor in question excelled. In ideal circumstances, the child is reared and socialized to realize these virtues. In this way, the connection between the living community and that of the living dead is preserved and strengthened. Through remembrance in naming, the vital force of the ancestors is transmitted to the entire clan. Likewise, naming people after events, seasons, locations, and other things preserves the connection between the rest of creation and humanity. It is also a reminder that the life force of humanity and that of nature are intertwined and inseparable.

In studying the peoples of western Kenya, Wagner has identified three types of names an individual might bear. The first is the

---

[29]L. W. Swantz, *The Role of the Medicine Man among the Zaramo of Dar es Salaam,* Thesis, mimeo (Tanzania: The University of Dar es Salaam, 1974).
[30]G. S. Were, *Essays on African Religion in Western Kenya* (Nairobi: East African Literature Bureau, 1977), p. 13.

person's childhood name. This informal name is usually conferred by the mother, grandmother, or any intimate relative of the
child, and is often a "pet" name or a name of endearment,
whether it refers to an ancestor, circumstances of birth, or perhaps is just a fond description of the child. Some of these names
also express a person's perception of her/his social environment.
Among the Kiga of Uganda, for example, such names as
Tibanyendera or *Tibenderana* (They Do Not Want Me, They Do
Not Love One Another), or among the Haya in Tanzania *Tiben-
dakarungi* (They Do Not Want a Good Thing), signify envy.

The second type of name is the adolescent name. One confers
this name on oneself or it is given by one's peers. These usually
laudatory "nicknames" often replace the names conferred at
birth. They either describe one's beauty or prowess or have no
meaning at all, having been chosen because of their sound or, in
the case of boys, merely for their coarseness. Since they are names
taken after initiation, they indicate an individual is in a new stage
of life and enjoys a certain amount of independence that has to
be reckoned with.

The most important name, as Wagner has noted, is the one cer-
emoniously bestowed upon the child some days after its birth.
This is the ancestral name, variously referred to as the "name of
the stomach," "the name of the umbilical cord," "the inner
name," or "the spirit name." Its significance is that it effectively
incorporates the child into the clan and lineage. With this name,
the child is finally "taken possession of" by the clan. The name
is sacred, touching the very core of the person; it may not be
bandied about, particularly in jest, as it belongs first of all to the
ancestors and elders who deserve respect. Perhaps that is why it
is not frequently used except for serious occasions.[31]

The ancestral name is chosen with great care, very often with
the aid of a diviner or an elder taking on the role of a diviner. The

---

[31]See Wagner, *The Bantu of Western Kenya*, pp. 313-22. J. Maquet, *Civilizations of Black Africa*. Trans. by J. Rayfield (New York: Oxford University Press, 1972) explains it in this way: "An individual is defined by his
name; he *is* his name. This is an inside name which is never lost, and is distinguished from the second name given on the occasion of an increase of
strength, such as the circumcision name, the chief's name received at investi-

ancestors themselves, as we have seen, give some indication that they would like to be named through dreams or other forms of revelation. The most usual one is through crying, a means the ancestors use to disturb the child and call attention to themselves. So the elders respond, referring to an ancestor: " 'Situma, if you are the one disturbing the child, leave him alone!' If Situma was the one causing the trouble the child would often stop crying. Similarly if it was Walubengo the child would stop crying."[32] It would then be named after that particular ancestor.

Wealth, health, strength, mental vigor, power, and eloquence are characteristics sought in naming and invocations at naming ceremonies amply illustrate this. In West Africa, a child is shown the moon with the words: "Look at the moon, little one; we bless you at the coming of the new moon. When you see the moon, you see riches, prosperity, and long life."[33] In northern Nigeria, a parent may offer a sacrifice and pray to an ancestor: "I give you this cock and this infant; watch him; take care of him; see that his mother and he be always in good health."[34] And a medicine man of the Thonga of South Africa may present the child to the ancestors with a similar invocation: "This is the child! May he grow! May he become a man by means of this medicine of mine! May his perspiration be good; may impurity go away . . . "[35] As Wagner writes, "Once the spirit has accepted the role of guardianship . . . the latter has no more to fear from him." The conviction is proverbially expressed that "A spirit after whom a child has been named never harms his namesake." But what if expectations for the child's health do not materialize? As Wagner notes, this would be due to other malevolent powers:

---

ture, or the diviner's name received upon his possession by a spirit. The inside name is the indicator of a person's individuality within his lineage. For no man is isolated: he 'constitutes a link in the chain of vital forces, a living link, both active and passive, fastened by the top to the link of his ascending line, and supporting at the bottom the line of his descent' " (p. 106).

[32] Were, *Essays on African Religion in Western Kenya*, p. 14.

[33] Quoted by Parrinder, *West African Religion*, p. 97.

[34] Quoted by W. C. Willoughby, *The Soul of the Bantu: A Sympathetic Study of the Magico-Religious Practices and Beliefs of the Bantu Tribes of Africa* (Garden City, New York: Doubleday, Doran & Company, 1928), p. 186.

[35] Quoted by Junod, *The Life of a South African Tribe, Vol. I*, p. 55.

Should the child get seriously ill . . . it does so owing to the evil work of a sorcerer or another spirit and in spite of the protection granted by its name-spirit, but not because the latter has withdrawn his protection or even reversed his attitude by sending harm to the child. The kind of protection which the name-spirit will offer is the same as that granted by other spirits whose good will one has secured by the performance of sacrifices. He tries to dissuade other spirits from sending harm to his ward and even summons them for assistance if harm threatens the child from other mystical agents, such as sorcerers and witches.[36]

Among the Bantu of western Kenya, "A person does not enter into any communication with the spirit after whom he has been named, nor is it necessary to make regular offerings to him. When sacrifices are offered to the ancestral spirits, the name-spirit is called along with the others to partake of the meal, but there are no special sacrifices addressed exclusively to him."[37] This is understandable. Since the communion between the ancestor and the descendant are so close, in fact, since they are to all intents and purposes one person, sharing an identical power of life, appeasement does not make sense.

INITIATION: CONFIRMATION OF THE VITAL FORCE

Between birth and puberty much goes on in a person's life: many rites are performed and many prayers are said to enhance the individual's vital powers. The individual also learns the traditions and patterns of life of the family, the village and the clan, through the pure curiosity of a child, but also through various forms of instruction from the parents, the neighbors, the grandparents, and the peers. The Fang people of Gabon in West Africa insist that it is important for adults to enhance in every possible way the "strength, intelligence, capacity for work, and ability to exercise authority" in children. As James Fernandez discovered,

---

[36]Wagner, *The Bantu of Western Kenya*, p. 318.
[37]Ibid., p. 318.

for them "the instruction the individual received in childhood was crucial in determining whether these capacities would be exercised in prosperous tranquility or would instead be frustrated and lead to heart-sickness and disorder."[38] But the most significant instruction on the life of the clan, the individual's rights and responsibilities in society, and the transition from childhood to adulthood is achieved only at or around puberty during the process of initiation. This is the time when the individual's vital force and the power of life generally are formally confirmed and imprinted indelibly in the individual's rational consciousness. If there is a time in the African person's life during which a veritable "forest of symbols," to use Victor Turner's phrase, is employed for the sake of instruction, it is during this period of initiation.[39]

Initiation, of course, does not refer exclusively to induction into physiological maturity, as is often reductionistically thought. It refers inclusively to all those rites that Arnold van Gennep[40] calls "rites of passage," or which can otherwise be referred to as "moments of crisis" that span the period from birth to death. In African religion, initiation also refers to the process of induction into certain groups and societies, blood-friendships, oaths of secrecy, or commitments to a certain cause, and so on. Thus van Gennep usefully distinguishes between "physiological puberty" and "social puberty," the former having to do with physical maturity and the latter with social maturity (the age of majority) or binding social arrangements.[41] In a sense, the two coincide, since every type of initiation has physical, psychological, and sociological elements, but in most African societies, distinctively social initiation rites usually follow the puberty rites of physical maturity. Yet, their moral implications are more or less identical.

Beginning with initiation into physiological adulthood, the

---

[38]J. W. Fernandez, *Bwiti: An Ethnography of the Religious Imagination in Africa* (Princeton, New Jersey: Princeton University Press, 1982), p. 197.

[39]V. Turner, *The Forest of Symbols: Aspects of Ndembu Ritual* (Ithaca and London: Cornell University Press, 1967). This is one of the most useful books on this subject.

[40]A. van Gennep, *The Rites of Passage*. Trans. by M. B. Vizedom and G. L. Caffee (Chicago: The University of Chicago Press, 1960).

[41]Ibid., pp. 65ff.

process of initiation usually includes five significant steps: seclusion, instruction, physical impression (either actual or symbolic), integration, and covenant. Jomo Kenyatta has argued quite correctly that this process, appropriately called *mabura* in Gikuyu, denotes "divine services," incorporates the moral code of the ethnic group, and "symbolizes the unification of the whole tribal organization."[42]

At the beginning of the process of initiation, the initiates are usually physically removed from the mainstream of society and sent to a secluded place where they have practically no contact with people from their community. This is a time of great physical and psychological stress as the initiates do not know their status in society. The community is telling them in a very radical way that without membership in a community a person is nothing. The individual, alone, literally does not exist; their seclusion signals their state of limbo. Not having received formal instruction, they do not properly understand the significance of the community's socio-religious customs. They certainly do not know what awaits them in the future. This situation of ambiguity gives the impression that the initiates have neither family nor community support: "What would I do if I suddenly became sick? If we were attacked? If my folks back in the village needed my help?"

Learning the values of cooperation and sharing and the central importance of belonging to a family, a clan, and a community as an integral and responsible member constitutes this initial phase of the initiation process. Just as one is nothing without belonging to a community, the community disintegrates somewhat without the membership and contribution of everyone. Therefore, seclusion signifies the death from which the initiates will be delivered only by integration into the community after the initiation process.

These symbolic and practical lessons are followed immediately (and in some cases simultaneously) with formal, pointed, and clear verbal instruction concerning the duties, responsibilities, and rights entailed in belonging to a community. The wis-

---

[42]J. Kenyatta, *Facing Mount Kenya: The Tribal Life of the Gikuyu* (London: Secker and Warburg, 1956), p. 134.

dom of the community is imparted during this stage—the wisdom of the ancestors, religious wisdom, wisdom for living well and fully for one's own sake and for the sake of the community. The proverbs, riddles, songs, and dances, as well as other sources of ancestral wisdom used in this period, exude moral guidance. They are, in the words of Aylward Shorter, "especially associated with the socialization of the young and this learning process continues through life by means of the occasional songs which help to communicate and perpetuate the traditional understanding of the world and people's attitudes towards it."[43]

A primary purpose of this instruction through ancestral wisdom is, once again, to impress upon the initiates the intimate connection between human life and the rest of creation. This is evident, first of all, in the genre of the method of instruction. Shorter explains how "The proverb borrows an image, often from the world of nature, and applies it to a particular human situation . . . [and how] didactic songs employ a wide range of images taken from the vegetable, animal and human worlds."[44] Instruction underlines the relationship between a human community and a given physical environment, the truth that human life "resembles nature, from which neither the individual nor society stands independent."[45]

The phase of formal instruction stresses five areas of ethical concern in the life of the individual and society: religion, the mystery of life and death, domestic and social virtues, sex and sexuality, and forms of self-identity.[46] The connectedness of these five concerns is emphasized. The most central theme among them is, of course, the absolute value of life. God as the Great ancestor gives life, but human ancestors guard it. The ruler must protect life in the immediate community by seeing to it that the community observes the ethical demands of religion. The ruler must himself or herself be an initiated person who stands as an example of

---

[43]A. Shorter, *Songs and Symbols of Initiation: A Study from Africa in the Social Control of Perception* (Nairobi: Catholic Higher Institute of Eastern Africa - Monograph One, 1987), p. 1.
[44]Ibid., p. 1.
[45]Van Gennep, *The Rites of Passage,* p. 3.
[46]Shorter, *Songs and Symbols of Initiation,* pp. 5-6.

the vitality of life, for the ruler's vitality signifies and influences "the necessary conditions of life, rain, harvests, forest produce and peace."[47]

It is not surprising that one of the areas emphasized in instruction is sexuality. Instruction in this area is exhaustive as the transmission of life and the preservation of the life force depends on sexuality. Coded language is almost always used, but there is little doubt about its meaning: sexual enjoyment is good, but it must be accompanied by sexual responsibility. This responsibility, applied strictly in the initiation camp, extends to the village as well during this time as a reminder. As Junod describes it among the Thonga, "Sexual intercourse is strictly prohibited to all initiates, men as well as shepherds [i.e., those guarding the initiates, elsewhere called 'tutors,' 'sponsors' or 'guardians']; breaking this law would kill the circumcised [or those to be]. Therefore the men must not go home, or at least as seldom as possible . . . [during the whole period of initiation]. Married people in the village may have sexual relations; but there must be no noise, no quarrels between jealous co-wives."[48]

Most African ethnic groups find it necessary to impress the lesson of the concern for life physically on the body of the initiate at least once in a lifetime. Some others do it symbolically at each crisis moment in life. But for those in the first category, this is the most intense and concentrated moment in the initiation process. As a rule, it involves some sort of surgery. Circumcision or scarification of parts of the body are the usual types of operation for boys. For girls initiation may involve clitoridectomy, the excision or enlargement of the labia, perforation of the ears or lips, scarification of parts of the body, or a combination of these. At any rate, the operation is always deliberately intensely painful.

The main features of this initiation surgery are similar throughout Africa. Wagner and Kenyatta describe clearly what takes place. At the circumcision of the boys in western Kenya, according to Wagner, "The operator's attire is very much the same among all the tribes. He dresses himself up so as to look as

---

[47]Ibid., p. 6.
[48]Junod, *The Life of a South African Tribe, I*, p. 80.

fierce and awe-inspiring as possible. His face, the upper part of his body, and his arms and legs are painted with streaks of white, red, and black paint; round his face he ties a head-dress of colobus monkey-skin (*enduviri*), round the waist a leopard-skin, and iron rattles round his legs." Everything is calculated to inspire fear; yet what is indented on the part of the boys is courage. Thus, "While the candidates line up to be circumcised the operator dances about wildly, jumping up and down in an abrupt rhythm and dashing towards the boys brandishing his knife, thereby showing his impatience 'to be let loose' on the boys. The candidates, however, must not be intimidated by his antics. Among the Vugusu they are even expected to rush forward individually and try to beat the operator with their *dzinundu*-sticks [a kind of clubbed stick or knobkerrie] to show that they defy his challenge."[49]

The boys are watched "for any signs of flinching or faltering," notes Wagner. "If one of them tries to catch the operator's hand or to run off at the last moment he is held by his clansmen and afterwards has to listen to songs of derision, sung by the girls and women who dance in front of the initiates while they sit in the shade of a tree waiting for the wound to stop bleeding. Moreover, to stamp such a boy as a coward, the operator bedaubs his face with streaks of blood which he must not wash off for several days."[50] Among the Kipsigis of Kenya, a boy who shows signs of fear finds that everyone, "men and women, will shrink from him, and his life will be one of continual humiliation; so that eventually he may make up his mind to move to a far-away place, where nobody has heard of his shame."[51]

The case among the Gikuyu is similar. Kenyatta has described the operation of the girls among his Gikuyu people. When the time comes, the girls are prepared very well by their sponsors, and precautions are taken to minimize bleeding. Each girl is expected not to show emotion or any sign of fear during the oper-

---

[49]Wagner, *The Bantu of Western Kenya*, p. 348.
[50]Ibid., p. 351.
[51]J. G. Peristiany, *The Social Institutions of the Kipsigis* (London: George Routledge & Sons, 1939), p. 14.

ation, for that would be a disgrace to her. "When this preparation is finished, a woman specialist, known as *moruithia,* who has studied this form of surgery from childhood, dashes out of the crowd, dressed in a very peculiar way, with her face painted with white and black ochre. This disguise tends to make her look rather terrifying, with her rhythmic movement accompanied by the rattles tied to her legs. She takes out from her pocket (*mondo*) the operating Gikuyu razor (*rwenji*), and in quick movements . . . proceeds to operate upon the girls. With a stroke she cuts off the tip of the clitoris (*rong'otho*)."[52]

Once again, it must be emphasized that this ritual is a celebration of courage; that is the purpose behind inflicting pain. E. C. Baker, a colonial administrator in the North Mara district of Tanzania (then Tanganyika), captures this aim very well in his description of the operation among the Bakuria youth. What he noticed among those attending the ceremony was the community emphasis on physical and, by implication, moral courage. He characterizes the attitude required of the initiates as "stoicism."[53] In the same vein, the Gikuyu, on their part, sing immediately after the operation: "Our children are brave . . . Did anyone cry? No one cried."[54] And, in many cases, this is not the end of pain inflicted on the initiates. Junod describes the "trials" that Thonga initiates have to undergo before integration. They include blows "on the slightest pretext," withholding drinking water from them, serving them unsavory food, and so on.[55] Similarly, among the Bambuti Colin Turnbull found a series of ordeals for the initiates that lasts for a considerable amount of time after circumcision. The initiates are frequently beaten and made to run, regardless of the fact that they have not yet fully healed from the operation. They are not supposed to show any signs of flinching when they are thus treated, otherwise they are whipped even

---

[52]Kenyatta, *Facing Mount Kenya,* pp. 145-6. For initiation processes among the peoples of West Africa, see Parrinder, *West African Religion,* pp. 95-114.
[53]Baker, *The Bakuria of N.M. Tarime,* mimeo., n.d., p. 103.
[54]Ibid., p. 146.
[55]Junod, *The Life of a South African Tribe, I,* pp. 84-5.

more.[56] Without courage among the youth, the life force of the clan withers and will eventually die. For if the young men of the community are cowards who will then defend the people? Similarly, will there be live births if the mothers-to-be cannot bear pain, namely, the pain of childbirth?

An additional purpose of this stoicism or, to use Aylward Shorter's expression, "sublimation of pain,"[57] is to teach a lesson in self-giving. It is to impress upon the initiate, in one intense, unforgettable moment, the reality of life and its requirements for the living. An initiation operation gives a clear message that to be self-giving and to sacrifice oneself for the sake of the community is an essential aspect of life, even if this means pain or may even demand extensive suffering. Furthermore, the operation is intended to tell the initiate that to know oneself and to appreciate the worth of others demands self-denial and a certain amount of suffering. Even to enjoy pleasure—and this is the lesson intended among those ethnic groups where an open expression of pain during the operation is permitted—some suffering is inevitable. This is why, then, that in many cases the surgery is performed on the sexual organs or parts of the body that are generally very sensitive, on the one hand and, on the other, are associated in one way or another with fertility.

The initiation operation also establishes the young person's identity as a member of a certain ethnic group and unites him or her in a very special way with the group's ancestors. The initiates are also united very closely themselves, forming an age-set or age-group. By mingling and sharing their blood by way of the initiation knife, or because they shed it at the same time, they become truly brothers or sisters, and must be ready to defend one another as brothers and sisters would do. This bond of relationship cannot be easily broken. Thus, the initiation operation leaves an indelible mark on a spot of the body not easily ignored that

---

[56]C. M. Turnbull, "Initiation Among the Bambuti Pygmies of the Central Ituri," in S. and P. Ottenberg, eds., *Cultures and Societies of Africa* (New York: Random House, 1960), p. 427.

[57]Shorter, *African Culture and the Christian Church*, p. 190.

reminds a young person of his or her place, responsibility, and rights in society.

Among those ethnic groups that do not use an initiation operation, the period of seclusion tends to be longer and is used for instruction in communion and solidarity with the ancestors and with the clan. Among the Zaramo, Lloyd Swantz observed that seclusion takes anywhere from one to three years for girls, "from the time of their first menstruation until the coming out ceremony, which is generally the day of their marriage."[58] This is not unusual among other African peoples. The instructions given and rites performed during this time concern fertility, maintaining the best in a human being as an individual and for the community to which one belongs. A myth recited to the Zaramo adolescent girls illustrates this value, which is pervasive in the initiation process. It involves the earth, which is equated to "Nyalutanga, a proto female who is said to have come from the earth, the origin of life. The earth was the great womb which gave birth to Nyalutanga, the first human being. She gave birth to the people who populated the earth and began the custom of instructing the adolescent girl. Without this instruction they would not grow up to be human, nor would they be able to bear children."[59]

The lessons that the Zaramo wish to impart during the initiation period are the same as those of the Temne of Sierra Leone and of African Religion in general: discipline and cooperation. As Vernon Dorjahn has reported with reference to the Temne's *Poro* society, discipline entails "submission to authority without question," and cooperation, "keeping secrets, . . . [and] abiding by established rules."[60] Everything of value to the life of the individual and society is imparted here: moral requirements; legal expectations; techniques for survival, such as farming and gardening; social and aesthetic requirements, most of which are not known to non-initiates and are under strict embargo until this time.[61]

---

[58]Swantz, *The Role of the Medicine Man,* p. 141.

[59]Ibid., p. 49.

[60]V. R. Dorjahn, "The Initiation and Training of the Temne *Poro* Members," in S. Ottenberg, ed., *African Religious Groups and Beliefs: Papers in Honor of William R. Bascom* (Chanakya Puri, Sadar: Archana Publications, 1982), p. 46.

[61]Ibid., pp. 46-7.

After the operation, when the initiates are healing or have completely healed, they are reintegrated into society. Integration or incorporation, which forms the last stage of the formal initiation process, implies a rebirth, a resurrection. It is meant to signify and effect the initiates' physical and moral maturity, that they have been approved by the ancestors of the clan and ethnic group. They are now part and parcel of the community of the living, the living-dead, and the yet-to-be-born; this community is one union whose whole purpose is, once again, the maintenance and furtherance of life. Integration means that the initiates are ready to get married and have children. This is what has been taught verbally and symbolically during initiation, through action, riddles, stories, songs, dance, and even instructive silence—those with children have nothing to fear here or hereafter.

A version of the instruction given by a father to a newly initiated son sums it up. Using partly coded language, the young man is first told that he now is ready for adult responsibilities, the most important of which is marriage. "My son," he is admonished, "you have left behind 'the mother's cloth' (i.e., the prepuce), but now you are given the father's cloth . . . If you come to a house and it is closed do not open it to enter. The closed door is not for you, only the open door is yours. If you find an old woman who has one eye [i.e., unmarried], go and build (a hut) for her. She will cook food for you in peace." Then the importance of respect for age in general is impressed upon him: "If you see an old man call him father and treat him as a father. If he tells you to go on an errand for him accede to his request. If you find him cutting or carrying the grass help him. If you 'sit in the beer' (i.e., if you are attending a beer-drink) and you are a strong boy and you see another boy troubling an old man, help the old man and fight the strong boy who is troubling him. If an old man calls you 'my strength' reply to him, 'Here I am, your strength.' " Age in general is to be respected, but this is even more true of old age in women, because women are mothers. Thus the young man is advised: "If you meet an old woman carrying water or wood or other heavy things, help her as you help your mother and call her 'mother.' If she begs you to cut grass for her or to help her digging do not say, 'Who are you, old woman, do not trouble me!' but go and help her in peace." Finally, the instruction underlines the importance of good social conduct, peace-making, and self-respect. The young man is reminded: "A good boy will always eat the secret things [reserved pieces of choice]. Friendship is always better than (to have) many things in the house or the possession of many cattle. Now you are a man. If you see the people quarreling tell them: 'Do not quarrel,' and if you find people hurting each other stop them. Now you are a man. No longer ride a cow or an ox! Do not dance about standing on one leg, because this is childish and a disgrace for a man."[62]

The initiation process, which turns a youth from a boy or girl into a man or woman, points to marriage as the most basic expression of the desire to maintain life. Without its consummation in marriage, initiation remains incomplete. Whatever else a person has or is, without marriage and children, one is nothing. Indeed, such a person is seen to be damned, a lost soul. Without marriage and children, a person is most likely already "rotten" in religious terms, that is, completely dead. Thus, marriage and procreation have the greatest importance in the moral thought of African Religion.

AGE-SETS, BLOOD PACTS, SOCIETIES, AND JOKING RELATIONSHIPS

Besides the confirmation of life by connection with the ancestors through formal induction into the ethnic group, initiation is also intended to instill courage, endurance, good manners, faithfulness to the clan, and to be an unforgettable reminder to the individual concerning the fulfillment of religious requirements for the perpetuation of life. But initiation also underlines the realization that within the social organization an individual is required to show special loyalty to certain personal or group-relations as a way of strengthening the whole society. This applies more particularly to the menfolk of a group, since they remain in

---

[62]Recorded by Wagner, *The Bantu of Western Kenya, I,* p. 365.

the same clan throughout their life, and therefore these relationships are more relevant to them. Women's group-relations exist
in some societies, but they do not hold the same significance.
They are normally of short duration, lasting only as long as the
group of females is unmarried. At marriage, as R. G. Abrahams
observed among the Labwor of Uganda, women automatically
share the status of their husband's group, "for example with
regards to some forms of dance, song and ornamentation, and
secondly to the extent that male age-group assemblies assert the
right to deal with some sexual offenses and to discipline the
unmarried girls of the community . . . "[63]

The most significant group-relation, established by the very
fact of initiation, is the institution of age-sets, sometimes referred
to as age-grades, age-classes, or age-groups. This ascribed and
compulsory relationship is usually formed through social and not
strictly biological maturation. It is to be distinguished, but not
separated, from generation grades that rely on genealogical generation.[64] Age-sets are also to be distinguished from voluntary
pacts of blood friendship, secret or open societies or organizations, and joking relationships. (Chapter seven will include a discussion of the political significance of these relationships.) The
socio-religious importance of age-sets is that they are used to
manage social complications that could be detrimental to the
force of life. Thus, they promote the overall life of society.

Among some ethnic groups, age-set systems involve compli-

---

[63]R. G. Abrahams, "Aspects of Labwor Age and Generation Grouping and
Related Systems," in P. T. W. Baxter and U. Almagor, eds., *Age, Generation
and Time: Some Features of East African Age Organisations* (New York: St.
Martin's Press, 1978), p. 39.

[64]"A genealogical generation is one which consists of men who share the
same genealogical level, that is one which consists of men who are all of the
generation of fathers and uncles and are followed by their sons and nephews
who form the succeeding generation. An uncle and a nephew cannot ever be
of the same genealogical generation. What we call here a shifting social generation consists of men who are grouped, in effect, into clusters of similar
age, status, etc. Uncles and nephews many be members of the same shifting
social generation . . . In many generation-systems the larger groupings are
genealogical generations and the age-groups into which they are internally

cated technical chronology and stratification.[65] Briefly, however, all males of a given ethnic group are usually classified into three or four categories: children, initiates, young initiated adults (warriors), and elders. In some cases, the initiates and young adult men are fused into one category of warriors. Obviously, this classification has something to do with a person's age.[66] But the most significant determining factor for an age-set in African Religion is the socio-religious institution of initiation. Initiation is the time when new members are inducted into the ethnic group and when a person's status and responsibility in the clan begin to be clearly determined, delineated, and consciously appropriated. All young people initiated together form an age-set. Jomo Kenyatta has shown that such people enjoy a special social and moral bond of "loyalty and devotion" with one another. "Men circumcised at the same time stand in the very closest relationship to each other," no matter where age-set members were initiated or currently may be. "When a man of the same age-group injures

---

segmented are narrow-span shifting social generations. Moreover each sort of generation has arbitrary features which create anomalies. Genealogical generations group men of disparate, even contradictory, ages, stages of development and social positions. Social generations must have hazy boundaries because men slide imperceptibly from one into the other. Self-definition of generation is likely to vary with situation, so that the same man may seek at one time the deference due to grey hairs and at another the privileged camaraderie of youth. Also assessment by others is unlikely to be unanimous, to a twenty year old a man of forty is an elder whereas to someone of seventy he is still a youngster." P. T. W. Baxter and U. Almagor, "Introduction," in Baxter and Almagor, eds., *Age, Generation and Time*, p. 7.

[65]There are numerous anthropological studies on this point. See, for example, the monumental study by H. C. Fleming, *The Age-grading Cultures of East Africa: An Historical Inquiry* (Ann Arbor, Michigan: University Microfilms, 1965); Baxter and Almagor, eds., *Age, Generation and Time*. Also G. W. B. Huntingford, "Nandi Age-Sets," in Ottenberg, *Cultures and Societies*, pp. 214-26; also in the same volume, M. Wilson, "Nyakyusa Age-Villages," pp. 227-36; G. Wagner, *The Bantu of Western Kenya*, pp. 373-8; and G. Schroder and D. Seibel, *Ethnographic Survey of Southeastern Liberia: The Liberian Kran and the Sapo* (Newark, Delaware: University of Delaware, 1974), pp. 97-116.

[66]Particularly among those ethnic groups that do not have a stringent initiation process, such as the Nyakyusa. See Wilson, "Nyakyusa Age-Villages," pp. 227-36.

another it is a serious . . . offence. They are like blood-brothers; they must not do any wrong to each other. It ranks with an injury done to a member of one's own family."[67]

Therefore, age-set members have the serious responsibility of looking out for one another and protecting each other's name and property. They are one in a very special way, having spilled their blood (the energy of life) to cross the threshold of adulthood (to acquire an even stronger life force) together and at the same time. As a rule they are called and refer to each other as brothers, and often as twins. The members of a given age-set consider the parents of each one of them as "father" and "mother," and their female siblings usually as "sisters," and accord them appropriate respect. However, the wife of one of them is, in principle, considered to belong to all of them, not normally in a sexual sense of right of intercourse (although in strictly prescribed situations this may happen among some individuals in certain ethnic groups), but in a social sense.

E. E. Evans-Pritchard illustrates more clearly the relationships that age-sets create among the Nuer, noting that family relationships determine the perception and language of relationships between age-sets. The idiom of family and kin relationships—father, mother, brother, and sister—is also used for age-set relationships. This means, therefore, that "The members of a man's father's age-set are his 'fathers' and the members of his father's brother's 'age-sets' are . . . also his 'fathers.' The sons of a man's set are his 'sons,' and they may fall into several sets. The wives of members of a man's father's set are his 'mothers,' and the wives of members of his sons' sets are his 'daughters.' " A person considers and refers to all members of his own set as brothers. Nevertheless, the dynamics of the relationship in this latter case do not exactly correspond to those of blood brothers: with blood brothers there exists a strict hierarchical relationship of seniority and juniority translating to an attitude of almost superiority and inferiority. But this is not the case here.[68] Unlike family or kin-

---

[67]Kenyatta, *Facing Mount Kenya*, p. 115.
[68]E. E. Evans-Pritchard, *The Nuer: A Description of the Modes of Livelihood and Political Institutions of a Nilotic People* (Oxford: The Clarendon Press, 1940), pp. 258-9.

ship relationships, therefore, this terminology applied to age-set relationships is not a "differentiating one," as Evans-Pritchard notes, and does not necessarily determine specific age relationships. For "a man commonly addresses all persons much senior to himself as 'father' and 'mother,' all persons much junior to himself as 'son' and 'daughter,' and all persons of about the same age as himself as 'brother' and 'sister.' " Apart from the set of his father or the one immediately preceding his own, all other senior sets constitute a man's fathers- and mothers-in-law, for it is a daughter of the people in these age-sets that he will some day marry. Accordingly, he is very careful in his demeanor in dealings with them.[69]

Age-sets supersede other forms of social organization, particularly that of kinship relationships, in very important life-enhancing ways. As noted above, kinship relationships are always determined by juniority and seniority. Denise Paulme has explained that "within the family there is no equality; instead relations between real brothers [as already indicated] are always in terms of an elder—that is superior—and a younger brother. In external relations lineages present a unified front, a block; within the lineage the elder brother claims his rights and expects mute obedience from his juniors."[70] This structure often causes quite pronounced friction and resentment among siblings. But relations within a given age-set are determined and regulated in terms of the strictest equality, loyalty, group solidarity, and trust. This is one of the most important unifying functions of initiation. For according to G. Dieterlen, "It is only this period of circumcision which can turn a disparate group into a coherent whole, a class of persons within which it is incumbent on everyone to show friendship, confidence and assistance in all spheres of social and private life."[71] Age-set relationships do not stand on ceremony with regard to the status of any of the members. Members of an age-set must always be on familiar and friendly terms, no matter

---

[69]Ibid., p. 259.
[70]D. Paulme, "Blood Pacts, Age Classes and Castes in Black Africa," in P. Alexandre, ed., *French Perspectives in African Studies: A Collection of Translated Essays* (London: Oxford University Press, 1973), p. 76.
[71]Quoted in ibid., p. 78.

what position they hold in society.[72] We may refer to age-sets as levelers, and their purpose is to promote social bonding and cohesiveness. Members of a given age-set celebrate together, perform functions together, help one another in all aspects, and even share punishment when inflicted. In a very real sense, the relationship is that of "all for one and one for all."[73]

Between the different age-sets, relations closely follow the kinship structure, with similar social attitudes. Senior age-sets are to be respected as elders whose vital force is consequently much more significant for the life of the community. Junior age-sets must be subordinate in every way to their seniors. The Nandi (of Kenya) age-set system illustrates this. "Behavior between sets, and the rights and privileges of the warrior set are carefully and jealously guarded, and any attempt on the part of the younger people to infringe them is sternly dealt with. In sexual matters the warriors have rights which are accorded to no other set. The uncircumcised are not supposed to indulge in sexual intercourse at all, while the members of the warrior set are allowed free sexual license."[74] Again, jealousy and bitterness of the junior toward the senior age-sets are naturally present, but they are of short duration and no harm is usually done. When a junior's circumcision time arrives, he "realizes that no harm has been done to him [by being required to be subordinate], and that what he has had to put up with is what many others have been through and sur-

---

[72]There are rare but possible exceptions. Abrahams says that among the Lobwor, for instance, "it is possible in certain circumstances for a person to be promoted into a higher age-group than the one to which he was initially recruited, and a type of situation commonly cited . . . in this context is the one in which three brothers are initially recruited into the same age-group. In such cases it is felt that the eldest of the three should move eventually and probably in middle age into the next group above and, although he is likely to have been a fairly senior member of his original group, such promotion can, it seems, occasionally lead to his belonging to a group senior to that of some persons who were initiated before him. I may add that such promotion will also usually mean that the person concerned becomes a relatively junior member of this new group, and some men refuse promotion for this reason" ("Aspects of Labwor Age and Generation Grouping," p. 42).

[73]See ibid., p. 78.

[74]Huntingford, "Nandi Age-Sets," p. 222.

vived. The effect of the age-set system is a strong factor in discipline, for it must be obeyed and there is no appeal against it."[75] This system maintains the cohesiveness of the society through the structured relationship of humanity to the ancestors.

A relationship that imposes similar demands and duties on the individuals or groups involved, but which is entered into voluntarily, is the blood pact or pact of blood brotherhood. The details of this ritual may differ, but the essentials are the same as those Richard Burton witnessed among the Zaramo (of coastal Tanzania): "The two 'brothers' [-to-be] sat face to face with legs outstretched to the front overlapping one another. Their bows and arrows were placed across their thighs whilst a third person waved a sword over their heads calling curses on anyone that would break the brotherhood. A slaughtered sheep, or more often its heart, was brought roasted to the pair. The two men sealed their vow by making a dagger incision on each other's chest close to the pit of the stomach and smearing a piece of the meat with the other's blood and eating it."[76]

The essential aspect of the pact, as its name implies, is an exchange of blood in some form, either by mixing it with food and eating it or by sucking one another's blood from an incision. Again, the exchange and sharing of blood makes those concerned brothers or even twins and allows one person to live the life of another by "giving one's life over to that other." Blood symbolizes and expresses life. In West Africa, a Malian myth of the origin of blood friendships explains this symbolism. While running away from an enemy, one Diallo gave his tired companion Diakunte a piece of his own flesh to eat, thus assuring the survival of both of them. Through this act of generous self-giving on the part of Diallo, he and Diakunte became brothers, sharing the same blood.[77]

The promotion of life is again the only reason for blood pacts. Between and within groups, they assure complete cessation of hostilities if performed by the legitimate representatives of the

---

[75]Ibid., p. 225.
[76]Cited in L. W. Swantz, *The Zaramo of Tanzania: An Ethnographic Study* (Syracuse University, M.A. 1956, mimeo), pp. 23-4.
[77]Paulme, "Blood Pacts, Age Classes and Castes," p. 74.

groups. They guarantee safe passage in one another's territory and they preclude stealing from or destruction of one another's property. Between individuals, a pact guarantees complete parity, solidarity, and reciprocity, a tie that is usually stronger than kinship ties. Paulme is correct in saying that, "A blood brother . . . is often held to be a closer relation than a real brother; he is the only person to whom you may confide a secret without any fear that he will divulge it."[78] The king of the Swazi, for instance, always has two such "blood friends," called *tinsila*. One is called the *tinsila* of the right side and the other of the left. By sharing the royal blood, they acquire the "power to 'sniff out' any danger which may threaten the king's person; without any conscious effort, but at the risk of their lives, they intercept all evil powers directed against him."[79] The death of one or both of the *tinsila* has to be kept strictly secret because it is tantamount to the death of the king himself. In different ethnic groups sexual relations between the wives of blood friends are permitted or prohibited. In either case, however, the fundamental implication is the same and relates to the fact that a blood pact engenders a very close relationship between individuals or groups. With such a pact two (people or groups) become effectively one; again, they become "twins."

In a very loose sense, but for the same practical purpose, joking relationships between individuals, ethnic groups, blood covenant partners, or certain kin establish some sort of twinning or an intensification of an already existing friendship. As opposed to blood pacts (where blood is involved), we may refer to these relationships, as Angela Cheater does, as "bond friendship." Cheater suggests that the distinction may be seen in terms of the "jural" nature of the former and the "non-jural" character of the latter.[80] In the latter case, as both Paulme and Swantz

---

[78]Ibid., p. 77.
[79]Ibid., p. 85.
[80]A. P. Cheater, "Bond Friendship Among African Farmers in Rhodesia," in J. Argyle and E. Preston-Whyte, *Social System and Tradition in Southern Africa: Essays in Honour of Eileen Krige* (Cape Town: Oxford University Press, 1978), pp. 118-9.

explain,[81] the intention is to diffuse conflict from the very beginning through an institution whose purpose is precisely not to take offense. Thus, the coarsest insults are traded, property is confiscated, and menial services are expected and given between the individuals or communities concerned, but all in good humor. Joking relationships (called *sanaku* among the Malinke and *utani* in Kiswahili of the Zaramo) are thus expressions of more than general intimacy. G. Calame-Griaule describes this relationship as being "characterized by a preference for subjects [for conversation] which are normally forbidden (sexuality, for example) and it attempts to perpetuate an outrage against the person concerned (by personal insults), his family, his property. Nonetheless it is formally prohibited to hurt each other physically or to have sexual relations with persons even if they would otherwise be licit. In other words joking relationships aim at replacing offenses with words which are only seemingly insulting (since they are exchanged 'in the air' so to speak and without having been provoked through any quarreling)."[82]

Besides diffusing *a priori* ambivalent and even potentially conflictual relationships without interfering with the established roles—such as that between cross-cousins, brothers- and sisters-in-law, clans of equal status and military power, and nobles and caste groups or servants—Swantz indicates how in joking relationships there is "On the more serious side . . . a mutual sharing of property. Those with *utani* relations may without asking take food, cow or hen, or clothing. In theory no article may be refused; but, an object might be redeemed for a few cents. Then there always might be an opportunity for the person unduly treated to come to the other's home and take back even more. There is no evidence that this privilege of taking things is misused."[83] As in blood covenants, joking relationships also ensure safe passage through each other's territory, provide assistance for such activities as burials (where dealing with them might be forbidden within the family), receiving privileged consideration in the

---

[81]See Paulme, "Blood Pacts, Age Classes and Castes," pp. 85-95, and Swantz, *The Zaramo of Tanzania*, pp. 22-3.

[82]Quoted by Paulme, "Blood Pacts, Age Classes and Castes," pp. 85-6.

[83]Swantz, *The Zaramo of Tanzania*, p. 22.

bride-wealth where marriage was permitted, and handling medical or religious functions for one another.[84] Between bloodbrothers, joking does not destroy equality and intimacy, but reinforces it. Between a social superior and an inferior, "joking stresses distance and at the same time kindles solidarity." It uses falsehood "in order to render the truth more manifest."[85]

Within the community, voluntary associations or societies, usually secret, preserve its accumulated knowledge, customs, and traditions perhaps more than any other group. K. L. Little quite correctly characterizes them as "cultural specialists"[86] who see to it that right order is maintained within the community in regulating behavior toward sexual relations, in overseeing political and economic well-being, and in various social services such as entertainment and medicine.[87] Initiation into one of these groups is mandatory, and it can be one of the longest and strictest of all forms of initiation. The maintenance of good order in society is stressed during the initiation period, but as in age-sets and blood pacts, comradeship among the members of the association is the fundamental point. The strength of the bond of initiation can be seen in the example of a West African rite. In the Poro society of the Temne, which we have already referred to, "A fowl is seized, its head placed on a large stone and severed by another stone. It is then thrown to the members ... While the head is being severed, a Poro official says a ritual word and to which the boys give the appropriate reply. This is repeated over each fowl in turn, and the ceremony is a warning to the boys to expect the same kind of treatment, if they divulge any Poro secrets to nonmembers."[88]

Dancers and singers, medicine men and women, and people

---

[84]See ibid., p. 23.

[85]Paulme, "Blood Pacts, Age Classes and Castes," p. 95. See also A. R. Radcliffe-Brown, *Structure and Function in Primitive Society: Essays and Addresses* (New York: The Free Press, 1965), pp. 90-116.

[86]See K. L. Little, "The Role of the Secret Society in Cultural Specialization," in Ottenberg and Ottenberg, eds., *Cultures and Societies of Africa*, p. 199.

[87]See ibid., p. 200. See also Dorjahn, "The Initiation and Training of the Temne *Poro* Members," pp. 35-62 and Parrinder, *West African Religion*, pp. 128-36.

[88]Ibid., p. 201.

with special skills often form their own associations. On account of their initiation, or at times prior to it, they claim in most cases to be connected with the spirit of their profession or association, and to act through its power. Some are not loath of boasting of their power. A Sukuma medicine-man, Ng'wana Mang'ondi, described himself as having had to spend "nine years at his master's home sleeping only at the entrance of the house. The result of that is that his master gave him the highest type of magic-medicine by which he can penetrate through any restrictions [obstacles]."[89] The inference of this coded language is that he can now heal all ills.

In conclusion, there is no other purpose to life but fostering life. Herein lies the mystique of life. All rites and rituals from birth to adulthood are meant to solidify this life. All of them connect human beings with other visible elements of creation and with the invisible world of God, the ancestors, and the spirits. All of these forces working together in harmony result in harmony and balance in the world and assure humanity of its good conduct. The opposite is also true. When there is disorder, humanity is to blame and must correct itself. In short, the vital force must be preserved and the way to do so among humanity is through procreation.

---

[89]Pambe, *Symbols and Change in African Beliefs*, p. 206. Also C. R. Hatfield, *The Nfumu in Tradition and Change: A Study of the Position of Religious Practitioners Among the Sukuma of Tanzania, East Africa* (Ann Arbor, Michigan: University Microfilms, 1969), pp. 129-238.

Chapter 4

TRANSMITTING THE VITAL FORCE

The entire process of initiation is, as we have seen in the previous chapter, mainly directed toward marriage and procreation. If the purpose of initiation is to impress upon the initiate the centrality of life in all of the affairs of humanity, and the human person's relationship to the universe, marriage is understood universally in African Religion to be the institution that makes possible the practical expression of the cherished fecundity. It is the acceptable social structure for transmitting life, the life that preserves the vital force of humans, families, and clans. All forms of marriage and its rituals, therefore, are intended to assure that procreation occurs according to the wishes of God and the ancestors, and as abundantly as possible.

MARRIAGE AND KINSHIP

For African Religion marriage involves not only interpersonal relations but also in the final analysis inter-community relations. In marriage, the communities involved share their very existence; in reality they become one people, one "thing," as Africans themselves would put it. Benezeri Kisembo quotes an address by a Zulu pastor to a newly married couple that accurately describes this aspect of African marriage and its social-ethical expectations. Adhering to the principles of African Religion on this matter, the pastor advises the couple that through their marriage, their families and clans are also united, so that what is done to one of their members is done to all. The marriage also means that the partners' responsibilities are not limited to themselves alone, but have a much wider application. Their own personal identity and identification are equally extended. The pastor says to the bride: "Mapule, you should bear in mind . . . that you are married not to your husband Paul, but to his family. That means you have to identify completely with all his relatives, look after them, care for them, go out of your way to make them happy. If you do that, you will have no cause for regret." And to the groom he says: "You, Paul, will have to do likewise with Mapule's relatives. Her people are your people and vice versa. Both of you will notice that old people in the community will tend to visit you, even for a brief moment . . . to show their interest in your welfare."[1]

The survival of kinship in the social structure of Africa depends on marriage. Without going into great detail about these kinship and clan structures, it is important to say something about the relationship between marriage and kinship. What establishes clan relationships to begin with is consanguinity, which is considered to be the primary and most important relationship in the social structure. It is recognized, however, that consanguineal relationships (effected through birth) are not possible without affinal relationships, that is, relationships effected through marriage. In the long run, marriage always establishes very strong bonds between the individuals belonging to different families and clans, particularly when children are born.[2]

Descent configurations among various clans will, of course, greatly differ, as will the terminologies of kin relationship among different clans. These differences will be clearly visible in the various kinship structures.[3] But whether descent structures are patrilineal or matrilineal, unilateral or bilateral, and whatever kinship-relationship terminologies are used, marriage bonds

---

[1]See B. Kisembo et al., *African Christian Marriage* (London: Geoffrey Chapman, 1977), p. 182.

[2]E. E. Evans-Pritchard, *Kinship and Marriage Among the Nuer* (Oxford: Clarendon Press, 1951), p. 96.

[3]Among the numerous works on the subject of kinship in Africa, see A. R. Radcliffe-Brown and D. Forde, eds., *African Systems of Kinship and Marriage* (London: Oxford University Press, 1950) and Evans-Pritchard, *Kinship and Marriage Among the Nuer.*

remain basic to effective relations, which, to various degrees, include relatives of both sides of the marriage partnership. For example, the Bantu of western Kenya, studied by Gunter Wagner, are strongly patrilineal in their clan organizational structure. "However, despite the strong emphasis placed on patrilineal descent the group of relatives with whom the individual maintains effective relations shows a bilateral orientation. The maternal kin is by no means overshadowed by the group of paternal kinsmen."[4] This is equally true among other African peoples such as the Swazi of Swaziland,[5] the Tswana of Botswana,[6] the Yako of Nigeria[7] who have a double descent or double unilineal kingroup system, as well as the Nyakyusa of Tanzania[8] whose village organization is based on age-sets.

Even among matrilineal and matrilocal peoples, as for example among the Akan-speaking Ashanti of Côte d'Ivoire and Ghana, or the rural Bakwaya of Tanzania, bilateral orientation remains a strong feature. In his study of kinship among the Ashanti, Meyer Fortes found that the basis of all social relationships is the bond between the mother and her child. Between the father and the child exists only a bond of love, as a father has no legal rights whatsoever over his children. Instead, this is the prerogative of the mother's brother. Thus, the Ashanti say, "your mother is your family, your father is not." Yet the father is recognized as playing an indispensable role even in this kinship structure. Generally he names his children after his own ancestors, an important religious function, as noted above. Furthermore, by the very fact of his paternity, he is recognized to bequeath his personality or spirit to his children, without which they cannot thrive or succeed in life. He takes pride in bringing up his children and in supervising their moral and civic training.

---

[4]G. Wagner, *The Bantu of Western Kenya: With Special Reference to the Vugusu and Logoli, Vol. I* (London: Oxford University Press, 1949), p. 83.
[5]H. Kuper, "Kinship Among the Swazi," in Radcliffe-Brown and Forde, *African Systems of Kinship and Marriage*, pp. 86-110.
[6]I. Schapera, "Kinship and Marriage Among the Tswana," in ibid., pp. 140-65.
[7]D. Forde, "Double Descent Among the Yako," in ibid., pp. 285-332.
[8]M. Wilson, "Nyakyusa Kinship," in ibid., pp. 111-39.

It is a shame and disgrace for all involved—that is, mother, child and the man—for the latter, as genitor of a child, to deny paternity under any circumstances. On the contrary, kinship bonds and the flow of life are established when paternity is claimed, even in cases of birth out of wedlock. Thus, such a situation is not seen to be so wrong or shameful. On the other hand, it is a crime, of often unpardonable proportions, for a child to disrespect one's father in any serious way, particularly to abuse him verbally or physically assault him.[9]

The Bakwaya of the northeastern part of Lake Victoria are basically a matrilineal people, but among them the bilateral ties of kinship are demonstrated clearly in the influence that both the paternal aunt and the maternal uncle have and claim over a child. Even though the biological father has the responsibility to bring up the child, the allegiance of the child is owed much more strongly to its maternal uncle (mother's brother). Boys are also entitled to inherit from them. Thus the Bakwaya have a saying to the effect that your own child lives only temporarily in your home and that the time will come when it will go where it belongs, that is to its uncles. While your own child is seen to be "a wild cat," your sister's child, however, is "a tame cat" because it will eventually come back to you. Still, reflecting the bilateral ties of kinship, in most major decisions in a child's life, it is the paternal aunt (the father's sister) who has the most, and sometimes the final say. Her title is *seenga* or "female father." Among the Bakwaya, the paternal aunt claims the most exceptional respect of anyone in the family or clan system of relationships. She must be visited frequently by her nieces and nephews; she must be given gifts and choice parts of meat at a feast or whenever an animal is slaughtered for any purpose, such as a funeral or simply to entertain a visitor. Her curse against her brother's children is particularly effective because of her privileged position in the clan structure.[10]

---

[9]M. Fortes, "Kinship and Marriage Among the Ashanti," in ibid., pp. 252-78.
[10]H. Huber, *Marriage and the Family in Rural Bukwaya (Tanzania)* (Fribourg, Switzerland: The University Press, 1973), pp. 193-216.

Because of these relationships established by marriage, as noted by Kisembo and his colleagues, the family created by marriage is the "fundamental element" and the "basic sphere of action" in African relationships. The family is the person's channel of integration into the clan and the wider society. Consequently, "in marrying his wife, . . . [the man] accepted responsibilities towards another family, and she likewise."[11] This social and communitarian character of African marriage means that the two communities are bound so closely together through a marriage that certain conditions, such as a rift between the two communities, can actually nullify a marriage between two persons. Enmity between the clans, notwithstanding any amount of cordiality and love between the two individuals, can not only nullify a marriage, but make it impossible in the first place. The value of marriage is communal, and the couple's consent has validity only in this communitarian social context.

Isaac Schapera investigated marriage and premarital preparations among the Tswana[12] and Kgatla[13] peoples in the southern part of Africa. In both cases he found that families and communities take care to seek out a "wife" or to accept as a "son-in-law" an individual that is suited to their expectations. The qualities preferred in a marriage partner are principally moral qualities. Even though physical qualities are not totally disregarded, they certainly take second place in marriage considerations. As the Kgatla put it, "A pretty girl either steals or wets her bed." They mean by this that physical beauty alone is not the most important thing to look for in a wife.[14] Industry in physical work, a respectful demeanor toward elders, and a generally good reputation as defined by that ethnic group, are the most significant characteristics for both partners. These characteristics are assessed by the qualities of the parents themselves. Wealth on the part of the boy's parents is of course a factor in his favor, but that

---

[11]Kisembo, *African Christian Marriage*, p. 182.

[12]I. Schapera, *A Handbook of Tswana Law and Custom* (London: Oxford University Press, 1955).

[13]I. Schapera, *Married Life in an African Tribe* (Evanston: Northwestern University Press, 1966).

[14]Ibid., p. 40.

is less important than personal character. If any of the men in his family is known or rumored to be sexually inadequate in any way, he is most unlikely to be accepted for marriage. Fertility is the central requirement in marriage. A marriage proposal would be even less likely if there were cases of barrenness among the female members of a girl's family. This might cast doubt on the ability of the whole family to transmit life. But the most serious impediment to marriage is witchcraft, of which impotence, sterility, barrenness, or a generally bad reputation may be considered to be symptoms.[15]

In order to be properly understood, the sexual, reproductive, and relational ethics of African marriage must be located and viewed within the context of relationships that affect the life of two families and communities involved in the marriage union. By "life" is understood not only biological life, but life in its comprehensive sense of the strength of vital forces. It involves love and fidelity, faith and trust, and the promotion of everything that fosters an ever-closer union between the spouses. This is important because it prevents dissension and promotes harmony in a marriage and in this way protects the vital forces. But beyond that, and perhaps paramount to and above everything else, life involves community survival through ancestral fecundity (that is, the preservation of harmonious relationships between the living and the departed). This is what is meant by references to ancestral wisdom. This is a precondition for preserving the harmony of the universe.

Thus marriage concerns not only social factors, but of necessity also economic, political, and religious factors, all of which are inextricably intertwined. The logic of strengthening the force of life at all levels demands that investigations prior to marriage stress all these aspects of life so that the flow of life will not be interrupted. This is also why there is such emphasis on the very serious obligation of everyone to marry. "Since the traditional family had to be large in order to guarantee the material well-being of all its members, of children, of the sick, the disabled and the old," A. K. H. Weinrich explains, "and since this required

---

[15]Schapera, *A Handbook of Tswana Law and Custom*, pp. 127-30.

continuity over time, every person had a moral obligation to marry and to contribute to the social reproduction of his kinship group. This most basic value, to beget or bear children, was instilled in all members of the society from early childhood onwards. Nobody was allowed to shirk this duty . . . "[16]

It is the responsibility of the whole clan to honor this obligation and to help all family and clan members to fulfill it. That is why solidarity within each family and between the families or clans involved in marriage is a basic element of relationships. Solidarity is at the foundation of community. Whereas it may often remain rather dormant, it comes palpably alive and to the fore in the sphere of marriage. Kisembo and his colleagues note that in marriage "the individual family member could count on the moral and material support of his family community whenever he was in need." The authors correctly assert that "It was especially in the vital area of marriage and child-rearing that the family, as a community, exercised its control . . . These things affected the growth and development of the family and its social relations with other family communities in society as a whole."[17] These most vital elements of community life make possible the transmission of life in both its physical and moral expression.

Because of its importance in preserving and transmitting the life-force, proper order is to be maintained every step of the way in marriage preparations and the marriage itself. Proper behavior and procedure are required of the living, but this is even more significant in the relationships between the living and the ancestors. All pertinent rituals and taboos must be observed. The ancestors, guardians of the vital power of their descendants, have a special stake in this step of a person's life, and so they are involved in a very special way. Whatever is done at a marriage ceremony is done in their sight and is, in a sense, dedicated to them. To be abundant, life depends on the ancestors who guard it on behalf of God, wherein lies its origin, and for whom the ancestors are intermediaries. African marriage is ultimately

[16]A. K. H. Weinrich, *African Marriage in Zimbabwe and the Impact of Christianity* (Gweru: Mambo Press, 1982).

[17]Kisembo, *African Christian Marriage*, p. 183.

anchored in God, the main sustainer of life and the principal pre-
server and transmitter of the vital force. For this reason, much of
what takes place in marriage has overtly religious characteristics
and significance.

The living head of the family or clan visibly represents God
and the ancestors. The role of this elder is clearly seen in the significant moments of the marriage process. From the first steps
leading toward betrothal and, in some cases, well into the marriage itself, the rule of avoidance is applied among many groups.
The bride-to-be or bride and her in-laws-to-be or in-laws are forbidden to come into direct physical contact. The same is true of
the bridegroom-to-be or bridegroom. At the very least, there
must be extreme respect, restraint, and distance between them.
The children-in-law must not speak too loudly in the presence of
their parents-in-law; they must not be seen to be gluttons or
drunkards; they may not appear to be irascible or quarrelsome.
On the contrary, they are obliged to be overtly generous and helpful to their in-laws. In many cases, the bride and groom are not
even allowed to speak the proper names of their in-laws.[18] They
address them only as "father" or "mother," which they now
become, other than simply on account of age alone.[19] Among the
Luo, for example,

> If a man meets either of his parents-in-law on a path he
> makes a detour, and if he has to speak to them he does so
> with his back turned to them, especially when he speaks to
> his mother-in-law, who also turns her back to him . . . A
> man who neglects these rules is said to be *wangatek*, to have
> strong eyes, and he makes a gift in compensation for his
> negligence. A man respects the whole lineage into which he
> has married. He can face the younger people but not their
> elders. He respects also the older people of the lineage of his
> wife's maternal uncle, for they are also his *ore*, his in-laws.[20]

[18]Huber, *Marriage and the Family in Rural Bukwaya,* pp. 158-63.
[19]See discussion on age-sets above.
[20]E. E. Evans-Pritchard, *The Position of Women in Primitive Societies and
Other Essays in Social Anthropology* (New York: The Free Press, 1965), pp.
242-3.

Even when some sort of physical contact is allowed, as among the Kran and the Sapo peoples of Liberia, it is for ritual reasons, and then only to emphasize even more the element of respect. Gunter Schroeder and Dieter Seibel explain this custom among the Konobo in that region of Liberia. The father-in-law washes the bride's face and anoints her with chalk on the wedding day to symbolize that she is joined to him through his son and her children are therefore of his lineage.[21] The rite says clearly that, as the person closest to the ancestors in the immediate surroundings, reverence is due him.

In the name of the ancestors, the paterfamilias or a representative designated by custom who has similar social and ethical qualities, blesses and sanctions the marriage. At the reception of cattle for the bride-wealth in Zimbabwe, for example, the father of the bride "called on his ancestors to announce to them solemnly that the cattle had been handed over to him for his daughter, that his daughter would go to another village to bear children for that lineage, and that the ancestors should bless her and make her fruitful."[22] Among the Vugusu and Logoli, very detailed instructions of married conduct are given to the bride at the appropriate time (usually before she goes to her new home) by the senior uncle, maternal uncle, or another senior person in the clan. The young bride is told not only what to do, but is warned about the consequences of not doing so. An example is the warning reported by Wagner of a Vugusu paternal aunt to a bride to emphasize what her maternal uncle had just said: "If you do not understand what your *xotja* [uncle] has said to you, you will be a bad wife and one day you will sleep on the trees and in the bush (i.e., you will have no home)."[23]

Similarly, the Kwaya anointing ritual illustrates the ancestral representation of the elders in the marriage process. On the day before her departure from her father's home, the bride's paternal aunt initiates the ritual by calling the bride to her mother's house.

---

[21]G. Schroeder and D. Seibel, *Ethnographic Survey of Southeastern Liberia: The Liberian Kran and the Sapo* (Newark, New Jersey: Liberian Studies Association in America, 1974), p. 137.

[22]Weinrich, *African Marriage in Zimbabwe,* p. 39.

[23]Wagner, *The Bantu of Western Kenya, Vol. I,* p. 425.

Legs stretched out, she has her sit down "on her mother's sleeping mat, preferably on the one upon which she had been delivered."[24] Her father anoints her first, and then her aunt. The prayer formulae used in this ritual are revealing. Invariably they signify that the bride is soon to be an "elder" in her own right and she is wished blessings in that "task" of keeping life alive and transmitting it. Huber quotes some of the formulae used. To begin with, the bride's father blesses her with words such as these: "My daughter, I have given you a house. Go and live in harmony with your husband! May your womb be clean [i.e., ready for healthy births]!" Then the aunt takes over with a similar injunction: "Today I give you full greatness in your own house, since now you have left childhood and girlhood. Now you have become a woman, you will be called a wife and head of a house. Hold the house, mother! It is greatness that I have given you. May you hold the house!"[25] The central intention is, of course, the maximization of life, "fertility and healthy deliveries," as the aunt finally utters, cursing anyone, even among her own relatives, who might wish otherwise: "We the sisters of the bride's father who have performed the bride's ceremony, should anyone of us hurt the girl spoiling her womb or delivery, such a person, aah! let her die! *Namuhanga* [God] is our witness!"[26]

MARRIAGE AS A MEANS TO ATTAIN FULL HUMANITY

The characteristics constituting the efficacy of African marriage are therefore different from those that apply to marriage that is merely of a statutory nature. Of course, as in all kinds of marriage, significant moments and ceremonies mark the process of African marriage, but the finality of the marriage itself goes far beyond ceremonies. It certainly goes beyond the declaration or ascertainment of personal love and the consent of two individuals. First of all, marriage in Africa is not merely a contract to be

---

[24]Huber, *Marriage and the Family in Rural Bukwaya*, p. 112.
[25]Ibid., p. 112.
[26]Ibid., pp. 114-5.

signed and done with; rather, it is seen as a step-by-step, progressive development undertaken in a community framework. In other words, it is not an end in itself, but a means to an end. At the 1980 Synod of Bishops in Rome, Bishop Andreas Kaseba from Zaire described it as "a very gradual development, a living process, which unfolds stage by stage, each following on the preceding one, right up to the arrival of the bride at the home of the bridegroom." This goes far beyond only one ceremony at one time. There are, on the contrary, numerous ceremonies and rituals of various importance over time and at different locations: "certain stages are celebrated at certain times in the home of the future bride's relatives, at other times in the home of her maternal uncle (in matrilineal societies), at other times again in the home of the young man." Bishop Kaseba points out the ritual, mystical, and pedagogical purpose of this process:

> Each of these stages has a specific reason, and is a constitutive part of the gradual elaboration of the marriage bond. At each stage, the two parties acquire a certain status, with special rights and duties. Whatever the actual number of these stages in various ethnic groups, *the gradual ripening of the union is always taken with the utmost seriousness: the people concerned are all involved in this process of growth which has the aim of leading them to a more solid and lasting union . . . It is the whole process that makes marriage a reality.*[27]

Bishop Kaseba sees this process as "a dynamic whole" whose purpose, among other things, is to create an alliance, "a gradual growing together of partners and families."[28] Aylward Shorter describes it as "diachronic," and notes that it "may be interrupted if the partners prove incompatible, or if essential conditions, such as fertility, appear not to be present. This interruption is not regarded as divorce or dissolution, but simply as the recog-

---

[27]A. Kaseba, "The Marriage Bond as the Result of a Process," in *AFER* 23:1&2 (1981), p. 40. Emphasis in original.
[28]Ibid., p. 40.

nition that a marriage has been attempted but has not come into existence."[29] It is to assure the true meaning and purpose of marriage that the process is taken with such seriousness and that such caveats are in place, for without children—who are proof of the transmission and preservation of the force of life—marriage has no meaning.

As has been mentioned, the stages in the marriage process differ from one ethnic group to another, but their intention is the same. Perhaps it is helpful to describe briefly the more significant of these stages in one ethnic group so as to make their significance a little clearer. I take as an example the practice of the Luo of Kenya, drawing on descriptions of Edward Evans-Pritchard.[30]

Relationship between the sexes in youth is extremely free so young people can get to know one another. There is no stigma for unmarried girls to visit unmarried boys in the latter's huts and to make love-play with them. As among the Gikuyu, it "is considered right and proper and the very foundation stone upon which to build a race morally, physically and mentally sound."[31] But this form of sexual contact (called *ngweko* in Gikuyu) must not be complete intercourse as the loss of the hymen lowers the status of the bride on the day of her marriage. (Among other ethnic groups, such as among the Nuer and Azande[32] and to a lesser extent among the Kgatla,[33] full sexual intercourse was not frowned upon as long as it did not result in pregnancy.) Next begins the courtship stage among the Luo. It is followed by the "abduction" of the bride by a party of the groom's friends. Although there is much resistance and wailing on the part of the girl, and mock battles between the young men from both sides, this is not a real abduction, but pre-arranged. Resistance is a sym-

[29]A. Shorter, *African Culture and the Christian Church: An Introduction to Social and Pastoral Anthropology* (Maryknoll, New York: Orbis Books, 1974), p. 183.

[30]In his work *The Position of Women*, pp. 228-44.

[31]See J. Kenyatta, *Facing Mount Kenya: The Tribal Life of the Gikuyu* (London: Secker and Warburg, 1956), p. 155.

[32]Evans-Pritchard, *Kinship and Marriage Among the Nuer*, pp. 49-58. Also E. E. Evans-Pritchard, ed., *Man and Woman Among the Azande* (New York: The Free Press, 1974), passim.

[33]Schapera, *Married Life in an African Tribe*, pp. 43-55.

bol of the girl's honor and a sign of her reluctance to incorporate her children into another clan. Had it been possible, this is intended to say, she would have preferred to remain with her people and to build up her own clan. Consummation takes place soon after this ceremony at the groom's home.

In reality, this is still courtship; it has not yet become marriage. For about two weeks after the abduction, there are other ritual activities, now at the home of the bride's parents, now at the groom's. By this time the bride has returned to her parents' house and she remains there until some of the bride-wealth has been paid. When enough has been paid, and the groom insists that he can pay no more, the bride's parents let him take her. During this *riso* ceremony, the girl is received at her new home with much rejoicing. She receives many gifts as the new wife of the clan. From now on, she no longer frequents her father's home; she only goes back after some months to ask permission to cook for her husband in her own house, instead of her mother-in-law's, and to collect some household utensils. Both are usually gladly given. At this stage, the courtship is over and married life has begun. But the marriage is not complete until a child has been born. After the birth of a child, preferably a male child, marriage "should not in any circumstances be broken"; the marriage makes binding demands that extend beyond the present life. For now, in the event the wife dies, "she ought to be replaced by her sister." Alternatively, if the husband dies, one of his brothers or relatives must take the widow to raise up offspring for him.[34] These sororate and levirate practices are often demanded by certain expressions of African Religion.

At the conclusion of the marriage through the birth of a child, husband and wife belong completely to one another, and the bond between the two families and communities is sealed. The wife gains a new status, a certain elderhood, among her husband's people. The rules of avoidance are now relaxed, and parents and children-in-law on both sides begin to relate in a more informal manner.[35] The couple's lives are qualitatively more com-

---

[34]Evans-Pritchard, *The Position of Women in Primitive Societies*, pp. 241-2.
[35]Ibid., p. 243.

plete: they have fulfilled the most basic responsibility of their existence as human beings, to themselves and to their communities, by becoming parents.

This journey began after initiation with the primary steps of courtship. The betrothal of a boy or girl created a communion between two families and clans. For the marriage process to continue, all social or political frictions between the two sides must cease. The order of the universe, which demands balance and a sense of harmony, has to be maintained for the marriage arrangement and ultimately the marriage itself to have any meaning. The rituals and ceremonies that take place throughout the process are intended to initiate, establish, and solidify those ties of mutual knowledge and understanding necessary for kinship. The two persons, families, and communities thus begin "to expand," "to be more," and thus to realize their humanity much more because they are now able to live in a larger circle of human beings: "You are a person with others, alone you are an animal." The expansion of the community circle results in togetherness as those involved actualize their full humanity. But what truly completes the humanization of a person in this world is the mystical union with the ancestors, which is achieved only through the generation of children. The moral requirement to transmit life is achieved and the ethical need to preserve life is attained through the actual re-presentation (or making present) of the ancestors through naming. Any "marriage" that does not result in all of these things—in social unity and ancestral communion—is seriously flawed. In fact, as far as African Religion is concerned, it is no marriage.

STABILIZATION OF THE VITAL FORCE BY LEGITIMATION OF CHILDREN

How are the children born of a union made to belong, so that they can enjoy the economic, social, and spiritual status of a certain family or clan? The question is important in every case, but it is highlighted in a situation where the *genitor* and the *pater* are different or, in other words, the physical father is not the same person as the social father. To which family and to which lineage does such a child belong, if belonging is one of the chief elements in being a full person? Which ancestors is the child socialized to look up to? Which spirits are expected to supply it with strength of life and to protect it from malice?

The marriage process normally assures this through the giving and receiving of bride-wealth. Bride-wealth is given not to purchase the woman to be married, as all the negotiations and manner of its "payment" or delivery make clear. It is not possible to discount the economic character of bride-wealth, but as Evans-Pritchard has shown among the Azande, its social and religious implications are much more significant. Among the Azande, the bride-wealth is paid over a long time after the initial token cattle have been given. The rest comes with the birth of children to the woman and, preferably, is completed with the birth of girls. In actual fact, then, in the Zande system, it is these children that provide the bride-wealth for their mother just as, in ideal circumstances, their own daughters will do so for them. Thus, the economic significance of the bride-wealth is largely overshadowed by its unitive, social power and value. For the Azande, therefore, bride-wealth cannot be given all at once because at the beginning the marriage is only a "marriage in embryo." But "as it matures the payment of the bride-wealth and all other customary observances between members of a marriage group become more pronounced."[36] After the birth of a child, the rules of avoidance are relaxed or removed, as we have pointed out, and the woman is truly incorporated among her husband's people, so much so that in the event of her death she must be "replaced" (giving rise to sororate unions). Conversely, if she survives her husband, one of his brothers or relatives must take her in the name of the deceased (levirate unions). And, even in these circumstances of the death of one of the spouses, bride-wealth may continue to be paid. Death does not alter or end marriage relationships.

In terms of kinship, therefore, bride-wealth both cements and expresses kinship ties. "The two families," as M. Angulu Onwue-

---

[36]Ibid., p. 182.

jeogwu argues, "by giving and accepting [it] have created a new pattern of relationships and behavior fully expressed in the avoidance" rules.[37]

Among the Tswana, to take another example, bride-wealth is called *bogadi*. The manner of its delivery is somewhat different from that of the Azande. Whereas among the Azande the payment of the bride-wealth is staggered over a long period of time, the Tswana *bogadi* must all be delivered at once. Although the Tswana system obviously provides a different or alternative approach to the custom of bride-wealth payment, its social and religious value remains the same as in most other ethnic groups in Africa. It is, of course, a form of thanksgiving to the wife's people for the care they have taken of their daughter. It fosters and solidifies bonds of relationship that are difficult to sever. And even though the children belong to another clan, *bogadi* usually gives the woman's children some privileges at her home of origin: they can be sent to grow up there with their maternal grandparents. But, as Schapera notes, the basic point of the bride-wealth has to do with life, the proper identification of the offspring and their confirmation into and within a certain clan whose life is increased on account of their birth. Thus, "No man can claim, for any purpose, the children he has by any woman, until he and his family have agreed to transfer, and under certain circumstances until they have actually transferred, *bogadi*." Schapera continues to show how *bogadi* establishes this legal paternity, which, because of it, always takes moral precedence over biological fatherhood. He notes a fact common throughout the continent that "all children borne of a married woman, no matter who their actual [biological] father may be, are held to be the legal offspring of the man on whose behalf *bogadi* for that woman was given out."[38]

This inner meaning of the bride-wealth expressed among these two ethnic groups, or certain modifications of either, is funda-

---

[37]M. A. Onwuejeogwu, *The Social Anthropology of Africa: An Introduction* (London: Heinemann, 1975), p. 63.
[38]Schapera, *A Handbook of Tswana Law and Custom*, p. 139. See also his *Married Life in an African Tribe*, pp. 82-92.

mental. Studies of the Gikuyu of Kenya,[39] the Kwaya of Tanzania,[40] the Kipsigis of Kenya,[41] the Akan of Ghana and Côte d'Ivoire,[42] and the various peoples of Ethiopia,[43] have shown this. Henri Junod found it among the Thonga of South Africa, and observed that it serves the above functions: it fosters solidarity among and between the two societies concerned in that the *lobola,* as it is called here, is given and received communally; it makes the marriage difficult to break on account of its social, psychological, and ritual significance; and it gives the children of the union legitimacy and identity[44]— all standard expectations of bride-wealth. Consequently, Shorter is right to apply these elements of the meaning of the bride-wealth universally to the entire continent. Where African Religion is concerned, he once again underlines the point that bride-wealth is not so much an economic transaction as it is a social and ritual symbol; in many cases the amount of the bride-wealth is so insignificant that it would be ridiculous to perceive it as "wife-buying." Furthermore, the idea of "purchase" is contradicted by the fact that the woman always belongs to her own parents, clan, and lineage, even after marriage. That is why the true, uncorrupted purpose of this practice can be summarized correctly as twofold. First, it establishes "the right of exclusive sexual access to the woman by the husband and for the power to bequeath status and property to the children of the union as to the descendants of the husband's group." Second, it "legitimates the children within the father's lineage." It is this legitimation that stabilizes the vital force of the clan and that makes the giving and receiving of bride-wealth so crucial from a religious point of view.[45]

[39]Kenyatta, *Facing Mount Kenya,* pp. 163-74.

[40]Huber, *Marriage and the Family in Rural Bukwaya,* pp. 77-94.

[41]J. G. Peristiany, *The Social Institutions of the Kipsigis* (London: George Routledge, 1939), pp. 56-75.

[42]See W. R. Bascom and M. J. Herskovits, eds., *Continuity and Change in African Cultures* (Chicago: University of Chicago Press, 1959), p. 191.

[43]See A. R. Tippett, *Peoples of Southwest Ethiopia* (South Pasadena, Calif.: William Carey Library, 1970), pp. 138-41.

[44]H. A. Junod, *The Life of a South African Tribe, Vol. I: Social Life* (New Hyde Park: New York: University Books, 1962), pp. 278-9.

[45]Shorter, *African Culture and the Christian Church,* p. 168.

Without such recognition and legitimation by bride-wealth, even if of a symbolic nature in the form of offering—hoes, spears, or even some beverage—the status of children born of a union becomes extremely ambiguous to themselves and dangerous to the community. In such circumstances, to which ancestral allegiance do the children belong? Which ancestors do they invoke? Can the ancestors look at them with favor? Since they may have no particular allegiance to the clan of the father, will they carefully observe its customs and taboos? To solve these issues, until legitimation is finalized by bride-wealth, as a rule children born of an illegitimate union are identified with and legally associated with the mother's clan and lineage. However, children born of an adulterous liaison by a woman whose bride-wealth has been paid are in a different socio-religious category altogether. They are the legal children of her husband and enjoy the same status in his clan as anyone else.

Aside from the question of children, the status of the woman in a relationship without bride-wealth having been exchanged is even more ambiguous. The question here is, without it, will she be blessed with ritual fecundity? Will her children be able to confer on her the full status of motherhood and, consequently, ancestorship, since she technically "has no husband"? Will she be loved and valued as a "wife" by the man with whom she has children? Will the relationship last? What about her duty to her ancestors and her need to placate them with the portion of the bride-wealth that is usually offered them? What about her responsibility to avail her brothers and other members of her own clan of the wherewithal to offer bride-wealth for their own wives? Will she be able to assure the members of the man's clan that the children born of her are really full members of their clan, that they are "their very own blood"? These are serious ethical questions that are faced by women in irregular unions, that is, without bride-wealth.

It is clear then that a marital arrangement without bride-wealth is highly irregular and offensive, and that a woman who accepts cohabitation with a man without bride-wealth does an injustice to the two clans concerned as well as to any children. Because bride-wealth forms part of the process of the covenant that breaks down barriers between clans and peoples and establishes unions of life, love, harmony, peace, and security beyond certain frontiers,[46] the woman in question is acutely aware that her situation is shameful. She is in fact a mistress and, as far as her own "spiritual" future is concerned, practically "dead." In normal circumstances, even though she might at first elope without the usual formalities, she is not content until some form of bride-wealth is sooner or later given by her "husband" or, in the case of his death, by the deceased man's relatives. This posthumous giving of bride-wealth is not rare in such situations. Otherwise, it is not uncommon that she would threaten to return to her parents' home and, in many cases, actually does so. There are no strong ties to her "husband" or his clan to prevent her from taking this step.

In various places throughout Africa, one of the prayers said by the father (or any other designated elder) of the bride-to-be at the reception of the bride-wealth is to implore the ancestors to take care of their daughter and bless her with children. Since bride-wealth is used also to facilitate the marriage of the brothers and other relatives of the bride, the clan elders of the Shona of Zimbabwe, for example, carry the received bride-wealth into the cattle byre and say to the ancestors: "Here is the cattle which will continue our line." And with the Gogo of Tanzania, to take another example, it is the custom for the elders to take the couple outside, after the process of the marriage has been marked by the reception of the bride-wealth, face them in the direction of the setting of the sun—probably the abode of the ancestors—and narrate to them "the clan histories of the four 'sides' (*zimbavu zose ine*; lit., [the] four ribs) concerned in the marriage: the fathers (*wasongwe*) of the bride and groom, and the clans of their mothers (*wokucekulu*), so that 'wherever they are, they may know this.' "[47] In both cases, this is to make sure that everyone

---

[46]See M. T. Hata, "African Marriage: Personal and Communitarian," in *AFER* 23:1&2 (1981), p. 36.

[47]P. Rigby, *Cattle and Kinship among the Gogo: A Semi-pastoral Society of Central Tanzania* (Ithaca and London: Cornell University Press, 1969), p. 222.

appreciates that the ancestors have a hand in the event and that the bride-wealth has a greater significance than is apparent. Similar prayers and rituals express the purpose of the bride-wealth throughout the continent.

The bride-wealth, however, is not the private property of one person or one family. Instead, it is meant to be a uniting element. In most African societies elaborate rules define its distribution among the various relatives of the bride. In fact, one or two animals comprising the bride-wealth (or a little of whatever is given to the bride's family) are used by both sides during the ensuing feasting as a demonstration of unity, communion, and the casting away of dissension and friction between the two groups. The Sonjo of Tanzania serve to illustrate how the dispersal of the bride-wealth in many ethnic groups symbolizes unity. Robert Gray noted this distribution of the bride-wealth as follows: "the girl's father receives approximately one quarter of the goats; another quarter is divided equally between her two grandfathers; another quarter is divided equally between the eldest brothers of her mother and father; the remaining quarter is divided among the other brothers of her father and mother, and their sisters may also receive one or two goats each if the bride-price is sufficiently large." What is sought in all this is fairness. "The basic principle is that after the father's share has been subtracted, the remaining goats are divided equally between the relatives of the father and mother. That is, individuals of the same degree of relationship on either side of the family receive the same number of goats. The total number of goats claimed by each side, however, need not be equal. Thus if one of the parents has more brothers and sisters than the other, that side of the family would receive more goats altogether."[48]

When all is said and done, by far the most fundamental meaning of bride-wealth is that parenthood is foundational of human existence. As emphasized above, the husband-wife status, although chronologically prior, is actually qualitatively sec-

---

[48]R. F. Gray, *The Sonjo of Tanganyika: An Anthropological Study of an Irrigation-Based Society* (London: Oxford University Press, 1963), p. 72. See also Evans-Pritchard, *The Position of Women in Primitive Societies*, p. 239.

ondary to the father-mother status. It bears repeating that the marriage is sealed by the birth of a surviving offspring, because then the purpose of marriage—transmitting and therefore preserving life—has been achieved. The marriage has enabled the four most important things in human life to be realized concretely: 1) it has re-presented (made present among the living) the life force of departed ancestors by way of naming; 2) it has given the parents the assurance of life with the ancestors in that they will in their turn be remembered by being named after; 3) it has ensured the continuation of the life of the clan in this world by increasing its vital force through the new members; and 4) comprising all the above, it has tied the bond of communion between the living, the living-dead, and the yet-to-be-born.

On account of this, marriage solemnized with bride-wealth becomes a profoundly sacred reality. Solemn prayers, sacrifices, and blessings are always offered over the marriage by the clan. Dissolution of the marriage bond understandably becomes extremely rare after a marriage has resulted in offspring; in other words, it is serving the purpose of life. Physical separation may occur in certain situations, such as cruelty, lack of care for the wife, or evidence of witchcraft in either spouse, but this separation does not necessarily imply that the marriage bond is broken. As noted above, ordinarily the bond of marriage continues after the death of one of the spouses. Polygamous, leviratic, ghost, and sororate marriages are sometimes required as a logical consequence of this unbreakable bond, when conditions such as death without children demand them. Woman marriage and widow inheritance also serve, at least in part, the same purpose of social and ritual bonding and children. These forms of union are also established for life-fostering purposes.

THE VALUE BEHIND DIFFERENT FORMS OF MARRIAGE

Abundance of life is the reason behind all forms of marriage and unions, and this is why African Religion sanctions many variations of union. Even when these forms are situated within certain social-economic contexts—that is, social prestige or the assurance of hands to work the fields (which motivations are always present, given the unity of life)—they all serve to preserve and prolong life, to provide for ritual fecundity and physical procreation.

The reasons for marriage also hold for polygamous[49] marriage: kinship- and alliance- formation, solidarity, and the bonding of the visible and invisible worlds that is effected through the birth of children. In Africa, polygamy is almost universally preferential or voluntary, in the sense that it is rarely, if ever, "legally"[50] mandated. Rather, there exists what Eugene Hillman describes as a strong "relationship of mutual support and reinforcement" between it and culture, tradition, public opinion, and other social structures.[51] Nevertheless, summing up the results of a 1948 survey of African marriage forms, Arthur Phillips points out that for African men "monogamy is, for the majority who are in fact monogamists, a matter of necessity rather than of choice."[52] This is to say that the majority of the population in Africa is monogamous because of certain constraints. The social and religious preference (if not ideal) is polygamy. That is why the Gogo insist that *"Kutola mitala kuswanu muno,"* which translates as "It is very good to marry more than one wife."[53] Unless there are clear restrictions imposed on an individual, such as the husband of a female chief who cannot by law marry a second wife, or an economic, psycho-sexual, physical, or other inability to take care of more than one wife, Phillips says, having "a number of wives is normally a mark of importance and success in life, and—for this among other reasons—is something which the . . . African man would gladly achieve if he could."[54] Since one's power and influence in the clan and lineage and in society in general depends to some significant degree on the size of one's family and how well one manages it, a man will be drawn

---

[49]Strictly speaking, "polygyny" as distinguished from "polyandry."

[50]We shall discuss the concept of "law" in African societies in chapter seven.

[51]E. Hillman, *Polygamy Reconsidered: African Plural Marriage and the Christian Churches* (Maryknoll, New York: Orbis Books, 1975), p. 88.

[52]A. Phillips, "An Introductory Essay," in A. Phillips, ed., *Survey of African Marriage and Family Life* (London: Oxford University Press, 1953), p. xiv.

[53]See Rigby, *Cattle and Kinship among the Gogo,* p. 180.

[54]Ibid., p. xiv.

into acquiring many wives because of the <u>potential to have a greater number of children</u>. This structure of marriage also provides more protection for widows, because it makes sure that women remain within the lineage after the death of their husbands and that they are materially provided for.

Polygamous unions for reasons of concupiscence on the part of African males are not sanctioned by African Religion. Concupiscence does not guarantee the permanence and stability that African polygamous unions demand and assure. By its nature, concupiscence does not seek fidelity or everlasting loyalty. However, these are the hallmarks of African polygamous unions. Further, concupiscence shows no concern for the integration of offspring into the clan or their responsible socialization. John Njenga has used the analogy of friendship to explain the seriousness of the covenant relationship in African polygamous marriages. In these unions, he explains, "the husband sincerely felt that each of his wives had a unique relationship with him, a relationship that was of husband and wife . . . [This] conjugal relationship was, in a manner, analogous to friendship, viewed as capable of being realized among various persons (wives) and not exclusively tied up with one person (wife) . . . "[55]

An important aspect of marriage that we must briefly discuss is hospitality. Eugene Hillman has pointed out that "While both polygamists and monogamists subscribe to the hospitality patterns dictated by their common culture (and African hospitality tends to be very expansive), . . . the larger family more easily acquires the prestige associated with generous hospitality."[56] Generous hospitality, though, is only possible in part because one has the material means to afford it. As Monica Wilson explains, the many working hands of the polygamist make this more likely than the few hands of the monogamist.[57] And generosity and hospitality are not only admired as moral qualities, they are taken as clear qualities of leadership. This is illustrated by an

---

[55]J. Njenga, "Customary African Marriage," in *AFER*, XVI:1&2 (1974), p. 117.
[56]Hillman, *Polygamy Reconsidered*, p. 119.
[57]Cited by Hillman in ibid., p. 119.

anecdote from Ethiopia. Batul, a wealthy but monogamous man (by preference), was not given to entertaining people. For that reason, he was passed over for leadership in his locality because the people perceived his attitude to be unsocial. His younger, but polygamous and more hospitable, brother was chosen instead, because as the people saw it, his homestead was "big and warm."[58]

Morally, the responsibility of the husband to all the wives and children in a polygamous marriage is the same. What he is required to do to one in terms of affection and concern, he is morally bound to do to all. Otherwise, it is unethical for him to enter into this form of marriage, and he risks public ridicule and even censure for jeopardizing the quality of life in this way. Plural marriage is not to be entered into lightly, nor is it easy to organize a polygamous family. An intelligent, mature, and ethical man must seriously weigh his capability to take care of more than one wife and numerous children before entering into another marital union. He must be sure of his own ability to handle the inevitable difficulties of such union that arise out of normal human emotions, such as jealousy among his wives and conflict among his children. Only when he has satisfied himself in these matters and sought the advice of others, may he embark on such a marriage. Even if a polygamous marriage is desired and preferred, " 'polygyny is a state into which most African men enter with a certain trepidation.' Frequently, husbands are reluctant to seek additional wives because of the greater burdens and responsibilities that go with the management of polygynous households."[59]

A discussion of one of the ways polygamy is initiated may indicate some of the ethical reasons behind the practice. In many cases, polygamy is undertaken at the man's initiative, even against the initial refusal of the wife, for reasons we have discussed. But, not infrequently, polygamy is entered into through the wife's initiative, even against the initial resistance of the husband. A wife may complain that she is tired of doing all the work at the home and needs a helper. She may continue entreating her

---

[58]Tippett, *Peoples of Southwest Ethiopia,* p. 142.
[59]Hillman, *Polygamy Reconsidered,* p. 120.

husband and may even suggest or provide a girl of her choice for him to marry. It is difficult for the husband to resist these pressures, and he most often ends up accepting his wife's wishes. The senior wife retains a certain privileged position with her husband in any case, and her children enjoy priority in all major affairs, unless they disqualify themselves by misbehavior. This legal prominence of the senior wife is well illustrated by the practices of the Bakwaya of Tanzania, and applies more or less to the perspective of other peoples in Africa.

Among the Bakwaya, the first wife is described as follows:

As she has been the one who "stood for the entrance," i.e., who cooked the official porridge and who had the ceremonially required intercourse with her husband, when he founded his own compound, she is, in some way, regarded as the head (*omwene*) of the domestic affairs. Her house as the most prominent of all faces the gate-way. Her husband keeps therein his personal objects. When he comes from a journey he normally stops first at her hut. If he brings something along (as for instance meat) he hands it over to her and she will then share it with her co-wives. In all major ceremonial occasions which concern either her own children or her husband, she is the one who stands for the *nyangi*, i.e. who performs the ritually demanded marital intercourse and who cooks the porridge. She should be present if something important is discussed in the household.

Her preeminence is particularly obvious in the event of the husband's sickness or death.

When her husband falls seriously ill, he is taken into her house, which is regarded as the appropriate place for him to die. Even in the case of a sudden death his body is carried there before it is buried; and there also the principal funeral and cleansing ceremonies take place. Even if his senior wife has left him long ago to follow another man, at the occasion of his death she is called back for the ritual cleansing, provided that she had children by him. They might then, if necessary, construct a temporary hut for her for the corpse of her ex-husband. The cleansing is then performed therein. As senior wife she sometimes "tastes" the grave, i.e. starts ceremonially the digging, and cooks the porridge at the close of the funeral.[60]

Likewise, other forms of marital unions are entered into for specific reasons. The leviratic union is not a proper "marriage" in the African point of view. Instead, it is "a temporary adjustment in a continuing marriage in which a brother-in-law substitutes for the deceased legal husband"[61] to fulfill an obligation to a deceased brother. A man takes on the widow of a deceased brother or relative to permit the birth of children for the dead man. The children belong to the dead brother rather than the living one and are entitled to inherit from his estate. Nor does the woman consider herself to be married a second time: the dead man remains her husband and the living person with whom she cohabits is simply her caretaker. This has been amply demonstrated by Michael Kirwen in a survey of four societies in Tanzania.[62] Although there are some differing emphases, the widow has the right to be taken care of by the relatives of her late husband, and these relatives clearly have the responsibility to do so, including the responsibility to cohabit with her in the name of the deceased.

This practice is illustrated by an incident from the Luo people. After the death of his brother a young, single, Catholic Luo man from northern Tanzania asked a priest to unite him with his widowed sister-in-law "in marriage" according to the rituals of the Catholic church. On account of pastoral considerations (the widow was still young, and Luo custom not only allows but insists on the need for him to "take care of her" for his brother), the priest agreed, but with one proviso, on which the priest firmly

---

[60]Huber, *Marriage and the Family in Rural Bukwaya*, p.155.
[61]M. C. Kirwen, *African Widows: An Empirical Study of the Problems of Adapting Western Christian Teachings on Marriage to the Leviratic Custom for the Care of Widows in Four Rural African Societies* (Maryknoll, New York: Orbis Books, 1979), p. 9.
[62]Ibid., passim.

insisted. The proviso was the young man should never marry again, as his sister-in-law was now his legal and only wife in the eyes of the church. The young man agreed, signed all the forms, and the marriage was solemnized. After a few months, however, the man went to see the priest again, this time with another unmarried young woman whom he now wanted to marry. In his mind, he had remained unmarried, because the woman with whom he had been living was the wife of his deceased brother. He now wanted a wife and children of his own.[63]

In this sense, a levirate marriage is different from widow inheritance, when a man takes his deceased brother's or relative's widow as a wife. The children of a levirate marriage are his (rather than offspring of the deceased) and they inherit from his estate. Although the leviratic union and widow inheritance are different in conception and fact, their ultimate purpose remains the same: the need and desire to survive through the bearing of children. The same is the case with sororate, ghost, and woman marriages, which frequently take place and are perceived as a duty in certain expressions of African Religion. For example, what options does a barren woman have to promote life? She might ask a sister to be a co-wife with her so that the latter can have children for the man's clan and remove the shame of childlessness that would otherwise fall on her family and clan. This is known as a sororate marriage. In the same vein, a ghost marriage may be entered into if a man dies without children, and the clan finds a wife for him to "marry" so as to provide children for him. Further, if there are no males to inherit a widow, she may be treated as a "man" and allowed to "marry" a "wife." Whatever children the latter may have through sexual liaisons with other men are counted as the widow's children and she is considered their legal "father." This is known as a woman marriage. In these contexts, African Religion views any sexual relations as ethical because of the purpose they serve.[64]

---

[63]See L. Magesa, "The Future of Inculturation in Eastern Africa," in P. Turkson and F. S. Wijsen, eds., *Inculturation: Abide by the Otherness of Africa and the Africans* (Kampen: J. H. Kok, 1994), pp. 65-6.
[64]See Kirwen, *African Widows*.

SEXUALITY AND SEXUAL RELATIONS

Marriage and other forms of legal sexual unions are meant to ensure procreation and the preservation of life and the life-force through sexuality and its physical expression in sexual intercourse. This is recognized with great intensity by African Religion and this is why one of the most central aspects of the initiation process is to impress upon the initiates acceptance of the dignity of their own sexuality and the need to be both very responsible and very proud of it. From initiation on, people are expected to recognize the basic role of sexuality and sexual relations in the life of the family and the clan. No young person who has gone through initiation takes kindly to being considered a child any longer, and is even less happy to be seen as incapable of accomplishing sexual relations according to custom. According to Evans-Pritchard, unmarried Azande young men and women, for example, can offer gifts to one another and make love without shame. "A girl would beg her mother to give her a chicken and when it was given she would cook it [in oil] and take it to her friend in his little hut. If she found good meat she would prepare a meal with it for her lover." He would do likewise with food or ornaments and the parents would pretend "not to notice."[65] Young people desire and pray for fertility and virility. A young woman will want to select a virile young man for a husband to "give her children," and a young man will pray for a wife to bear him many children. This is why African Religion tries, through instruction and rituals, to ensure that each individual person accepts his or her sexuality and gender roles with grace and ease, without any undue embarrassment. The rather free social relationships across gender permitted among the young, within certain limits, are not interpreted as irresponsibility. Rather, they are seen as a pedagogical tool for the purpose of procreation.

This is why the actual use of the generative powers through sexual intercourse is closely controlled to ensure its full procreative potential. For example, the Lango of Uganda believe there

---

[65]Evans-Pritchard, *Man and Woman among the Azande*, p. 194.

is a cosmic power or force, which they refer to as *jok*, that is generated during copulation. It is a spark of this power that enters a woman at coition through the man's spiritual part (*tipo*) and conceives life. In fact, this *jok* that is released at orgasm remains with a man until he dies. Then it returns to the invisible world, which is its source. It is understandable, therefore, that "If the sexual act generates *jok* power, we may expect it to be ritually controlled."[66] As a result, there are numerous prohibitions and taboos on the sexual act to keep its practice within the limits required by good order and promotion of life; otherwise, it might jeopardize the wellsprings of life.

Benezeri Kisembo and his colleagues explain that the proper expression of sexuality resulting in the birth of legitimate children is indeed the cornerstone of life and happiness in the African community. For Africans, "Infertility and sterility block the channel through which the stream of life flows; they plunge the person concerned into misery, they sever him from personal immortality, and threaten the perpetuation of the lineage." But it is precisely because of this that sexuality and sexual expression are sacred and must in no circumstances be abused. Because sexuality contains and constitutes so much of life, it is liable, by the same token, to be extremely destructive of life if mishandled. Thus, as Kisembo and his colleagues further explain, "because the generation of life was a matter of concern for the whole community, there were strong sanctions against people who indulged in sex for selfish [i.e., destructive] reasons. Sexuality and its powers were understood as permeating every level of human existence: interpersonal relationships and matters of ritual. Sexuality was looked upon as mysterious and sacred. If it were misused, evil surely resulted. Initiation rites prepared the adolescent for the right use of his/her sexuality, to get married and raise a family."[67]

The rites that surround impotent and barren people are also indicative of the centrality of the purpose of sexuality in life: barrenness and impotence cannot be accepted as realities that sometimes happen to some people. Barrenness is universally abhorred among African women and it constitutes the greatest fear and shame for them. Impotence has similar psychological and moral effects among men. In both cases, everything possible is done to try to reverse the situation. For example, among the Lango of Uganda, impotence is interpreted either as a curse or a mishandling during birth, and must be undone. The rite to "undo" impotence in a man among the Lango people requires him to be "reborn." At the beginning of the rite, the man in question enters his mother's hut and remains in seclusion there for three days just like a baby at birth. During this time he must suckle his mother's breasts, cry, and do practically everything a baby does. Then the ceremony of outing is performed, and it is believed that he will have regained his full potency as a man. Or, in another rite, he enters a hut, constructed for that purpose, which is then completely sealed. It is set on fire and the man must come out by another entrance that he forces open as a sign of regaining his virility.[68]

In the view of African Religion, therefore, sexual relations are a means to an end and that end, once again, is procreation. However, to achieve this end, the use of sexuality must be "healthy" or life-promoting. It must not jeopardize the totality of the well-being of the community. And so, not surprisingly, sexual taboos must be strictly observed. Briefly put, however, and within prescribed limits, sexual relations in African Religion enjoy wide leeway and with little attached shame. Within these limits, sex is a good thing, and it is a subject of much unabashed conversation. It is the most obvious and pragmatic way of transmitting and preserving the force of life; it is because of sexuality that humanity continues to perpetuate itself and the ancestors are assured of remembrance and honor. But, because it is so fundamental to the preservation and transmission of the vital force, it must be strictly protected from any kind of abuse. This creates a somewhat contradictory situation: a wide ambiance of sexual freedom on the one hand, and on the other, severe curtailment of sexual relations by prohibitions.

---

[68]Hayley, *The Anatomy of Lango Religion and Groups*, p. 140.

Incest, for example, is completely proscribed. Even if offspring might ensue from an incestuous relationship, the relationship is not viewed as life-giving because the incestuous act greatly disturbs the well-being of the community in very serious ways. It confuses or disorders human relationships here and now in terms of family and clan lineages. But, even more important, it angers the ancestors whose remembrance through naming becomes even more disordered and confused. This ancestral anger may result in many still-births, not only in the family concerned, but perhaps across the clan. That is where the immorality of incest lies and why it is generally reprehensible.

In comparison, fornication, as has been shown among the Azande youth, and even, at times, adultery become less serious offenses. These remain offenses involving the living but they do not directly involve the anger of the ancestors, unless feuds and loss of life ensue. Barring such developments, however, children born of such liaisons—assuming that bride-wealth is in order—are perfectly acceptable to the ancestors concerned as re-presentations of them. As a rule, they are named after the ancestors without any hesitation.

Within the broad area of sexual relations, there seems to be a hierarchy of values in the religious perspective of Africa. Within the context of this hierarchy of values, for example, there might be an appreciation of the moral acceptability of such practices as sexual hospitality. Because hospitality and friendship rank very high on the scale of values that promote harmony and unity in an age-group or across friendships within which such hospitality is permitted, some expressions of African Religion may accept that sexual relations can be at the service of these values. A jealous husband who would not willingly accept this practice would, in fact, be the one who would be behaving against the interests of society by breaking important bonds that hold the society together.

Generally, all aberrations and abnormalities in sexual life, whether consciously willed or not, are seen as impinging negatively on life and are consequently morally reprehensible. In addition to impotence and barrenness, mentioned above, homosexuality is viewed as such an abnormality, an immoral state of existence. Barrenness and impotence are often attributed as moral shortcomings of the persons concerned. On the one hand, there is a realization that the individuals thus afflicted are not as a rule *personally* responsible for their condition. Nevertheless, a degree of personal culpability is, albeit often unconsciously, always attributed to them by the religious mentality of the community. The reasoning is that somewhere along the line, someone in the family, lineage, or clan—if not the individual in question—must have committed an offense against the ancestors or broken a taboo. Because of the strong sense of the corporate personality, barrenness or impotence strikes the person whose family, lineage, or clan has offended. When rituals that are used to try to reverse the situation fail, then woman marriage, sororate unions, or other sexual arrangements are employed to enable those "afflicted" persons to have children of their own. Active homosexuality is morally intolerable because it frustrates the whole purpose of sexual pleasure and that of a human person's existence in the sight of the ancestors and God. Thus, homosexual or lesbian orientations cannot be allowed to surface, let alone be expressed actively. It is clear how such an expression would be directly antagonistic to what the ancestors and the preservation and transmission of life stand for.

Paradoxically, however, people considered to be in such abnormal—that is immoral—states of life sometimes do play a unique social and religious role. In parts of the continent, barren and impotent people, by that very fact alone, possess special mystical powers that can be used for the good of the society. Divination, rain-asking, and mediumship are powers that these people are said to hold. In some places clandestine homosexual acts may be imposed as a condition to acquire wealth.[69] All of these cases demonstrate an obvious ambiguity in moral judgment.

A similar kind of ambiguity is present in the case of twin births. In many places, twin births are not only considered to be abnormalities but also inauspicious occurrences, bad omens. Webster notes that "Twins are sometimes regarded as an indication of unfaithfulness on the mother's part, because of the notion

---

[69]According to information given to me by some Kuria men in Tanzania.

that two children born at the same time cannot have one father. They are also sometimes supposed to have been engendered by an evil spirit, which entered the mother." So they have to be eliminated.[70] The Zulu, the Bavenda, and the Thonga of southern Africa all hold similar views, as do the Afungwe of Malawi and the Akamba of Kenya (the latter treating twins of cattle in the same way). In West Africa, the Edo and Ibo of Nigeria hold the same belief. In some places in Africa, the parents of twins are also placed under various kinds of temporary interdiction, as among the Nandi and Wawanga of Kenya and the Bassari of Togo. To be readmitted into regular society, they must undergo certain purification rituals. The logic behind this is the same: twins are a sign of disharmony in creation. As the Ibo reason (differently from the Akamba), only animals, not humans, give birth to twins by nature; according to them, "There must be a difference between mankind and brute creation. To function as an animal is to degrade humanity," which is what the birth of twins does.[71] In all cases, however, the birth of twins presents a mysterious intervention in life. In the absence of proper purification rituals, the event of twin-births may affect the whole society: rains may fail, animals may not give birth and things generally may turn bad.

In other places, however, the birth of twins is a good omen from God. In these latter cases, twins are seen to have powers not granted to anyone else, and it is hoped that they will use these powers for the good of the community. We may cite the Yoruba of Nigeria; the Ganda, Banyoro, and Lango of Uganda; the Kpelle of Liberia; and the Dogon of Mali as examples. Among the Kpelle, twins are born with the mystical powers of sorcery and must be treated with great respect from the beginning. With the Yoruba the situation is much the same: twins have spiritual powers that influence even siblings born after them. The mother of twins is congratulated profusely for having had them.

But it is perhaps among the Dogon and the various peoples of

---

[70]H. Webster, *Taboo: a Sociological Study* (New York: Octagon Books, 1973), p. 61.

[71]Ibid., p. 64.

Uganda, in particular the Baganda, that reverence for twins as auspicious and their parents as people with special blessings is most clear. Marcel Griaule reported that among the Dogon "the birth of twins is a notable event. It recalls the fabulous past, when all human beings came into existence in twos, symbol of the balance between the human and the divine." The birth of twins, according to the Dogon, is the reproduction of the birth of the first woman whose clitoris was transformed into a scorpion. The scorpion's eight feet equal the number of arms and legs of twins and this symbolizes that the scorpion is their protector. And so "no one dares touch them for fear of his sting."[72] Dogon twins also bestow sacrality on their mother; because she has been touched by a spirit she is able to conceive and bear them. Among the Baganda the birth of twins is also seen as an act of God. Twins must receive most careful treatment, for anything that might befall them may bring God's anger on the whole clan. In Buganda, the parents of twins are not interdicted, but, as Webster notes, "Both mother and father were made sacred, not polluted, by the twin-birth, and they remained so until an elaborate ceremony had been performed to remove the odor of sanctity attaching to their persons."[73]

Here, in the case of twins, although their interpretations of order and harmony differ substantially, two obviously contradictory perceptions have the same basic intention, that of preserving the vital power of the universe—the most significant factor in African Religion.

PRESERVATION OF LIFE THROUGH TABOOS

As mentioned briefly above, taboos play a significant role in the ethical duty of transmitting and preserving life and the breach

---

[72]M. Griaule, *Conversations with Ogotemmeli: An Introduction to Dogon Religious Ideas* (London: Oxford University Press, 1965), p. 198. The whole cosmology of the Dogon peoples rests on the concept of twinness, that is, perfection. We shall explore this in another connection in a later chapter, using a slight variation of the same cosmogonic myth.

[73]Webster, *Taboo*, p. 66.

of taboos endangers the health and well-being of society. Taboos relate to many areas of human life: such as things associated with death (for instance, corpses and certain diseases), sacred persons and things (chiefs or royal paraphernalia), and strange persona and phenomena (for example, lightning or hail). African moral thought would universally concur with the conviction of the Bakuria of Tanzania that, for example, "if satisfactory rainfall is to be obtained the land must be at peace and untroubled by dissention."[74] Similarly, the related ethnic group of the Bazanaki also affirm, "it was equally important that private individuals should be prevented from actions which might disturb the internal harmony of the community" if people were to enjoy the blessings of rain and other necessary gifts of nature.[75] Because taboos are also so intimately concerned with the expression of human sexuality, perhaps it is appropriate at this point to discuss their application in this area of life.

Among the numerous taboos concerned with sexuality, the two most significant are the taboo against intercourse during menstruation and taboo against incest (the latter having been referred to above). In this study, I have endeavored to show that all creation consists of the sacred and, in a sense, incorporates it. This is particularly true of humanity. In the human person, as in the rest of creation, this sacred power is generally diffused, but often concentrated in certain "privileged places," as Emile Durkheim has characterized these parts of the human body. One of these places is the blood.[76] It is not surprising, therefore, to find that many of the sexual taboos have to do with blood. Isaac Schapera found that among the Kgatla, "The restrictions on sexual intercourse are associated with the idea that at certain times a person's blood becomes 'hot,' and until it has 'cooled down' he is in a condition harmful to others with whom he comes into very

---

[74]E. C. Baker, *The Bakuria of N.M. Tarime, Tanganyika Territory,* mimeo, n.d., p. 89.

[75]Ibid., p. 89.

[76]See E. Durkheim, *The Elementary Forms of Religious Life.* Trans. J. W. Swain (New York: The Free Press, 1965), p. 159.

close contact."[77] Schapera continues to explain that, according to Kgatla understanding:

> Both men and women still capable of bearing children are "hot" immediately after intercourse, and, since they presumably lead active sexual lives, they are accordingly debarred from taking part in certain forms of ritual. Thus, in some of the rain-making ceremonies and similar occasions, only children who have not yet attained puberty or women who have passed the menopause can be employed, for they are not yet or no longer able to be "hot." Widows and widowers are also "hot" for about a year after their bereavement. A woman is "hot" during her menstrual periods, during pregnancy (especially in the early stages), and immediately after childbirth. If she has aborted, she is "hot" until she menstruates again. Her condition in all these instances is shared by her husband or the man responsible for her pregnancy.[78]

The expectations of the Mbuti of Zaire in this sphere hold generally true in African Religion. They demand that "a man with a pregnant wife, or whose wife has just delivered a child, must not hunt until her blood has absolutely ceased flowing and she has put on her loin cloth. In the same way, the husband of a menstruating woman must stay in the camp and cannot hunt."[79] Both sperm and vaginal secretions during intercourse are considered "blood," and so people who have just had sexual intercourse can be dangerous to others and must take certain precautions, because their blood is hot. In many instances, as, for example, throughout West Africa, human milk is considered in the same category as blood, so that a man is not allowed to have intercourse with his wife while she is still suckling a child.[80] But the

---

[77]Schapera, *Married Life in an African Tribe,* p. 194.
[78]Ibid., pp. 194-5.
[79]Ibid., p. 32.
[80]G. Parrinder, *West African Religion: A Study of the Beliefs and Practices of Akan, Ewe, Yoruba, Ibo, and Kindred Peoples* (London: Epworth Press, 1961), p. 179.

most stringent prohibition across the continent is against sexual intercourse during menstruation, for obviously loss of blood conflicts with acts of life.

In consequence, the Ga and Twi people of Ghana, the Bakongo of Zaire, the Gikuyu and Akamba of Kenya, and many peoples of southern Nigeria all forbid contact with menstrual blood. A menstruating woman is usually forbidden to handle food or water for others, or to touch clothing and other household articles. In some cases, she is not allowed to sleep in the same house or in the same bed as her husband, because doing so might harm him in various ways. A breach of this taboo is surrounded by all sorts of dangers not only to the people who come in contact with her, but also to herself. A man who has intercourse with a menstruating woman, for example, might become sick or even lose his virility. If, in the meantime, he has intercourse with another woman without undergoing purification, the second woman might die. An Akamba girl menstruating for the first time must be careful that her blood does not come into contact with anyone else, especially a man. If a stranger treads upon it and indulges in sexual intercourse before her menstrual blood ceases, the Akamba believe, she will never conceive.[81]

Another important taboo in the area of sexuality, even more serious than the blood taboo, is taboo against incest, which applies to both kinship and fictive relationships. Although expressed in various ways among different African peoples, its pattern is the same. It is generally forbidden to marry or have sexual relations within the bounds of blood friendships and pacts, and within the same totemic system. Kenneth Little has listed the extensive range of kin relationship included in this prohibition. A person must not have sexual relations with one's own parent or child; grandparent or grandchild; sister, half-sister, brother, or half-brother; aunt or uncle; the children of one's sister or brother or again their children; sister- or brother-in-law while either of the couple lives; the sister, brother, half-sister, or half-brother of

---

[81]Webster, *Taboo*, pp. 85-6.

a woman or man with whom one has had sexual relations; any woman whose milk a man has suckled.[82]

Whatever limits are set to the range of relationships within which sexual relations are not permitted, the horror of incest (within those limits) arises from the confusion it creates. Members of the same clan share the same totem and the same source of their vital power. (Blood friends also share their vital power by sharing their blood.) How can that power be mingled again by the act of intercourse? If this happens by accident, the clan- or blood-relationship must be ended immediately, if at all possible. The Gikuyu have a ritual for this. "The elders take a sheep and place it on the woman's shoulders, it is then killed, the intestines are taken out, and the elders solemnly sever them with a sharp splinter of wood . . . and they announce that they are cutting the clan, by which they mean that they are severing the bond of blood-relationship (of the clan) that exists between the pair. A medicine man then comes and purifies the couple."[83] What is otherwise required is to keep the clan distinguished sexually through exogamy. To do so is to maintain the plans of God and the ancestors as they were established.

In summary, taboos connect human life and the benevolence of creation to humanity. As such, they are an essential feature of the moral perception of African Religion. Beyond that, they indicate the relationship between humanity and the living God, from whom the gift of life ultimately originates; they also indicate the relationship between humanity and the ancestors, who are life's immediate mediators. Thus, for example, though rain emanates from God, it "can be controlled by human agency through the medium of ancestral spirits," and when these have been wronged

---

[82]K. L. Little, "The Role of the Secret Society in Cultural Specialization," in S. and P. Ottenberg, eds., *Cultures and Societies of Africa* (New York: Random House, 1960), p. 203. An interesting discussion in this connection is Y. A. Cohen, *The Transition from Childhood to Adolescence: Cross-cultural Studies of Initiation Ceremonies, Legal Systems, and Incest Taboos* (Chicago: Aldine Publishing Company, 1964), pp. 159-96.

[83]L. Levy-Bruhl, cited in F. Steiner, *Taboo* (London: Cohen & West, 1956), p. 112.

by transgression of a taboo, proper procedures of atonement must be initiated so that God's gifts may flow once again in abundance for the benefit of the life of humanity.[84]

The causal relationship between human life and the natural world is very clearly seen in the connection between totems and taboos. This relationship contains codes that distinguish the moral from the immoral way for an individual or a community to act and live. In other words, totems and taboos clarify for all to see those elements in human attitudes and behavior toward creation that enhance life and those that do not. Such taboos also consider the correspondence of the act of human sexual intercourse with the force of life in nature, and the interaction between humanity and nature. Sex and sexuality are the basic and primary vehicles for preserving and transmitting the ancestral vital force and thus are sacred. But even this most basic conduit of the force of life diminishes life when it is perversely used—this is to say, when taboos governing its use are disregarded or broken. Creation (or nature) also suffers as a consequence of such a breach, causing changes that are not favorable to human life.

For example, there are certain times of the year when sexual relations are not permitted because it is deemed that they would interfere and disturb the rhythm of nature and so result in harm to the individual and/or the community. It seems paradoxical that prohibitions against sexual intercourse coincide most often with events and situations in nature that are normally fecund in themselves, such as cultivation, harvesting, hunting, and so on. However, the purpose of the prohibition of sexual relations, as with the taboos of incest, is to safeguard life. By distinguishing and avoiding confusion of what seems to be "dangerously similar" in humanity and in nature, life in both spheres is guarded and protected. E. M. Zuesse explains: "If we were to extend the meaning of these taboo-norms into a general analysis of taboos, we would conclude that taboos separate the dangerously similar, that which is vulnerable to confusion of categories. In this way

---

[84]Ibid., p. 90.

the divine order is preserved in the face of threatening chaos."[85]

The rhythms of the life-force of nature and of humanity are always in communion, influencing each other for good or evil, and the delicate balance between them must be carefully preserved. The preservation of the balance ultimately depends upon human ethical behavior, including the observation of taboos and other prohibitions. This is why such anti-life attitudes as enmity among members of a family, lineage, or clan inevitably affect the rhythm of the universe. The weather may change adversely, perhaps causing suffering from drought or floods, cows might mysteriously die, lightning might strike, a house may burn down, a child might die. This is the case with other kinds of wrongdoing as well, such as theft or murder. Sex, birth, growing up, marriage, old age and death, and burial are related to rain, planting, the germination of seed, harvesting, eating and drinking. In a word, they are related to life, and good behavior on the part of human beings assures success and abundance in the sphere of nature. Abundance in nature affirms that the moral codes of the community have been observed. Conversely, in the event of a problem in nature, the cause undoubtedly lies in human behavior; it must be investigated, discovered, and rectified, for it is an enemy of life.

MORAL MATURITY IN DEATH AND THE TRANSMISSION OF ANCESTRAL VITAL POWER

Because of the intimate connection between life and death (and death and life) in African Religion,[86] it should not be surprising that a discussion of death is an essential part of this discussion of the transmission of life. Old age and death have

---

[85]E. M. Zuesse, *Ritual Cosmos: The Sanctification of Life in African Religions* (Athens, Ohio: Ohio University Press, 1979), p. 32. A very illuminating study on the meaning of taboos is Mary Douglas's *Purity and Danger: An Analysis of the Concepts of Pollution and Taboo* (London: Routledge & Kegan Paul, 1966).

[86]As was illustrated in the previous chapter by the funerary rites of the Bahema of Zaire (pp. 86-87).

important roles in African understandings of the vital force: they are moments in life compared to birth, initiation, marriage, and so on, insofar as all of them mark periods of passage in an individual's life. Accompanied by the appropriate rites, they are moments when the power of life is intensified for the individual and for the individual's society.

Longevity is a prized aspect of life. In fact, it is seen as a consequence and proof of having lived morally. The death of a young person in battle is understood, but apart from such circumstances, the death of the young is an inexplicable tragedy that points to moral disorder in the individual's life or society. On the contrary, death in old age is a dignified event. It is expected that old people must demonstrate courage and heroism when faced with death. Such behavior increases their honor and the influence of their vital force in the eyes of those they leave behind. As a result, the words a person utters at the moment of death have utmost significance. As Leo Simmons notes, "The prestige of the aged in death has been frequently enhanced by the significance attributed to their 'last words.' These final statements have often dealt with disposition of property, choice of successors, impartation of special knowledge or counsel, pledge of special favors from the spirit realm, and pronouncement of blessings—sometimes curses—upon close relatives."[87] Simmons cites examples of the Ashanti and the Akamba. The patriarchs of both groups of people bequeath their property at the time of death, with the injunction that harm will come to anyone who does not follow their instructions. A parent might curse "any son or daughter who incurred his displeasure by invoking upon them poverty, barrenness, and early death. A dying curse upon property was believed [by the Akamba] to retain its harmful effects to the third and fourth generations.[88]

---

[87]L. W. Simmons, *The Role of the Aged in Primitive Society* (New Haven: Yale University Press, 1945), p. 241.

[88]Ibid., p. 241. We need to mention that, even though respect for age is universal in Africa, the treatment of old and sickly people varied in the past according to the circumstances of the society. Abandonment of the aged was a practice, particularly among hunting and pastoral peoples. Simmons (p. 226) mentions the people of the Kalahari, as an example, who "forsook their

At death in physical maturity (that is, old age), as shown in the ritual of the Bahema of Zaire, the elder's power is not only transformed, but is handed over to the surviving elders to continue nourishing them, the family, and the community at large. Death is "perceived as a change of status, an entrance into a new and deeper relationship with the clan, tribe and family."[89] The end is also a conspicuous beginning. This beginning contained in death is, in many cases, symbolized and emphasized by a ritual sexual act, which is the most obvious life-generating act. As Monica Wilson noted, among the Nyakyusa of Tanzania this is done to assure the continuation of both physical health and the blessing of the shades (the ancestors) for the living, and it underscores the link between death and life.[90]

Death is also the beginning of an individual's deeper mystical relationship with the whole universe. In many myths, death is a consequence of the breakdown of communication between God and humanity caused either by an act of a human being or one of the creatures. It is explained "in terms of the [now] wider polar-

---

aged and decrepit when moving from place to place; but it was their custom to build little shelters for them, and provide them with firewood, a piece of meat, and a shell or an ostrich egg filled with water." This was not seen as an act of cruelty but of mercy. It was something done in the interests of life: by being thus abandoned, the old person would go quickly to join the ancestors, and the life of the community would be preserved by enabling it to move more freely about in search of sustenance.

I therefore subscribe to Dominique Zahan's interpretation of the ritual killing of chiefs, and often of other people associated with them in the past (as among the Ashanti), that "All these deeds denote a religious 'confusion' on the part of Africans between life and death, or rather an astonishing sense of life which in their eyes could only be fully realized if interrupted by momentary stopping points. Instead of diminishing and weakening life, these moments of rest give it a new vigor each time, to the extent that life continues reinforced and renewed after each ordeal." See D. Zahan, *The Religion, Spirituality, and Thought of Traditional Africa*. Trans. by K. E. Martin and L. M. Martin (Chicago and London: The University of Chicago Press, 1979), p. 47.

[89]L. Magesa, "Death as Moral Maturity: a Synthesis of Three Theological Theories," in *CHIEA African Christian Studies* 4:2 (June 1988), p. 41.

[90]M. Wilson, "Nyakyusa Ritual and Symbolism," in J. Middleton, ed., *Myths and Cosmos: Readings in Mythology and Symbolism* (Garden City, New York: The Natural History Press, 1967), p. 158.

ities between sky and earth, divinity and humanity, and [consequently] life and death."[91] Death, however, bridges these polarities and the human person becomes mystically closely connected to all of earth's creatures. In this way, death complements life,[92] and communication between the visible and invisible world is reestablished through *tradition*, that is, reference to the dead through prayer, sacrifices, offerings, and divination.

As Dominique Zahan has explained,

> Tradition as the "word" of the dead remains the most vital means of assuring the link between the dead and the living. Owing to this "speech," which is transmitted through the ages, the presence of the ancestors among men is assured at each instant. By conforming to the legacy of the dead, the living in turn recognize their authority and avoid "dangerous" undertakings. Presence on the one hand and submission on the other, this is the very object of the exchanges between two worlds whose reciprocal permeability is never contested by any African. On the contrary, the African lives with the idea of a perpetual osmosis between the two interfacing realities.[93]

Yet, the ancestors control this speech. That is why "To join the ancestors at death, especially to become one of them, is the goal of . . . African peoples."[94]

Mortuary rites in Africa show very clearly the belief that out

---

[91]B. Ray, "The Story of Kintu: Myth, Death, and Ontology in Buganda," in I. Karp and C. S. Bird, eds., *Explorations in African Systems of Thought* (Bloomington: Indiana University Press, 1980), p. 60. See also D. Zahan, *The Religion, Spirituality, and Thought of Traditional Africa*, pp. 36-52.

[92]Ray, "The Story of Kintu," p. 77.

[93]Zahan, *The Religion, Spirituality, and Thought of Traditional Africa*, p. 48.

[94]E. Dovlo, "Ancestors and Soteriology in African and Japanese Religions," in *Studies in Interreligious Dialogue,* 3:1 (1993), p. 50. See also C. R. Gaba, "Man's Salvation: Its Nature and Meaning in African Traditional Religion," in E. Fashole-Luke et al., *Christianity in Independent Africa* (Bloomington & London: Indiana University Press, 1978), pp. 389-401.

of death comes life, beginning with the prayers said during death and burial. Almost all prayers begin by sending away the spirit of the dead person, by asking it not to bring trouble to the living; they usually end by imploring the departed to bring life and everything that favors life on earth. Turkana (Kenya) burial prayers show this double intention very clearly. As the Turkana bury a male elder, they will address the corpse thus: "Now we must stop thinking...about you, we bury you. We must stop thinking about you, give us everything that is good..."[95] Or, they will say as they place the man's valuables in the grave with him: "Oh! Father leave us, here is your stool; here is your tobacco, chew it, this is your milk, drink it, this is your feather holder, take it. Here is your oil, drink it, this is your meat, eat it. Father help us now and give us life, make us rich and give us food."[96] The point here "is to separate the 'deceased' from the community without creating animosity between the parties. It is very important for the community and its welfare that the 'deceased' is properly treated..."[97]

Nearly all the other mortuary and funerary ceremonies emphasize these two characteristics of the death-event: the sending away, and the amplification of earthly life. As a rule, the former is meant to serve the latter. The shaving of the hair (one of the parts of the human body where life is seen to be concentrated) at the death of a relative signifies one's own death, but it also emphasizes the importance of strengthening life when the hair grows back. Similarly, the celebrations undertaken, the dances performed, the intense conversation engaged in, and the huge amount of food and drink consumed at funerals have the same purpose. With reference to the Nyakyusa on this issue, Monica Wilson admits that death is, indeed, feared and causes sorrow. But, "The fear and sorrow of death are only emotionally tolerable if their expression is followed by, or combined with, an asser-

---

[95] A. Barrett, *Dying and Death among the Turkana, Part I* (Eldoret: Gaba Publications, June 1987), pp. 34-5.

[96] Ibid., p. 35.

[97] A. Barrett, *Dying and Death among the Turkana, Part II* (Eldoret: Gaba Publications, October 1987), p. 13.

tion of life . . . Africans turn at burial to a realization of present life in its most intense quality, to the war-dance, to sexual display, to lively talk, and to eating of great quantities of meat."[98] But a third element is also evident in these rites and ceremonies. It is the relationship between life and nature. Turkana custom mandates that at a funeral, "Certain animals must be killed by special people and in a well-defined way. The deceased's favorite animal is killed. This is the animal whose name he bears; whose praises were acclaimed in song and dance. In the mortuary rites, man, animal, ancestors and *Akuj* (God) are brought together in a new relationship and the Turkana world is reconstituted."[99] This intention underlies the moral philosophy of other African peoples as well.

If, therefore, the basis of African morality is the promotion of human life, then the existential ethical *duty* of every African person is to see to it that life is transmitted as fully as possible from one generation to another. Fecund marriage in any of its many forms assures this; accordingly, marriage is an ethical duty. Certain funerary rites must also be performed because they avail the living of the deceased elders' vital power, without which life can only be impoverished. For the same reason, anything that threatens the full transmission of life in interpersonal or social relationships must be fought against. The practice of medicine and the forms of political organization aim to assure smooth transmission of the society's vital force through the generations.

---

[98]M. Wilson, *Rituals of Kinship among the Nyakyusa* (London: Oxford University Press, 1957), p. 30.

[99]Barrett, *Dying and Death among the Turkana, Part II*, p. 14.

Chapter 5

The Enemies of Life

In African Religion, as noted several times, morality and ethics refer to thoughts, words, attitudes, and actual behavior that promote the force of life. Conversely, when we speak of immorality and destruction, the reference is to those thoughts and attitudes—and, of course, people and other elements of creation—that act against the life force and eventually destroy life itself. In this chapter, there are several elements to consider that African Religion perceives as unambiguously anti-life forces. Even though they mutually interact, as is usually the case in African Religion, and it is therefore inaccurate to see them as separate entities, for the sake of clarity we will begin with the more visible and immediately experiential aspects of the diminishment and destruction of life. These are wrongdoing (wrong actions), illness, and witchcraft.

CONCEPTS AND UNDERSTANDINGS

In the beginning, it is important to be clear about the use and meaning of concepts in this realm. These involve both abstraction and concreteness of expression. What is elsewhere conceptualized and explained as "sin" or "evil," for example, is better expressed in African Religion by the concept of "wrongdoing," "badness," or "destruction of life." This does not imply that the more abstract notions of sin and evil are non-existent in African religious consciousness; it is to say, however, that the moral perspective of African Religion is quite concrete and pragmatic. The

161

concept "sin/evil" seems to give less emphasis to wrong or bad *actions,* which emanate from *bad people,* people who have an "evil eye" or "bad heart," which the African religious consciousness prefers.

In African Religion, sin is always attached to a wrongdoer and, ultimately, the wrongdoer is a human person. The sense here, then, is that sin and evil do not and cannot exist in human experience except as perceived in people. It is people who are evil or sinful, whether or not they are aided by invisible forces. For, even when invisible forces intervene in human life to cause harm, it is more often than not because they are "used" by evil people, or are manipulated by forces on earth. Otherwise, these spirits (though without physical bodies of their own) are personalized by the African religious mentality to express their badness in what they do as "bodied" beings. It is people or personalized beings who are evil, precisely because they actually entertain bad intentions, utter bad words, or engage in wrong deeds. In other words, they are incarnations of evil powers, at least for the time they behave in an anti-life manner, that frustrate the flowering of life and life-energies.

In the preceding chapter we noted that even if the life-force is understood to be diffused in all parts of the human body (as it is in all parts of the other elements of creation), it is perceived by African Religion to be more concentrated in some parts than in others. Thus, blood has a very high concentration of the power of life, so much so that it is often identified with life itself. Consequent are the many taboos surrounding blood as well as the function of sharing blood in cementing blood-pacts or blood-friendships, and in assuring transitions through the critical stages of life.

Hair is another part of the body with a high concentration of life force and is therefore symbolic of life. This is why, when a close relative dies, many traditions require shaving off one's hair completely as a sign, at least in one sense, of the extinction of relative's worldly life-force. When the hair grows back—and this is what the ritual also says—the life of the family and clan, now aided by the new life-force of the deceased relative, must continue and thrive. This represents the same understanding of death as the beginning of life that was explained earlier in the Bahema funerary rite of the paterfamilias and his surviving sons.[1] Saliva is also perceived to have a high concentration of the life-force, thus its frequent use in blessings or curses. In much the same sense, fecal matter and urine represent the life of the individual, and so are seen to contain special power to be used for harm.

Just as vital power is diffused in all parts of the body and yet more concentrated in some, so is the power that leads to wrong-doing. In this latter respect the head, the heart, the stomach, and the eyes are particularly significant. With various African peoples, harmful intentions originate from one or the other of these organs because, once again, this is where the concentration of forces for possible wrongdoing is to be found. Intentions are translated from these human organs, voluntarily or involuntarily, into words, attitudes, or actions that diminish life. Even ordinary conversation often indicates the ethical significance of these organs as possible enemies of life if not properly managed and controlled. When a person is referred to as having a "bad heart," what is meant is that the individual in question is un- or antisocial, perhaps greedy, and therefore readily capable of harming others. On the other hand, people who are afraid that something wrong may befall them due to external forces say that their "hearts ache." The same is the case with the stomach and head. If these organs are "dirty," it means that the individuals concerned are incapable of fostering life in various ways. And as Placide Tempels notes, anger induces "darkness before a person's eyes" (*Mu meso mufita fututu,* as the Baluba express it),[2] making the destruction of life immediately probable.

These organs are also the seats of "enmity, hatred, envy, jealousy, evil speech, even false praise or lying eulogy . . . "[3] To put it more accurately, they are seats of life-forces that have been perverted, for enmity, hatred, envy, lying and so on are nothing other than perversions of bonding, love, sharing, and honesty. Thus hair (growing on the head), blood (pumped by the heart), fecal

---

[1]See pp.86-87 in chapter 3, above.
[2]P. Tempels, *Bantu Philosophy.* Trans. by C. King, mimeo, n.d., p. 47.
[3]Ibid., p. 47.

matter (coming from the bowels or the stomach), and saliva (also emanating from the bowels, according to African conceptions) all signify life. It is not surprising, then, that they are also the materials most sought by those who wish to harm life. To be able to manipulate them through mystical powers is to have power over the body and life of the person from whom they come.

On account of their vital properties, the same elements in animals can also be used to harm humans. John Roscoe has shown this among the Baganda. "If a man wished to kill another," he writes, "he would take a fowl, dig a hole in the path leading to the man's house, kill the fowl there, let the blood run into the hole, cut off the fowl's head and bury it with the blood." If the person for whom it is intended walks over it, he or she will die.[4]

Before leaving this topic, let me say something about the eye, another organ of the body that is frequently seen to play a part in the destruction of the life-force. The phenomenon of the "evil eye" is a belief in many parts of the world, as Clarence Maloney asserts, and it means simply that "someone can project harm by looking at another's property or person."[5] In African Religion, the phenomenon of the evil eye shares the features that characterize it in other parts of the world. Maloney mentions seven such features. It is believed that,

> (1) power emanates from the eye (or mouth) and strikes some object or person; (2) the stricken object is of value, and its destruction or injury is sudden; (3) the one casting the evil eye may not know he has the power; (4) the one affected may not be able to identify the source of the power; (5) the evil eye can be deflected or its effects modified or cured by particular devices, rituals and symbols; (6) the belief helps to explain or rationalize sickness, misfortune, or loss of possessions such as animals or crops; and (7) in

---

[4]Quoted by J. O'Donohue, *Magic and Witchcraft in Southern Uganda* (Kampala, Uganda: Gaba Publications, n.d., no. 36), p. 30.
[5]C. Maloney, "Introduction," in C. Maloney, ed., *The Evil Eye* (New York: Columbia University Press, 1976), p. v.

at least some functioning of the belief everywhere, envy is a factor.[6]

A few peoples, such as the Amhara of Ethiopia, distinguish a certain class of people who are considered to have the evil eye. They call these people the *buda*. They are not part of the Amhara ethnic group, and they usually are potters. Despite themselves, the *buda* possess the power to curse or destroy others. Their power to "eat" people is demonstrated in several ways: they may change themselves into hyenas, find victims, gaze upon them at night, and then go back home and change into human form again. Eventually, the victims who have been "eaten" die. A second way the *buda* kill their victims is to tie a knot in a certain plant and squeeze it slowly. The victims also die. A third method is simply gazing at the victim, who slowly dies. *Buda* are believed to resurrect their victims and turn them into mute slaves or "helpers" for a period of years before the latter disintegrate.[7] This last method of attack—the power to harm people simply by gazing at them—is the most common in other parts of Africa. Using the victims as mute slaves is also done, for example, among the Sukuma-Nyamwezi of Tanzania. Unlike among the Amhara, however, a person with the evil eye need not belong to a specific class of people. On the contrary, such people are all around one and may even be one's kin. At any rate, there is the belief that malevolent energies subsist in all human beings, and anyone driven by envy or jealousy can, willy-nilly, cast the evil eye.

In such cases, a person with the evil eye may even have distinguishing physical characteristics. Among the Lugbara of Sudan, such people can sometimes be spotted "by a squint or by red eyes, and by a shifty and ill-natural glance."[8] People with the evil eye

---

6Ibid., pp. vii-viii.

7R. A. Remininck, "The Evil Eye Belief Among the Amhara," in C. Maloney, ed., *The Evil Eye*, pp. 87-91.

8J. Middleton, *Lugbara Religion: Ritual and Authority Among an East African People* (London: Oxford University Press, 1960), p. 241. See also J. Middleton, "The Concept of 'Bewitching' in Lugbara," in J. Middleton, ed., *Magic, Witchcraft, and Curing* (Garden City, New York: The Natural History Press, 1967), p. 60.

are usually greedy and grumpy and, as the Kipsigis of Kenya understand them, they are practically incapable of not feeling envious or jealous. Even if they want to be good, the Kipsigis say, people with the evil eye cannot. For, if a woman with the evil eye "sees a man being happy, she is jealous and casts a spell; if a child is fat, she casts a spell; if a cow has much milk, she casts a spell. Her eyes are 'bad.' "[9] While among the Kipsigis, most people with the evil eye are female, with the neighboring Luo they are exclusively female. Known in Luo as *jasihoho*, these women inherit their power through the maternal side. It cannot be acquired. They harm people and things by simply gazing at them, and their motivation is uncontrollable jealousy or envy at the success or good fortune enjoyed by others. Because it destroys life, the evil eye is understood in Africa as a type of witchcraft, which shall be described in more depth below.

WRONGDOING AS CONTRAVENTION OF MORAL CODES

In African Religion, wrongdoing relates to the contravention of specific codes of community expectations, including taboos. Individuals and the whole community must observe these forms of behavior to preserve order and assure the continuation of life in its fullness. To threaten in any way to break any of the community codes of behavior, which are in fact moral codes, endangers life; it is bad, wrong, or "sinful."

Many of these moral codes are very well known to the adult members of a given community and have been inculcated from childhood through the normal daily processes of socialization. During the initiation process they are imprinted on the body and mind of an individual in a very special and practically unforgettable way, as explained above. Some codes or taboos may be less well-known and a few known only to a limited number of people because they escape mention during the initiation period, or are simply taken for granted. But all moral customs, whether

---

[9] J. G. Peristiany, *The Social Institutions of the Kipsigis* (London: George Routledge & Sons, 1939), p. 226.

known or unknown, require observance. In fact, less well-known codes and taboos present greater danger since it is possible to transgress them without being aware of it. Ignorance, though, seldom exempts one from the consequences of a transgression, although it may occasionally lessen the force of the shame or ease the conditions of purification. Still, whatever the circumstances, any violation is wrongdoing. In the example of an incestuous marriage among the Gikuyu, referred to above, the young people concerned did not know they were related when they entered into marriage. Nonetheless, they were considered to be guilty of breaking the incest taboo. In that particular case, purification rites were undertaken so that the marriage could continue as a legitimate affinal relationship.

Even if the moral codes involved are small or insignificant, each is nevertheless important in the ethical system and the breach of any one constitutes an unacceptable act for the individual and often the entire community. Because of the inner dynamics and interconnectedness of African Religion's moral codes, to refuse to give due respect to the elders, for example, may ultimately be as serious a transgression as the deliberate refusal to marry and have children, the refusal to take care of a brother's widow or a sister's widower and procreate in their name, or the refusal or negligence to offer sacrifices and frequent libations to the ancestors. Disrespect for elders implies disrespect for the ancestors as well, for the elders are their visible "representatives" on earth. Sacrifices offered by disrespectful individuals or libations made by them to the ancestors cannot be genuine. But perhaps most seriously, such disrespect suggests that one refuses, by one's attitude, to have children. Such behavior may indicate, in fact, that one desires to be treated in such a manner by one's own offspring. And no one wants to have disrespectful children. Faced with any disrespect by youth, a potent curse by an elder would be: "May your own children do to you what you have done to me."

Relationships between the sexes often consist of important moral codes that may appear on the surface to be insignificant. In patriarchal societies, such as that of the Dinka of Sudan, women are generally expected to be respectful of men. This is most evident on occasions that manifest the presence of the sacred in some particular way. One such occasion is a meal. Francis Deng explains how, among the Dinka, girls and young women must show "exceeding deference" to the men, particularly when visitors are present. "A girl or woman approaches men well-poised and with her skirts properly held in place. Some yards away she kneels and approaches them on her knees. Sitting on her legs in almost ritualistic manner, she places the food in front of them, crawls backwards on her knees until she is some distance away, and then stands up to go, holding her skirts in place and walking with the self-conscious yet dignified poise with which she had come."[10] Some of these moral codes apply to men as well, such as the avoidance between in-laws preceding a marriage, as discussed above.

Although the conception of morality in African Religion demands that both individuals and communities refrain from wrongdoing, it demands much more than merely avoiding the transgression of rules and taboos: it requires people *to consciously pursue right behavior*. In fact, it is the pursuance of right behavior, rather than the avoidance of wrong, that is the distinguishing mark between an authentically good (or moral/ethical) person (*mtu, omuntu,* in most Bantu languages) and one who is not truly so. In other words, ethical behavior requires what we may call a "maximalist" approach to doing good, rather than a "minimalist" attitude of simply avoiding wrong attitudes and actions. For example, hospitality to strangers is an important ethical requirement. However, precisely *how* to be hospitable is left to each individual's discretion. A person might refuse a drink of water to a traveler, saying there is no drinking water in the house at the moment (even if there is) without incurring any major sanction. Similarly, one might ignore the code of welcoming passersby to a meal. Nevertheless, the possibility of being cast as a

---

[10] F. M. Deng, *The Dinka of the Sudan* (New York: Holt, Rinehart and Winston, 1972), p. 59. Because our purpose is to show the ethics of African Religion as it sees itself, we prescind here, as we do throughout the book, from discussing the question of whether or not this is an instance of cultural/religious oppression of women, and so on. As we indicated in chapter one, this question, important though it is, constitutes a different level of discussion.

"stingy" or "greedy" person for such behavior is never far away. Instead, the behavior that merits the praise of the community and showers upon one the blessings of the ancestors calls on a person to go out of the way to a neighbor's house next door to get water for a traveler if there is none in one's own house, or to call out to passers-by to come and share a meal. These are the signs of a good, morally upright person.

Moral culpability, the admission of wrongdoing by an individual or group of people, follows several interlinked steps between the wrongdoer and the community. It entails much more than personal, interior feelings of guilt. At most, such personal feelings constitute only an initial step in a wrongdoer's possible acceptance and confession of guilt. But the most decisive element in the recognition and acceptance of moral culpability involves the community. The community's perception of a person's act or attitude as contrary to accepted codes of ethical living may have two possible effects. On the one hand, it may trigger in the wrongdoer an awareness of failure, of having let down oneself and the community. If so, the wrongdoer feels remorse or "shame" for the wrong, a sense of personal shortcoming, of betrayal against oneself and the clan. If the matter in question is serious and the community insists that the wrongdoer redress the wrong, the guilty party may be led to admit and confess, a process that usually culminates in an appropriate rite of reconciliation with the community, the ancestors, and God. This may include some form of punishment for the wrongdoer. On the other hand, if the person presumed guilty by society does not feel shame and does not admit wrongdoing, means are sought to prove innocence or guilt. While they can be legal, for example, a trial before a chief, most often the means are religious. They may include divination or trial by ordeal and the verdict is believed to establish, beyond all reasonable doubt, innocence or guilt. These measures to reestablish the energy of life will be discussed in chapter six.

The role of shame has a very important significance in the African religious psychology of wrongdoing. Given the holistic perception of the human person predominant in African Religion, it is not possible to make a neat distinction between guilt and shame, as is done in contemporary Western psychology. In Western psychology, shame is associated with "being," whereas guilt is associated with "feeling," and these are seen as radically different. John Bradshaw is one of the authors who have popularized this distinction. "Shame is a being wound and differs greatly from the feeling of guilt," he writes. "Guilt says I've *done* something wrong; shame says there *is* something wrong with me. Guilt says I've *made* a mistake; shame says I *am* a mistake. Guilt says what I *did* was not good; shame says I *am* no good."[11] For Bradshaw, therefore, guilt is proper to wrongdoing, while shame is psychopathological, playing no positive purpose in moral development.

In African Religion, however, guilt and shame interpenetrate so closely that, even if we accept Bradshaw's distinction, it is understood that "feeling" results intrinsically and radically from "being," and "being" leads ineluctably to "feeling" and "doing." Thus, it is not possible for a person to have done wrong if there is nothing wrong with the person. An individual with the evil eye harms others because he or she *is* evil. Indeed, if a certain individual has made a mistake, to a certain degree that same individual *is* a mistake. Being and doing cannot be divorced in the African understanding of things. Guilt in African Religion, then, is the psychological/moral stage of development where a person "owns up to" personal worthlessness or shame. In this case, shame is the primary factor in the recognition and confession of guilt.

Shame, as described by Gershen Kaufman (and paraphrased by Bradshaw), agrees in a morally positive sense with African Religion's understanding of it:

> Shame is the source of the most disturbing inner states which deny full human life. Depression, alienation, self-doubt, isolating loneliness, paranoid and schizoid phenomena, compulsive disorders, splitting of the self, perfectionism, a deep sense of inferiority, inadequacy or failure, the

---

[11]J. Bradshaw, *Bradshaw on the Family—A Revolutionary Way of Self-Discovery* (Deerfield Beach, Florida: Health Communications, 1988), p. 2.

so-called borderline conditions and disorders of narcissism, all result from shame. Shame is a kind of soul-murder. Once shame is internalized, it is characterized by a kind of psychic numbness, which becomes the foundation for a kind of death in life. Forged in the matrix of our source relationships, shame conditions every other relationship in our lives. Shame is a total non-self-acceptance.[12]

For African religious psychology, all of these disorders or "non-self-acceptance," which need not be permanent, occur as a consequence of shame for doing wrong, which also means *being* wrong or worthless. They happen because one is, in a sense, "not accepted" by society because of a wrong that has been done. Because being human depends so much on communion with society, society's rejection can only bring about self-rejection. The question here is one of moral authority. "In the case of shame," as Agnes Heller has persuasively argued, "the authority is *social custom*—rituals, habits, codes or rosters of behavior—represented by the '*eye of others.*'" It is an "external authority," but this is not to say "that shame is [thereby] not internalized." Heller suggests that "the question as to whether *shame* is internalized becomes irrelevant once it is seen that shame is a feeling and, as such, an internal occurrence." She argues:

> The proper question then is whether or not the occurrence of the feeling signifies the internalization (not of shame) but of the external authority. If not, shame can only be reactive and would not imply the recognition of the validity of the norms of the external authority by the members of the community. But if the members of a community did not consider certain actions and modes of behavior as "shameful," the *fear* of being put to shame would not make people avoid transgressing against the external authority of conduct, and no one would be put to shame at all.[13]

---

[12]Ibid., p. 2.
[13]A. Heller, *The Power of Shame: A Rational Perspective* (London: Routledge & Kegan Paul, 1985), pp. 3-4.

Just as the people of New Guinea distinguish between "shame of the skin" for minor transgressions and "deep shame" for major ones,[14] many African societies distinguish between "shame of the face" and "shame of the heart or soul." To come into unavoidable physical contact with an in-law may be shame of the skin or of the face, but to commit incest is deep shame or a shame of the heart that calls for confession and retribution. If the person is to become whole again, the shame needs to be removed by specific rites.

AFFLICTION AS A CONSEQUENCE OF WRONGDOING

Wrongdoing can never be neutral. It always has consequences to the perpetrator, and very often to the perpetrator's community. Consequences come in the form of calamities: blight, failure to kill game or acquire food, murderous anger, and all kinds of anti-life phenomena that may emerge in society, whether they are personal, social, physical, psychological or natural. These calamities may be generically categorized as affliction, usually perceived as illness or disease. There is disease if rains do not fall so there is no food in the land, or if too much rain falls and crops are spoiled, or if cattle do not give birth so there is a shortage of milk. Any failure that befalls the individual or the community is interpreted as disease. Human illness, of course, forms the deepest core of this conception.

The causality of disease in humans can be explained in three ways, using the description of David Westerlund. There is the "religious (suprahuman)" causality, which presupposes "a belief that human beings in different ways are influenced by or dependent on suprahuman or spiritual powers such as God and spirits of nature." Then there is the "social (human)" causality, which "refers to relations between living human beings, which in Africa frequently entail a supranormal component." Witchcraft and curses serve as examples, even though, as will be shown below, "witchcraft" is often used as an all-embracing term for affliction-

---

[14]Ibid., p. 4.

causation. Finally, there is the "natural (mainly physical)" causation. "Natural, or mainly physical, explanations [of disease causation] refer to entities of nature, that is, the effects of, for instance, insects, germs, natural substances, forces or conditions, such as certain food, the weather or lack of equilibrium of some basic elements in the body."[15]

Religious, social, and natural causes of affliction cannot be seen in Africa as entirely separate and unconnected. Rather, they all constitute stages in the psychological/spiritual awareness of an immoral situation. The order of conceptual awareness and any attempt at analysis and understanding of an affliction usually, though not necessarily always, begins with a natural explanation of causation. Unless witchcraft, spirit, ancestral, or divine displeasure are immediately suspected, a natural cause is first sought and then initially accepted as the reason for a particular happening. As a matter of fact, natural causes are often very obvious, such as tripping on a stone and hurting oneself because one is drunk, or being bitten by a snake while hunting in tall grass, or being hit by a falling tree in a storm. Even when these causes are not very obvious, people know through experience that certain insects transmit certain diseases and that contact with certain invisible substances is harmful. Among the Zinza of Tanzania, for example, disease that happens in this way is "just a disease (*ndwararwara*)." As Bjerke explains,

> Such a disease will typically either be ascribed to an accumulation of too much blood in the affected area, a condition known as *muziga*, or more often, to the harmful activity of one or other of some peculiar type of snake of which everybody has a varying number in his stomach. Such snakes may cause various diseases when provoked and irritated by food which is not to their liking, or by

---

[15]D. Westerlund, *Pluralism and Change: A Comparative and Historical Approach to African Disease Etiologies* (Stockholm: Universitet Stockholm, 1989), p. 179. See also, S. Bjerke, *Religion and Misfortune: The Bacwezi Complex and the Other Spirit Cults of the Zinza of Northwestern Tanzania* (Oslo: Universitetsforlaget, 1981), pp. 112-32.

saliva, urine, stools, or the "bad smell" (*kinuko*) of people suffering from the disease in question.[16]

There are medicines intended to "drive the disease away." Although cupping, the use of a specially made animal horn to suck "bad" or "harmful" blood from the body, is used among the Zinza and other Bantu ethnic groups, herbs and roots with medicinal qualities are the usual means of treatment.[17]

If the particular affliction does not grow in seriousness, the natural explanation will suffice. However, when afflictions grow worse, as often happens, the second and third clusters of causality are never far away from the African's mind. In fact, it is more correct to say that social causality is already contained in the first understanding of affliction-causality. If one trips on a stone while walking, for instance, one will realize and accept the fact that one has just tripped. Yet lingering at the back of one's mind will be the questions, Why me? And, why did I trip at this particular moment? Why didn't the person I was walking with trip? Why did I take this particular side of the path where the stones are? It is never questioned that sometimes people hurt themselves on stones along the path or that some snakes are poisonous and can kill. The issue at the social level of affliction-causation is different. The issue is "why the snake bit the particular person and not the one walking immediately in front of or behind him; it is not why tuberculosis killed A but why the disease attacked A and not B?"[18] To answer these questions satisfactorily, we must resort to human or religious causality. It is on these levels that misfortune begins to make sense in the African moral perception of the world.

The reason here goes back to the African world view described in some detail in the second chapter. The world ought to be harmonious, balanced, and good. Accordingly, misfortune, which means imbalance and disharmony in the universe, does not just

---

[16]Bjerke, *Religion and Misfortune*, p. 113-4.

[17]Ibid.

[18]O. K. Mutungi, *The Legal Aspects of Witchcraft in East Africa With Particular Reference to Kenya* (Nairobi: East African Literature Bureau, 1977), p. 18.

happen. If and when it does, it is because there is a malevolent cause, either human or suprahuman. Morality demands that these causes of disruption and affliction in human life, and their motivations, be identified. Even if the wrongdoer happens to be the victim, it is still important that the fact be known and something be done about it.[19]

In the "religious" category, the ancestors may cause illness and suffering. This is often diagnosed by religious specialists (diviners) to be the case. On being consulted about the cause of a brother's illness, the diviner (*n'anga*) of the Shona of Zimbabwe, for example, might say: "I have seen your one in trouble. Your trouble is serious. The cause of the illness, I have seen, is due to his dead father, whose spirit is complaining that he did not brew beer for him and no longer remembers him."[20] Thus, the deceased father is angry for being neglected. The sick person, then, must realize his neglect of responsibility and correct the situation.

Ancestral spirits may cause affliction because they desire sacrifice and offerings. We mentioned earlier that as a rule, they do not visit death upon their descendants; they are interested instead with the development of the latter's life. But the living must fulfill their responsibilities to the ancestors, because that is the condition for order in the universe. A central element of order is peace, and peace is expressed by way of commensality. Human beings destroy this peace if they do not adhere to the principle of commensality where their ancestors are concerned. The Sukuma say, "If descendants suffer from maladies caused by the ancestors, it is because the descendants have neglected them. For instance, the living may have disregarded the possessions of ancestors, failed to observe lineage rules or neglected to conduct rituals in the name of the ancestors. A descendant may also suffer because of past grievances."[21]

The question of ritual is extremely important in this regard.

---

[19]See Bjerke, *Religion and Misfortune,* p. 114.
[20]See M. Gelfand, *The Spiritual Beliefs of the Shona* (Gwelo: Mambo Press, 1977), p. 78.
[21]Westerlund, *Pluralism and Change,* p. 188.

"Among the Sukuma, [as among many other African societies], certain sanctified objects and animals represent ancestors. Moreover, miniature houses are built for them. Such objects, animals and houses of ancestors must be handled with appropriate religious care..." With reference to the proper consecration and handling of these, S. Tcherkezoff writes about "the domestication of the dead. Without a due 'domestication' of and respect for the ancestors there will be rampant problems of disease."[22]

But the other side of the picture also applies. When, for unknown or unknowable reasons, the ancestral spirits cause misfortune, they also break the peace between them and their descendants. In other words, they become "estranged" from them. Thus, "there can be no commensality between the human members...and the spirits who brought about this state." And so, "From the cult point of view," as Bjerke notes, "this implies that no calendrical rituals in which the principle of commensality is expressed, may be performed until the state of peace has been brought back by means of critical rituals culminating in acts of commensality."[23]

Non-ancestral human spirits and nature spirits also may and do cause misfortune. Many are simply malevolent spirits who bring disorder for no good reason. They might be spirits of people who did not receive a proper burial at death, for instance, who are resentful and go about trying to avenge themselves and are never satisfied. Spirits of children who did not go through the initiation process also belong to this category. They are extremely dangerous in their potential to cause harm to the living. Nature spirits sometimes cause affliction because they have been harmed in the earthly elements they inhabit. It is known, for example, that certain things and places are their habitat and reserved for their use. Certain trees or caves or forests, for example, should neither be put to human use or trespassed; to do so invites their anger and brings about calamity. A previous chapter referred to a woman who ate fruit from a tree reserved for the forest gods

---

[22]Ibid.
[23]Bjerke, *Religion and Misfortune*, p. 122. See also Gelfand, *The Spiritual Beliefs of the Shona*, pp. 74-90.

(spirits), and one who collected firewood in the same circumstances. Both were punished for their transgressions. (Nature spirits also require sacrifices before a permissible undertaking involving their "territory." The sacrifice seeks permission to trespass that territory for the purpose of human existence. If the sacrifice is not undertaken, while there might not be immediate physical illness, there might be a calamity of a slightly different nature: for example, a hunting expedition or a fishing trip may not succeed in killing game or catching fish. But, as we have seen, in the long run this is also a form of illness.)

Whereas ancestral (and sometimes nature) spirits need to be placated through sacrifices and offerings, those spirits that are merely malevolent and unknown must be "expelled" or "driven away" so that they will not cause affliction. The services of a religious specialist are required for this. When such a spirit of affliction is diagnosed, it must be disowned and made to go "where it belongs," that is, to its proper family or habitat. "You go away, where you belong," the spirit may be scolded. "This is the wrong family . . . I do not want you."[24]

Agents of certain illnesses may sometimes be determined by the symptoms they cause in an individual. But this is not always an exact method of diagnosis, as John Middleton found among the Lugbara of Uganda. More often than not, "the nature of the sickness is determined not by its symptoms," he observes, "but rather by the identity of the agent as decided by oracular utterance." Nevertheless, it is still important to recognize that the symptoms of the illness are the first signs that enable people to classify the disease according to what kind of loss of vital energy is involved. For the Lugbara, for example, "A man aches and grows thin and so knows that the ghosts have sent sickness to him; he aches in his stomach or his bones in the early morning and knows that a witch or sorcerer has affected him; he aches in his head and knows a kinsman has cursed him; his wife does not conceive and he knows a grandmother has cursed him; and so on." There is a certain "inexactitude" in the terms used. In these descriptions, "growing thin," for instance, may not be "neces-

[24]See Gelfand, *The Spiritual Beliefs of the Shona*, p. 87.

sarily observable." Rather the symptoms described are "an assumed physiological concomitant to any general physical or even mental malaise," that is, a general loss of vital energy.[25] On being questioned about how one feels physically, one does not point directly to what ails one physically, but instead relates all the circumstances, including people, places, things, and times, surrounding the origin of one's malaise, all of which are significant to properly understand it.

Whatever the cause of an affliction, it must be placed into the category of an enemy of life. Illness is a statement about the condition of the physical body. Something has happened to it and, as a consequence, it is not in the state that it should be. Here already, elements of perception bring the understanding of illness into the realm of power and relationships. All illness, but particularly a serious one, means erosion of power, and a sick person is spoken of as "losing" or "gaining" power as the illness progresses or recedes. Thus, a person may become so sick that he or she loses the "power" to sit, stand, or even cough or breathe. This power is not merely the energy to perform those human functions, but the decline of one's being itself. This decline of power is symptomatic of broken relationships, and consequently of disturbed harmony and peace in the community. Whatever the cause of the affliction is, it ultimately means that there is no order or peace—either among human beings, or between them and the spirits, ancestors, or God, that is, the universe. Africans remain aware, particularly in the case of affliction, that ultimate power belongs to God. In other words, they strongly hold that God

is the manifestation of power in its totality, even though his power is not experienced in as immediate a fashion as the power of the ancestors. As the ultimate master of life and death, He may, occasionally, punish evil-doers; and it is generally recognized that a person cannot be sick without the connivance of God. If a person does not recover from

---

[25]See Middleton, *Lugbara Religion: Ritual and Authority,* pp. 79-80.

an illness, the lack of recovery may be caused directly by God Himself.[26]

It must not be forgotten that the destructive intervention of these invisible forces ultimately impels human beings to take steps to protect life. To a great degree, that is its purpose. It is meant to shock human beings into reestablishing the equilibrium in the universe required to preserve and continue life. Even those spirits of affliction that are clearly agents of diminishment of life have another function. Paradoxically, through their agency to diminish life, they indirectly become agents that can restore the abundance of life. Thus, while we cannot overlook their role as anti-life agents, we must at the same time acknowledge their indirect positive function. If humanity's moral duty is to enhance life, it is to be expected that other powers should intervene as reminders if this duty is neglected. More often than not, God and ancestral spirits are, therefore, "provoked" by human irresponsibility to visit people with pain and suffering. Mere malevolent spirits, however, even though they may serve a positive purpose in the end, need no provocation. As we have mentioned, the latter enjoy causing affliction. Their counterparts in the visible world are the practitioners of witchcraft.

WITCHCRAFT AS THE HUMAN EMBODIMENT OF EVIL

In African Religion, an understanding of witchcraft is central to understanding wrongdoing as evil. What is witchcraft? How does it influence the day-to-day life of the African religionist? To start with, it is again important to clarify our use of terms. If there is one area where a foreign expression used to describe African realities is likely to fall short, or even mislead, it is in this area of witchcraft. The English word "witchcraft," for example, as Cosmas Haule has argued, does not express all the nuances contained

---

[26]Westerlund, *Pluralism and Change,* p. 188.

in the various African names of the phenomenon.[27] The terminology that the Bantu and Luo peoples apply to the phenomenon we refer to here as witchcraft illustrates this point, and the distinctions they make apply with very minor variations throughout the continent.

Among the Bantu of Tanzania, witchcraft is called *uchawi*, with minor variations among the different groups. *Uchawi* is a generic term that includes a wide variety of practical realities. As Haule has shown, the word *mchawi* (or witch) "may be applied to a [malevolent] witch, a sorcerer, a witch-doctor, a herbalist," or anyone considered to have more power than that of the average person.[28] In addition to malevolent witches, sorcerers, medicine-doctors, and herbalists may possess the same powers as witches, but they are not necessarily malevolent. On the contrary, sometimes they use their power in benevolent ways. Because of the mystical power that they share with a "witch proper," they are also referred to as witches (using the vernacular).

Although discussion about herbalists and medicine-doctors belongs to the following chapter, it is proper to say something here about sorcery. David Tait investigated this phenomenon among the Konkomba of Ghana and Côte d'Ivoire. His findings apply as well to many other parts of the continent. The most important characteristic of the sorcerer, as opposed to the witch, Tait notes, is the fact that the sorcerer "does not kill at random." The sorcerer harms for a specific end: "Sorcery is a technique to be acquired, and the sorcerer kills with full knowledge of his evil intentions." What, then, characterizes the sorcerer, Tait asks? "He is always an individual working alone. He is one who chooses to make a deliberate approach to someone versed in sorcery to learn a technique. He is one who has asked a senior sorcerer to give him the medicine and by an act of will has eaten it in order to gain the mystical knowledge of sorcery. The sorcerer can, if he wills, cease to be a sorcerer. Indeed, to avoid the anger

---

[27]See C. Haule, *Bantu "Witchcraft" and Christian Morality: The Encounter of Bantu Uchawi with Christian Morality—An Anthropological and Theological Study* (Schonek-Beckenried: Nouvelle Revue de Science Missionnaire, 1969), pp. 20-26.

[28]Ibid., p. 20.

of God he must make that decision; and the problem of sorcery is therefore [also] a moral one."[29]

Because of the nature of its acquisition and use, sorcery is much more predictable than witchcraft, and thus protection against sorcery is more easily done. For instance, it is possible to secure one's homestead against sorcerers who fly by night to attack their victims by firmly closing the compound door at night. Similarly, a person on a late night journey usually makes his or her presence known by making audible noises of singing or whistling and thus scares away sorcerers. There are also "protective medicines" to use against sorcery, though "once the attack has begun, it is too late to use them."[30]

The Luo have the same thought patterns on this issue. Sorcerers of different kinds (*jandagla, jonawi*), herbalists, and various other kinds of medicine men/women (*jabilo, jamkingo, jasasia, jadil, ajuoga*), and witches properly so called (*jajuok* and *jasihoho*), all basically share in the same mysterious power. What distinguishes them is the way they use this power to harm life: the sorcerer is always conscious and intentional, whereas the witch acts automatically and often unintentionally.[31]

So, in African Religion, witchcraft in general must be understood as part of the mystery of the human person. Contrary to what the English word suggests, the reality of witchcraft in Africa is not primarily an "art" or a "craft." Haule correctly identifies it as "a mysterious power," indeed perhaps "the mysterious power" that resides in, and with, human beings.[32] As Africans see it, it is ubiquitous; it permeates all areas of life and is an ever-present reality in people's political, social, and economic organizations. Everywhere in Africa, as among the Azande, according to E. E. Evans-Pritchard, it plays a role "in agricultural, fishing, and hunting pursuits; in domestic life of homesteads as well as in

---

[29]D. Tait, "Konkomba Sorcery," in J. Middleton, ed., *Magic, Witchcraft and Curing*, p. 167.

[30]See ibid., p. 159.

[31]See A. B. C. Ocholla-Ayayo, *Traditional Ideology and Ethics Among the Southern Luo* (Uppsala: Scandinavian Institute of African Studies, 1976), pp. 153-65.

[32]Haule, *Bantu "Witchcraft,"* p. 21.

communal life of district and court." Its role and influence are not limited to activities of a social nature. Witchcraft influences personal life as well. Efforts to preserve and promote life cannot be understood without reference to the power of witchcraft, which is closely connected to and influences the establishment of law and the understanding of morality and ethics. As Evans-Pritchard notes further, there is, indeed, no aspect of culture, however small or insignificant, where the power and influence of witchcraft is absent.[33]

In the African mentality, everything wrong or bad in society and in the world, and, most particularly, various afflictions, originates in witchcraft. There is no kind of illness or hardship at all that may not ultimately be attributed to witchcraft. When natural or religious explanations fail to satisfy, the social explanation—witchcraft—is invariably invoked. As Evans-Pritchard observed among the Azande,

> If blight seizes the ground-nut crop it is witchcraft; if the bush is vainly scoured for game it is witchcraft; if women laboriously bale water out of a pool and are rewarded by but a few small fish it is witchcraft; if termites do not rise when their swarming is due and a cold useless night is spent in waiting for their flight it is witchcraft; if a wife is sulky and unresponsive to her husband it is witchcraft; if a prince is cold and distant with his subject it is witchcraft; if a magical rite fails to achieve its purpose it is witchcraft; if, in fact, any failure or misfortune falls upon any one at any time and in relation to any of the manifold activities of his life it may be due to witchcraft.[34]

The power of witchcraft is not a prerogative of only certain individuals. Every human being has this potential power, so that in fact, every human being is potentially a witch. In the great majority of people this power is latent, dormant, or "cool," as

---

[33]E. E. Evans-Pritchard, *Witchcraft, Oracles, and Magic Among the Azande* (Oxford: Clarendon Press, 1937), p. 63.
[34]Ibid., pp. 63-4.

the Azande themselves would express it. In some other people, however—regardless of whether they are consciously aware of it or not—it is active or "hot." Consequently, if confronted with the suggestion (or mild accusation) that one may be a witch, a Zande person can only feebly retort: "If I possess witchcraft in my belly I am not aware of it; may it cool," an admission that one is, in fact, a potential witch.[35] In an active witch, this power operates psychically. "A witch performs no rite, utters no spell, and possesses no medicines. An act of witchcraft is a psychic act."[36] The belief of the Ga people of Ghana attests to the same power. As Margaret Field reports in *Religion and Medicine of the Ga People*, the power of witchcraft to cause harm does not have any "palpable apparatus connected with it, no rites, ceremonies, incantations, or invocations that the witch has to perform. It is simply projected at will from the mind of the witch . . . Witches are people mentally afflicted with the obsession that they have the power to harm others by thinking them harm."[37]

Just as vital energy is concentrated in certain organs of the body—such as blood or hair—the power of witchcraft can also be concentrated as "witchcraft-substance" in certain organs of the human anatomy. For the Azande, it resides in the liver. "It is attached to the edge of the liver," they say, and you have only to cut open the belly of the witch, as in an autopsy, to find the witchcraft-substance there.[38] However, it bears emphasizing that those who possess this substance are not necessarily *aware* that they have it. Nevertheless, it gives them great power to act and to succeed in their actions. Among the Tiv of central Nigeria, it is believed that "All old people are supposed to have this substance, for that is what enabled them to live to old age. If the witchcraft-substance is good it can be used for personal advantage, and it inspires men to particular feats of talent. But it is potentially dangerous. Only with this substance can a man

---

[35]Ibid., p. 123.
[36]Ibid., p. 21.
[37]Cited in G. Parrinder, *Witchcraft: European and African* (London: Faber and Faber, 1958), p. 135.
[38]Evans-Pritchard, *Witchcraft, Oracles, and Magic*, p. 22.

bewitch another, send him evil dreams, and make poisons to kill him."[39]

Even in communities that do not identify specific organs as concentrating the witchcraft-substance, witchcraft is still a pervasive power in an active witch, a power that is compulsive and cannot be resisted by the individual in question. A witch is irresistibly driven to cause misfortune. Such power is so strong that it often palpably affects the physical appearance of the individual. Witches may be unusually old, strong, beautiful, or ugly. Often they are described as having red eyes. Extreme physical deformities may also be a sign of witchcraft, as are excessive social successes or failures. Consequently, a very rich or a very poor person, or a very popular or unpopular individual, may all be characterized as witches.[40]

Even though every person is potentially a witch in African thought, that is to say that all human beings have witchcraft power in them, active witchcraft is usually either inherited, bought, or acquired: "caught" is the general African description for this alternative type of transmission of witchcraft power. The Basuto and the Lovedu of Southern Africa and the Azande of Sudan are among the peoples who believe that witchcraft is inherited. With these groups, witchcraft is transmitted from parent to children and, as a rule, from mother to daughter, or from father to son. The transmission of witchcraft by females is by far the most predominant among these peoples. Children "drink in the witchcraft from their mother's milk," the Lovedu say. Among them, "The mother is said to begin the training, teaching the child to cling to the wall like a bat long before it can walk."[41] The idea that witchcraft is inherited is not totally absent from other African peoples who hold that witchcraft can be bought or caught. The Nupe of northern Nigeria, for example, say that witchcraft "is acquired by rubbing a medicine into the eyes or on to the body." Still, they accept, even so, that it often constitutes

---

[39]Parrinder, *Witchcraft*, p. 136.
[40]J. Middleton, "The Concept of 'Bewitching' in Lugbara," in J. Middleton, ed., *Magic, Witchcraft, and Curing*, p. 65.
[41]Parrinder, *Witchcraft*, p. 143.

a family trait. For the Ga of Ghana, active witchcraft power may be bought or even "imposed upon the witch against her will." But they simultaneously affirm that it may also be inherited.[42]

The activity of witches is characterized universally by secrecy and loathsome behavior. Witches do not want their revolting activities exposed to the ordinary person. They break all the accepted norms of society. They reject kinship ties and loyalties and will as readily harm a kinsperson as anyone else. In fact, a general condition of "graduating" into a witchcraft sorority or fraternity (coven) is to kill and eat the flesh of a close relation. Nor do witches adhere to sexual taboos: they commit incest and cause other people to do so, or at least, to have incestuous dreams. Likewise, they are known to engage in sexual intercourse with spirits and animals. This is possible because they possess the power to change themselves into spirit-like beings at night and go to witches' assemblies while their physical bodies remain at home. Witches can also change themselves into animal shapes such as hyenas, owls, or other nocturnal creatures. Alternatively, they ride on these creatures to their assemblies. Moreover, human beings who are thought dead may actually be used by witches as "familiars," to run the witches' harmful errands, causing misfortune in society. When secretly active at night, they prefer to be naked, performing their dances while holding or actually spurting fire. They handle excrement, urine, and vomit for purposes of harming people through the life force that these materials represent. They also enjoy soiling their neighbors' yards and other property with these materials.

One of the more heinous things witches are said to do is eat human flesh. Because of their craving for it, they are often found assembled in graveyards. This craving is also believed to be one of the reasons why they have the urge to kill people. Among the Ga, Azande, Ibo, Nupe and Lovedu, this "eating" is not physical but "spiritual," in that it is the soul or the psyche—the actual vital force—of the victim that is "eaten." But with the Basuto and many other Bantu peoples, it involves actual consumption of the

---

[42]Ibid., p. 142. See also L, Mair, *Witchcraft* (New York: World University Library, 1969), pp. 47-52.

flesh. In either case, witches engage in this abhorrent behavior to enhance their own witchcraft power.[43]

To summarize, Parrinder has described the conception of the witch in African Religion:

> generally [but not exclusively] female. She goes out at night and meets in an assembly with other witches. She leaves her body in her hut and flies to the assembly, often as an owl, other bird, or animal. The witch preys on other people and procures a victim for consumption in the assembly. The blood of the victim is sucked or its members eaten. This causes the wasting disease to his physical body, and the victim lingers until the heart, liver, or some other vital organ is eaten. Children are often thought to be eaten by witches. Any disease may be taken as a sign of their evil machinations. Some people believe that the witch is possessed by a witch-spirit, or has with her some witch-substance . . . [44]

This brief description of witchcraft indicates the central place it holds in the moral structure of African Religion. It can be summarized in one sentence: "Witchcraft is *the* enemy of life." Harmony, order, good neighborliness or good company, cooperation and sharing, propriety and equitableness, honesty and transparency—all of which constitute signs of how human and created order should be—are denied in the most fundamental way by witchcraft. It is no wonder, then, that a witch "is a person who does not control the impulses that good members of society must keep in check. Insatiable desires and hatreds account, separately or together, for the deaths that witches cause."[45] Witches are "morose, unsociable people; people who eat alone so that they need not share their food, but who can be dangerous if others do not share food with them; arrogant people who pass by others without greeting them; people who are readily

---

[43]See Mair, *Witchcraft,* pp. 38-40.
[44]Parrinder, *Witchcraft,* p. 138.
[45]Mair, *Witchcraft,* p. 38.

offended."[46] By their actions or mere intentions, they make other people ill. Nothing is too vile for a witch, nothing too shocking. The solidarity of society and the unity between the living and the dead, fundamental elements in the order and survival of the universe, mean nothing to people with active inclinations to witchcraft.

Thus, witchcraft is intolerable for any society that values ethical principles and life itself. For, instead of working to strengthen the force of life, as all moral persons are required to do by religious tradition, witchcraft disturbs this order and causes chaos. Order requires that people act openly in daylight; that they exhibit more or less equal physical and mental powers; that they identify with kith and kin and act in solidarity with them; that they avoid anything associated with death, which is (except in mature old age) the ultimate negation of life; that they observe all sexual and other taboos of the community; that they bear normal children; that they try to do whatever has been determined by society as being the good that builds up the life and life-force of the community. Such is the normal and moral way for human beings to conduct their lives. But witchcraft contradicts all of this and in this sense is "an abomination . . . [and] there is no reason adequate to justify or to excuse such action of superlative wickedness."[47]

Paradoxically, in the moral order, witchcraft also serves as a sanction. Insofar as every human being experiences emotions of envy, hatred, anger, pride, lust, and so on, everyone is a potential witch. Witchcraft is, in essence, a personal failure to keep these destructive emotions in rein. This is indeed the horror of witchcraft. At any moment it may overcome an individual, become active or "hot," and act to destroy life and the power of life. Human beings must always be on guard against the potential of witchcraft that is in each one of them. They must always go out of their way to show love, care and concern, and sharing and good company. As a sanction, witchcraft constantly warns individuals, through the community, against meanness, inhospitable-

---

[46]Ibid., p. 43.
[47]Haule, *Bantu "Witchcraft,"* p. 96.

ness, quarrelsomeness, rudeness, sullenness, disloyalty, false or reckless speech, and disrespect towards elders.[48] Witchcraft reminds everyone that such behavior risks two dreaded things: that one might be accused of witchcraft, or that one will be harmed by witchcraft. According to J. La Fontaine, "In Bugisu [Kenya] the eccentric is branded as a witch ... *and fear of being thought a witch is the sanction which enforces conformity.* Children grow up with the realization that the stigma of nonconformity is dangerous; too great a departure from the norms of everyday conduct will attract the suspicion of others and lead to isolation and eventually destruction."[49]

Having established early on that morality/ethics refers *both* to principles *and* to actual behavior, we can clearly see the role of witchcraft as sanction against immoral behavior. In addition to establishing rules for right living, morality/ethics concerns itself with the cultivation and social inculcation of practical attitudes approved by the rules, on the one hand, and the discouragement and sanction of behavior deplored by the rules, on the other. In African Religion, the approved principles or virtues that are expected to rule the way of every person's life are kindness, conviviality and solidarity. Selfishness, envy, and secretiveness are vices. To avoid accusations or suspicions of witchcraft, then, people seek to behave in the way sanctioned by the principles and laws of the community. As Haule notes, summarizing various authors, this has "the effect of increasing social solidarity and conformity, since it is the non-conformer, the unpopular person or the recluse who is often accused, and may reaffirm social values by ... 'dramatically' defining the bad and by attributing to witches such reversals of accepted behavior as nakedness and the practice of incest. Fear of being accused of witchcraft may also prevent moving around at night, and thus act as a sanction against clandestine affairs ... "[50]

If and when a person is convicted of witchcraft, the consequences are invariably grave. The Lamba of Zambia spear a

---

[48]See ibid., p. 97.
[49]Quoted in ibid., p. 98.
[50]Ibid., p. 99.

witch to death. The Akamba of Kenya execute proven witches by arrows. Some African communities kill witches by beating or strangling them to death, or by burning them alive. Another form of punishment is banishment from the community, which, in the African conception of human life, is the equivalent of death for the individual in question as far as that community is concerned. Quoting Monica Wilson's study among the Nyakyusa of Tanzania, Lucy Mair notes that, "when a man was convicted of witchcraft and did not admit it, he was compelled to move from his village, and often to leave the chiefdom altogether. Often his cattle and crops were taken by the chief."[51]

The response to a sorcerer who causes illness, on the other hand, often involves a ritual. Because, generally, sorcerers bring harm only to enemies (to people who themselves have done wrong), the sorcerer may be justified. The sick person or victim may be induced to beg for pardon from the sorcerer for his or her fault, in which case reconciliation will be effected between the sorcerer or the sorcerer's client and the victim.

False accusations of witchcraft are also severely punished, and are never lightly made. As we shall see in the following chapter, such false accusations may result in death by oracle or demand compensation for the accused person.

AFFLICTION AS A PIVOTAL THEOLOGICAL ISSUE

Faced with the need to explain the existence of beliefs in witchcraft and sorcery among different peoples of the world, various scholars have suggested the following hypotheses:

1. For some members of a given community, these beliefs provide an outlet for repressed hostility, frustration, and anxiety.

2. Accusations of witchcraft and sorcery are indices of tense

---

[51]Mair, *Witchcraft*, p. 141. Some banished individuals are lucky. Elsewhere, the banished individual's "new neighbors are not concerned with what he did in the past. Or his former neighbors may go and fetch him back, arguing... that repentant witches are good 'defenders.' Only if their behavior is such as to make them unpopular again is the past remembered" (ibid., p. 153).

social relationships between the accuser, on the one hand, and the presumed sorcerer or witch, on the other. Accounts that people give of attacks by sorcerers or witches reflect their insights into the incidence of social tension in their society.

3. Beliefs in witchcraft and sorcery serve as a medium through which real or imagined episodes dramatize and reinforce social norms, in that anti-social and socially inadequate conduct are attributed, sometimes retrospectively, either to the accused sorcerer or witch, or to his believed victim.[52]

These explanations may, no doubt, be the case, but there is a danger from the perspective of African Religion that "psychologizing" the phenomenon too much robs it of its essential theological character. Where African Religion is concerned, the fundamental reason for sorcery and witchcraft as explanations of disease and other afflictions is theological. To return to an earlier illustration, the question at stake in witchcraft is *why* bad things happen in the world.[53] "A man may be bitten by a snake; why was not another bitten instead? Why does it rain on one field and not on another? Why do the wicked prosper, building fine houses, having bumper crops, while others equally hard-working fail continually?"[54] Don't all of these occurrences upset the order of the universe as Africans know God and the ancestors intend it, and as it has been handed down to the community throughout the ages by tradition?

The primary theological character of African beliefs in witchcraft and sorcery must be understood within this order; the primary human task is the promotion of life. In this context "a proud man who treats his neighbors with disdain; a retiring man who always keeps silent in public; a person who is habitually surly, who builds his house in the bush far away from other people, who neither invites others to eat with him nor accepts invi-

[52]See M. G. Marwick, "Some Problems in the Sociology of Sorcery and Witchcraft," in M. Fortes and G. Dieterlen, eds., *African Systems of Thought* (London: Oxford University Press, 1965), p. 171. See also Parrinder, *Witchcraft*, pp. 191-203; Mair, *Witchcraft*, pp. 199-221; and Haule, *Bantu "Witchcraft,"* pp. 100-107.

[53]Christian theology would refer to it as the question of "theodicy."

[54]Parrinder, *Witchcraft*, p. 193.

tations from neighbors to share their food and drink" is not merely unsociable. Such a person is deeply immoral. With that kind of behavior, he or she denies all that is essential in maintaining the connection between humanity and the ancestors and God. Such a person denies life and embraces death, the utmost affliction.

Chapter 6

RESTORING THE FORCE OF LIFE

The logic of the moral/ethical orientation of African Religion is unmistakable: wherever and whenever there is a diminishment or a destruction of the force of life, something must be done to restore it; whenever there is a breach of order in the universe as established by God through the ancestors, humanity must see to it that harmony is restored. Failing this, humanity will suffer. Thus, the causes of wrongdoing, illness, and witchcraft, as elements that diminish life, need to be exposed and counteracted, but this is particularly true in the case of witchcraft. For witchcraft is not only a symptom of the diminishment of the power of life (as wrongdoing and illness may be perceived to be), it is also seen to be the very embodiment of evil in the world. In a very particular way, then, it is essential that witches and witchcraft be detected and dealt with if life in the community is to continue and flourish.

APPROACHES IN DEALING WITH AFFLICTION

African Religion recognizes various ways to deal with affliction, and has different religious experts whose task is to discover the reasons for disharmony in the universe. These experts are generally expected not only to know the causes of calamities, but to prescribe antidotes or cures for these problems. Their responsibility is to advise on measures to be taken to restore the force of life. In a previous chapter we referred to these religious experts as the "moral theologians" of African Religion. They are cer-

193

tainly the moral conscience of African society. With trained minds and keen eyes for breaches in the moral order, they show and help people how to act so as to avoid or, more often, to repair such breaches. Because they often speak for the ancestors, they are expected to be listened to. To defy their directives is to court disaster. Anyone who does not listen to what they counsel is usually perceived as immoral.

Michael Kirwen cites a poignant instance of such defiance by a stubborn incestuous couple who married. Against all counsel, the couple refused to break up their union. When the wife died of injuries sustained during a domestic quarrel, the community was angry at the parents of the husband who had failed to make their son abandon the incestuous situation. "What kind of human beings are you," people derided them, "that don't even know how to raise your children to respect the sacred laws of the clan, that tempt the anger of the ancestors? Are you, in fact, a family of witches, perverted human beings, antihuman, perverse, eaters of human excrement?"[1] The disappointment of the community was not so much that the young couple had made a mistake by marrying within the forbidden relationships. It was mainly because they had obstinately refused to yield to their elders' words of counsel to dissolve the union. It was also because the parents of the boy had allowed their parental authority to be thwarted by their son in such a fundamental matter.

It is not possible to appreciate the role religious experts play in restoring the power of life without considering such procedures as prayers, sacrifices and offerings; protective and curative medicines; shame and guilt; ordeals and punishment; therapeutic dances and reconciliation rituals. Some of these procedures to remediate various afflictions are performed by any leader; however, others, performed in certain situations, require special expertise. This chapter will focus primarily on the latter, the major elements and persons responsible for maintaining or restoring the force of life. Although we will discuss personal and

---

[1]M. C. Kirwen, *The Missionary and the Diviner: Contending Theologies of Christian and African Religion* (Maryknoll, New York: Orbis Books, 1987), pp. 29-30.

public efforts separately here, they are essentially united and mutually interdependent. Even though prayers may be personal and are not necessarily accompanied by public sacrifices or offerings, the opposite is not the case. For offerings and sacrifices, prayers are a necessary element. And even though prayer is part of an adult's daily life, sacrifices and offerings are public acts and require religious officials, whether they be household heads or people with particular expertise or status in the wider society.

IMPLORING MYSTICAL POWERS IN PRAYER

Prayers, sacrifices, and offerings are elements considered central to an ethical life and feature prominently in the practice of African Religion. First, let us consider the element of prayer. When Tokunboh Adeyemo describes prayer as "the commonest act of worship"in Africa, he is quite correct.[2] Rarely does any important moment pass during each day of an adult's life without a verbal or mental recollection of the power of God and/or the ancestors. An accidental bruise or a gift received evokes a prayer. Sickness or good health in the morning, a feast or a funeral, good or bad news—all are recognized by appropriate prayers. John Mbiti characterizes the practice of prayer as "one of the most ancient items of African spiritual riches."[3] So are sacrifices and offerings, as will be shown, not only because they are always accompanied by prayers, but also because the occasion for prayer may also indicate the need for sacrifices or offerings.

When life is threatened or weakened, prayer is most abundant, both private and public prayer: prayer is a means of restoring wholeness and balance in life. In African Religion, prayer is comprehensive, requesting the removal of all that is bad and anti-life in society, and demanding restoration of all that is good. Nothing less satisfies the African religious mind. It is significant to

---

[2] T. Adeyemo, *Salvation in African Tradition* (Nairobi: Evangel Publishing House, 1979), p. 35.

[3] J. S. Mbiti, *The Prayers of African Religion* (Maryknoll, New York: Orbis Books, 1975), p. 2.

note, though, that the very act of prayer sheds light on the centrality of relationships in the African moral vision.

African prayer acknowledges the mutual interdependence of the visible and invisible worlds. Prayer, however, emphasizes more the *dependence* of the living on the ancestors and God. Prayer says that there comes a time when order and harmony in human life and in the world depend on powers greater than human power. This is especially so when humanity has done wrong or harbors anti-life elements within it. Praying places the individual or the community in the hands of greater invisible and mystical powers and intends to overcome or to assuage their displeasure. This is why the individual or the community at prayer is often humble before God and the ancestors, referring to itself as a "worm" or an "ant."[4] Nonetheless, as Africans approach prayer, they find it proper to be confident even in humility, precisely because the powers addressed in prayer are God and the ancestors, who have obligations towards their "children," the living. It is perfectly legitimate for the living to express their deepest emotions of frustration, confusion, and anger in prayer to these invisible, mystical powers when things are not going well in this world.

There are some, but very few, formulas in African prayer. Normally, African prayer expressions are not standardized; rather, every prayer is uttered to fit the occasion and the current frame of mind of the one who utters it. This is what determines whether it is angry or joyful, hopeful or despairing. Despite the tone, "the items mentioned in these prayers have a personal dimension, a community orientation and a universal application."[5] They hinge upon feeling and experience. Prayer is the time to express oneself in an uninhibited way; it is the time to let go of one's whole being, to be more forthright and honest than usual. Africans realize that prayer is a time to communicate and commune with the spiritual beings that are most intimate with, and most caring for, humanity. Not to open oneself up completely to the mystical powers in prayer can do nothing

---

[4] See ibid., pp. 13, 16-21.
[5] Ibid., p. 18.

but bring more harm. Without honesty, they might not appreciate the extent of suffering or take action. Not to express oneself
completely in prayer is dangerous, moreover, because it implies
a further breach of trust between the visible and the invisible
worlds. The consequences for the living are invariably disastrous.

One important characteristic of African prayer is petition. In
this respect, Africans are pragmatic. They ask for practical needs
that comply with their religious perception of a full life. Protection from all affliction, or removal of it, is a primary concern.
They also desire to be protected from all sources of badness that
we have described in the preceding chapter. These include evil
spirits and witches and all ill-wishers. As a corollary, they pray
for longevity, abundance of food and drink, animals, and above
all offspring.[6] If a final reward is expected from God and the
ancestors, it is that they provide the means to affirm life in the
world.

It is useful to cite some recorded prayers that highlight this
characteristic. A Meru (Kenyan) prayer for life is especially illuminating of the theology and basic expectations of African
prayer:

> Kirinyaga [God], owner of all things,
> I pray to Thee, give me what I need,
> because I am suffering, and also my children,
> and all the things that are in this country of mine.
> I beg Thee, the good one, for life,
> healthy people with no disease.
> May they bear healthy children.
> And also to women who suffer
> because they are barren, open the way
> by which they may see children.
> Give goats, cattle, food, honey,

---

[6]E. B. Idowu, *Olodumare: God in Yoruba Belief* (New York: Frederick A.
Praeger, 1963), p. 116.

And also the trouble of the other lands
that I do not know, remove.[7]

After a good harvest season, and for the continuation of good harvests the Gikuyu (Kenya) pray in the following vein:

Mwene-Nyaga [God], you who have brought us rain and given us a good harvest, let people eat grain of this harvest calmly and peacefully. Do not bring us any surprise or depression. Guard us against illness of people, or our herds and flocks; so that we may enjoy this season's harvest in tranquility. Peace, praise ye, peace be with us.[8]

The Nuer of Sudan pray for "coolness" of the soul in times of hostilities in words like these:

Our Father, it is thy Universe,
it is thy will, let us be at peace,
let the souls of thy people be cool;
Thou art our Father, remove all evil from our path.[9]

And the Kono of Sierra Leone might use these or similar words to ask for forgiveness for wrongs done to the spirits:

O Fanu [spirits], if I am for you and you are for me, and all the people are for you, therefore, you should not be vexed at the people. Here are the things that they have brought that you may forgive their wrong deeds.[10]

This sample of prayers shows that although petition is the main element of prayer in Africa, there are other underlying motivations as well, including thanksgiving and memorializing.

---

[7]A. Shorter, ed., *The Word That Lives: An Anthology of African Prayers*, mimeo, n.d., p. 32.

[8]Ibid., p. 20.

[9]Ibid., p. 36.

[10]Ibid., p. 22. For an extensive collection of African prayers for various occasions and needs, see Mbiti, *The Prayers of African Religion*.

Prayers and sacrifices, or offerings of thanksgiving and memorial, are a common form of prayer made in return for favors received from the ancestors and God. Yet, the dominant motif is still petitions for the protection and flourishing of life. The Gikuyu prayer of thanksgiving for a good harvest (above),[11] for example, concludes as a petition to God to maintain the situation: "Do not bring us any surprise or depression," the people finally implore. "Guard us against illness of the people, or our herds and flocks, so that we may enjoy this season's harvest in tranquility."

A very common feature of African prayer is petition to protect a specific undertaking, as shown in two prayers, one from the Ngombo of Zaire and another from the Ga of Ghana. A Ngombo prayer asking for blessing on a journey entreats:

> Akongo [God] of my father,
> Akongo of my mother,
> Akongo of my mother's people,
> Akongo of my sisters,
> I killed a male wild-pig for you, my uncle,
> I killed an otter as well;
> I caught fish for you;
> One day I caught twenty for you.
> I killed a *katukatu* as well . . .
> When I go [on my journey],
> Let there be no obstacle;
> May I meet with nobody on the way,
> May I arrive at the town where I am going;
> Hard things may I avoid;
> May I come back safely.[12]

The following is a typical Ga prayer for universal blessing:

> Hail, hail, hail! Let happiness come!
> Our stools and our brooms . . .

---

[11]Fn. 8, p. 198 above.
[12]See Mbiti, *The Prayers in African Religion*, p. 158.

If we dig a well, may it be at a spot where
water is.
If we take water to wash our shoulders, may we
be refreshed.
Nyongmo, give us blessing!
Mawu [God], give us blessing!
May the town be blest!
May the religious officials be blest!
May the priests be blest!
May the mouthpieces of the divinities be blest!
May we be filled going and coming.
May we not drop our head-pads except at
the big pot.
May our fruitful women be like gourds
And may they bring forth and sit down.
May misfortunes jump over us.
If today anyone takes up a stick or a stone
against this our blessing, do we bless him?
May Wednesday and Sunday kill him.
May we flog him.
Hail, let happiness come!
Is our voice one?
Hail, let happiness come![13]

The religious specialists of many African communities include
prayer leaders. Prayer leaders are generally held to the strictest
personal moral standards, as is true of most African leaders.
Among the Meru of Kenya, for example, the office of prayer
leader is held by the *Mugwe*, who is required to be no less than a
perfectionist. The *Mugwe* must be born of a good family (the
position is usually hereditary), he must not break any taboo during his life, and he must be able to prove that he has followed the
customs of the tribe to the letter. Furthermore, as James Kihara
explains, "the *Mugwe* is expected to keep sober. He can, of
course, drink fermented beverages, but he must not be an addict.
For the same reason, he is not supposed to go around from one

---

[13]See ibid., pp. 160-1.

beer party to another. The *Mugwe* must be kind to his people and everyone, even his enemies."[14]

SACRIFICES AND OFFERINGS

We have mentioned how prayers, sacrifices, and offerings are closely interconnected in African Religion. Apart from the frequent ejaculatory prayers of individuals, which we may characterize as private, all other prayers are public or semi-public and accompany rituals. When it is an issue of restoring or maintaining the power of life, such rituals take the form of sacrifice or offering. Both sacrifice and offering involve the setting apart of an item, usually associated with human use, for the supernatural powers. Animals and food products are most often used for sacrifice and other forms of dedication (offerings). Although in practice sacrifices are not often distinguished from offerings, it is important to clarify the distinction. The item in a sacrifice is killed or destroyed by ceremonial immolation, by fire, or by "abandonment." The emphasis is on separation by *destruction*. Items for offerings are not, as a rule, directly destroyed by the person or community offering them. Instead, these items are simply dedicated to the recipient. They may remain in the household or village; less often, they may also be cast away, like sacrificial items, depending on the nature of the offering. The emphasis here is on separation by *dedication* (not necessarily involving destruction). So, generally, sacrifices are usually made of items of value and the ritual is "bloody," whereas items of offering are symbolic and the ritual is usually bloodless. In either case, however, the item is meant to be removed from human possession or use and transferred to the mystical powers, who become the new "owners" of the sacrificial or offered item. If the sacrifice is meat, human beings may partake in consuming it, but according to specific rules. During the sacrifice and after the dedication, they do so essentially as "guests," for the purpose of obtaining blessings.

---

[14]J. Kihara, *Ngai, We Belong to You: Kenya's Kikuyu and Meru Prayer* (Eldoret: Gaba Publications, December 1985), p. 6.

These blessings are bestowed from the sacrifice, which now is a gift *from* the invisible, mystical powers.[15] The sense here, in the words of R. H. Nassau, is that "the offering [more precisely, the sacrifice] is presented to the god whole, but the worshipers help to eat it. The god gets the savor of it which rises in the air towards him while the more material part is devoured below."[16]

With few variations, the structure of personal (that is, semi-public) or collective (public) sacrifices has four general features listed by Evans-Pritchard as "presentation, consecration, invocation and immolation." If other features are added, "such as libations and aspersions and, mostly in sacrifices to spirits, hymn-singing," he explains, they are not essential to the form of the sacrificial rite but supernumerary. That is to say, they do not form a necessary part of the fundamental "canon" of sacrifice.[17] These four features incorporate the basic purpose of sacrifice, which has been described by Anthony Barrett, observing the Turkana people of Kenya, as involving three theological motifs: "separation," "recombination," and "reconstruction." The act of taking an item from one's personal use and giving it over as a "gift" to God or the ancestors constitutes the separation motif. Immolation brings about the recombination motif in that the sacrificial item is united with God or the spirits. These two acts generate or construct a new relationship, or add new elements into the relationship, between human beings, God, and creation. The ritual thus effects its ultimate purpose, which is to reestablish the pristine divine order in the universe.

There is some variation in the prayer formulas used in destroying the item of sacrifice, but they all convey handing over: "This is your animal, take it," "Take your ox," "Take your animal." But then, in return, "Give us life, health, animals, grass, rain and

---

[15]Adeyemo, *Salvation in African Tradition,* pp. 33-4.

[16]R. H. Nassau, *Fetishism in West Africa: Forty Years' Observation of Native Customs and Superstitions* (New York: Charles Scribner's Sons, 1904), p. 95.

[17]E. E. Evans-Pritchard, *Nuer Religion* (Oxford: Clarendon Press, 1956), p. 208. See also L. de Heusch, *Sacrifice in Africa: A Structuralist Approach.* Trans. by L. O'Brien and A. Morton (Bloomington: Indiana University Press, 1985).

all good things." In Turkana sacrifice, described by Barrett,

> The act of giving or presenting is creative, for it constructs a tripartite relation between Akuj [God] (spirits and ancestors), man, and animal. In the quotidian affairs of life, these three "elements" occupy separate domains. When the animal is immolated, dissected, roasted, thrown to Akuj and the ancestors; and eaten by the men, as smoke and smell ascend to Akuj; then there is being constructed a new entity or super-entity of interrelationships with coolness and happiness. What used to be three separate entities are now transformed through ritual activity into substantial totality and not just a metaphorical likeness.[18]

Sacrifices and offerings gain value because of what the items represent. The offerer identifies himself or herself with the sacrificial item by touching it or making a similar gesture before the victim is destroyed or dedicated. In other words, the offerer "becomes" the sacrificial victim. In a blood sacrifice, then, it is the offerer who sheds blood and gives up chyme, the symbols of life. It is the offerer who gives him- or herself in propitiation or expiation, and in this way asks to be reintegrated properly into the order of the universe. The fundamental meaning of sacrifices and offerings lies in their efficacy to restore wholeness. If wrongdoing causes a dangerous separation of the various elements of the universe, sacrifices and offerings aim to reestablish unity and restore balance. In the words of Evan Zuesse, sacrifices and offerings have as their goal "to give the cosmos dynamic continuity."[19] They are pragmatic ways by which the living acknowledge their limitations before the ancestors and God and their indebtedness and gratitude to the mystical powers.[20]

---

[18]See A. J. Barrett, *Sacrifice and Prophecy in Turkana Cosmology.* Ph. D. Dissertation (Chicago: The University of Chicago, mimeo, 1989), pp. 31-3.
[19]E. M. Zuesse, *Ritual Cosmos: The Sanctification of Life in African Religion* (Athens, Ohio: Ohio University Press, 1979), p. 125.
[20]The purpose of sacrifice elaborated here explains all the motivations for sacrifice advanced in the theories of various scholars. Barrett summarizes them as the gift theory, the thanksgiving theory, the communion theory, the

It can be said that God is the *final* recipient of all sacrifices in African Religion. Although in certain cases, particularly in the case of expiation of a major wrongdoing or for the purpose of averting a major affliction, sacrifice is made directly to God, more often sacrifices are offered to specific spirits. But insofar as these "may be regarded as hypostases, representations, or refractions of God," as is the case in Nuer thought, "we can say that a sacrifice to any one of them is a sacrifice also to God."[21] Still, it is useful, for purposes of clarity, to distinguish the various groups of spirits to whom sacrifices and offerings are directed, and to try to understand why this is so.

Harry Sawyerr isolates at least six categories of spirit-recipients of sacrifices and offerings in African Religion: spirits of affliction and death; spirits of the power of witchcraft; the ancestors; spirits who are bringers of good; nature spirits; and "vocation" spirits. As Sawyerr himself admits, this classification is not exhaustive; however, in terms of understanding the relationship between sacrifices and the restoration of the power of life, it is very useful.[22]

All spirits are capable of causing suffering, disease, and even death. Some spirits are more capricious in this respect than others, as we saw in the last chapter. Among the Dinka of Sudan, the most notorious spirit, *Macardit*, has the status almost of a god. But, unlike God, *Macardit* goes around killing people. The situation is similar among the Igbo, where the class of evil-doer spirits is called *Ulu Chi*. *Ulu Chi* personify misfortune and exist to block people's good fortune. They act against the wishes of God. Among the most feared are those spirits that enter a young woman's womb and cause a miscarriage. They are usually spirits of children who died in their infancy without benefit of the

---

covenant or alliance theory, the substitute theory, and the diversion of human violence through a scapegoat theory. See A. J. Barrett, *Sacrifice and Prophecy in Turkana Cosmology*, pp. 14-34. See also J. v. d. Loo, *Religious Practices of the Guji Oromo* (Addis Ababa, Ethiopia), pp. 113-9.

[21] Evans-Pritchard, *Nuer Religion*, p. 200.

[22] H. Sawyerr, "Sacrifice," in K. A. Dickson and P. Ellingworth, eds. *Biblical Revelation and African Beliefs* (Maryknoll, New York: Orbis Books, 1969), pp. 64-5.

naming rites. Malevolent spirits also include young men who died without being initiated, and adults who died without children.[23]

At one time or another, then, this or that particular spirit or category of spirits must be appeased or "expelled" if normal life is to be maintained by the individual, the family, or society. As is to be expected, such appeasement requires special rituals. To propitiate *Macardit*, or to neutralize it by keeping it in the forest far away from the community, the Dinka sacrifice to it takes place at the edge of the village. The Igbo offer sacrificial food to *Ulu Chi* with the left hand, to signify that it is despicable and unwanted.[24] In situations of affliction that defy explanation, the Gikuyu of Kenya actually engage in symbolic battles against the spirits. "At the sound of the war horns," writes Ikenga-Metuh,

> the entire village rushes out with clubs and sticks and starts to beat down the bushes of both sides of the paths that lead to the stream in the attempt to drive the evil spirits down the stream. At the stream, the war horn is sounded again and the people throw their sticks into the stream, and shout victoriously simultaneously: "Evil spirits and your illness we have crushed you. We now sink you in the river. Let the water drive you far away from us. You will go forever and never return again."[25]

J. H. M. Beattie discusses a ghost cult in Bunyoro in Uganda where ghosts, the disembodied spirits of people who have died, are often perceived to be extremely malevolent.[26] All kinds of misfortune is attributed to them. If they possess a person, doctor

---

[23]See E. Ikenga-Metuh, *Comparative Studies of African Traditional Religions* (Onitsha, Nigeria: Imico Publishers, 1987), pp. 155-7.

[24]Throughout the continent the left hand is usually associated with negative connotations.

[25]Ikenga-Metuh, *Comparative Studies of African Traditional Religions*, p. 157.

[26]See J. Middleton, ed., *Gods and Rituals: Reading in Religious Beliefs and Practices* (Garden City, New York: The Natural History Press, 1967), pp. 255-87.

diviners (*bafumu*) employ different means to destroy them, send them away, or keep them at bay. In some cases, a sacrifice is required. As Beattie explains, "The ghost of a close relative or of a spouse cannot be destroyed, but must be enabled to enter into an enduring relationship with the living by means of a possession cult."[27] This is how it is done: the diviner induces the ghost in question to state what it wants. As a rule, it wants a goat—a male goat for a man's ghost and a female goat for a woman's ghost. The animal is ritually killed and the meat is cut up and distributed among the people present. The goat's head, however, which belongs to the ghost, is buried. Depending on the wishes of the ghost (as diagnosed by the diviner), additional sacrifices may be necessary, including, perhaps, the dedication (that is, offering) of a favorite animal. In addition, ghosts of kinspeople may require the erection of special huts for them or they may further command "the carrying out of specific obligations and commitments which have been neglected." One Isoke, for instance, refused to carry out his brother's death-bed wish to distribute his goats among his sisters. The living brother fell ill, and recovered only when he had fulfilled his brother's wishes.[28]

Intrusive nature spirits are often approached in the same way as ghosts. People try to keep them at bay with sacrifices because they too can cause suffering. The Banyankore (Uganda) accompany such sacrifices with invocations like this:

> Come and go with yours—
> This is your goat —
> This is your road —
> Go and don't return.[29]

If the spirits have already caused suffering, they must likewise be placated through sacrifice. In the following sacrificial prayer, the Kono of Sierra Leone implore God and the spirits at the same time to refrain from causing further affliction:

---

[27]Ibid., p. 267.

[28]See ibid., pp. 268-74. A similar illustration of this important obligation among the Ashanti is provided in the following chapter.

[29]See Mbiti, *The Prayers of African Religion,* p. 106.

O Meketa, Seven Heavens, Seven Earths, Fakumu
    Faiyande, Heavenly Children:
Whether or not I know how to make this sacrifice,
you will trouble the one who does not know how,
but the person who knows how will have no trouble.
Therefore, I ask you to hold all evil from us.
Make it blind; make it lame; carry it to the spirit in
    the mountain.
Put it in a deep pit; place a stone upon it;
let the good wind from the north and the south
and from the rising to the setting sun blow
upon it. Let it be so for you are able to do this.
The Heavenly Children are offering this sacrifice.
They are calling.
Whether or not I know how to make this sacrifice,
you know when I am free.
You are my helper, my lifter.[30]

To be efficacious, sacrifices must be performed according to specific requirements. For example, when sacrifices are offered in order to obtain the good will of nature spirits before a hunting expedition, certain sexual taboos must be observed so as not to alienate the spirits of the forest. This applies also to fishing expeditions, the beginning of the cultivation season, the end of the harvest season, and so on. Yet, these sacrifices in themselves might not be totally efficacious; at every step in the process, further sacrifices may be required. Among the Mende of Sierra Leone, for example,

> when a farmer decides to cultivate rice on a plot of ground, on arriving at the farm and before commencing to clear it, he first offers a sacrifice to the spirits of those who had previously formed the plot [now become part of the natural environment there]. He then proceeds to prepare the soil; but before he sows the seed, he offers some seed-rice to the same spirits. Then, when the harvest is due, he offers the

---

[30]Shorter, *The Word That Lives*, p. 21.

first-fruits of the crop, which are ground into flour, to the spirits. Finally, at the end of the harvest, he makes a large feast as a sacrifice to round off the exercise.[31]

With nature spirits, it seems, one can never be too careful.

Sacrifices to ghosts are obviously similar to sacrifices, offerings, and libations to ancestors. Of course, because of their solicitude for the living, the intent of sacrificial rituals for the ancestors is not to banish them or to keep them at bay, but to keep them happy and to win more favors from them. In addition to the usual and often incessant libations to the ancestors already mentioned,[32] there are more formal sacrifices. A dream about an ancestor may be cause for a sacrifice. With the Turkana, if the dreamer is the head of a household, he immediately goes into the goats' enclosure and spears an animal. It is left at the spot until morning "to allow the ancestors to eat its cool 'fat.' " The meat of such an animal is not eaten by anyone, but is thrown about for the ancestors.

Sawyerr uses the term "personalized agencies" to describe the various spirits that assure more than the ordinary life force—such as success or fame.[33] They are "personalized" spirits because they are usually approached by individuals rather than a group, and they are "agencies" because the people who approach them are, as a rule, already quite successful or famous. Nevertheless, offerings and sacrifices are made to guarantee more of the same good fortune. The Igbo of Nigeria refer to this category of spirits as *Chi* (spirit of destiny) as opposed to *Ulu Chi* (spirit of affliction). The spirits of destiny can further be classified into categories, with the

---

[31]Sawyerr, "Sacrifice," p. 59.

[32]For example, Barrett, in *Sacrifice and Prophecy* (p. 135) explains: "Children get a lot of illness and the reason for this, according to the Turkana, is they constantly pick up food that falls on the ground. They refuse to share with the ancestors, therefore the *ngikaram* [ancestors] inflict them with illness. This is meant to be a corrective to 'meanness'... When children become ill, the mother makes delectable food and places it in a shallow hole in the ground; the sick child lies on its belly and eats from the hole and thus effects a cure."

[33]Sawyerr, "Sacrifice," p. 65.

most important spirits being those that initiate and enhance divination, mediumship, rain-asking, and medicine. Periodic offerings are required for their continuing effectiveness. They also
receive offerings and sacrifices of loyalty and trust, such as those
made in oaths, initiation, or renewal of blood-covenants. Any
blood shed, whether it be human or animal blood, represents the
life power of the parties to an oath or covenant. A party to an
oath, initiation group, or pact who contravenes its stipulations is
certain to be hounded by the spirits in question to death, unless
a countervailing offering is made.[34]

Finally, at certain times an individual or society may offer sacrifices to the ancestors to gain strength against the power of
witches. These sacrifices are often carried out when procuring
medicines or talismans, or at shrines to the ancestors and other
spirits constructed for this purpose. It is important that the
proper medicine or talisman be used for the proper purpose. Is
the medicine intended for protection or cure? And of what?
Homes, cattle, farms, children, oneself? And from what affliction? In other words, "diagnostic" procedures must precede
treatment. But before discussing how African Religion determines sources of affliction, some understanding is needed of the
nature of medicine itself.

MEDICINE: PROTECTIVE AND CURATIVE

Specialists in medicine, known as herbalists or medicine-doctors,[35] are people with knowledge of herbs, roots, or even fruits
with the power to prevent or cure disease or other afflictions.
Because medicine-doctors, men and women, often rely on divination for their practice, it is sometimes difficult to distinguish
between diviners and "pure" medicine-doctors. It is also important to note that medicine-doctors who use their medicines to
harm others are regarded as sorcerers. While the distinction

---

[34]See ibid., pp. 65-73.
[35]These are the "witch-doctors" or "magicians" of the old ethnographical
works on Africa.

between diviners, sorcerers, and herbalists is sociologically quite thin, from a religious point of view it is quite significant: divination is prognosis in order to right wrongs and enhance the vital life force; sorcery diminishes the force of life by the use of medicine; and herbalism also uses medicine to protect or restore life.

Practitioners of herbal medicine usually depend on spirits for their knowledge and they must make sacrifices and offerings to those spirits from time to time. Their extensive medicinal powers and knowledge of curative and protective herbs are generally inherited, acquired through friendship, or purchased. Individually owned, they span the range of life's situations, as Alden Almquist noted among the Pagibeti of Zaire: "One person may know the medicine for healing broken bones," he writes, "another for relieving neck-stiffness, another for making infants walk, another for curing spirits possession, another for giving an enemy sickness, and another for seizing thieves of garden crops or trapped forest animals."[36] There are medicines for good fortune, love, success, security of person and property, and so on, and there are also medicines against sorcery and witchcraft.[37] But, significantly, all medicines contain (or are) a power that ought to be used for the benefit of humanity, but can also be put to detrimental use by immoral individuals.

Even though the power of nature in medicine seems obvious, it is important from a religious point of view to note that such medicine underlines the interconnectedness of, and interdependence between, humanity and the rest of creation. Roots or leaves or parts of animals or birds boiled in water or pulverized in fire form the basic ingredients of medicine. All of these elements—plants, animals, water and fire—represent the major forces of nature. The vapor and smoke produced in boiling and pulverizing these medicines symbolize the air. In applying them to the human body, the link between nature and humanity is established in a very intense way and it generates the power to protect and

---

[36]A. Almquist, "Divination and the Hunt in Pagibeti Ideology," in P. M. Peek, ed., *African Divination Systems: Ways of Knowing* (Bloomington & Indianapolis: Indiana University Press, 1991), p. 103.

[37] See E. E. Evans-Pritchard, *Witchcraft, Oracles, and Magic Among the Azande* (Oxford: Clarendon Press, 1937), pp. 387-539.

heal. This linkage is also implied in the use of charms and amulets, which are medicines that protect.[38]

PROCEDURES FOR DIAGNOSING SOURCES OF AFFLICTION

Shame and guilt play major roles in diagnosing most forms of affliction. As noted earlier, shame becomes guilt when a wrong-doer is identified, either by a segment or the whole of the community. In other words, shame becomes guilt when wrongdoing becomes public. At this stage, an admission of guilt and a confession are demanded, and an appropriate "punishment" in the form of retribution or ritual purification is imposed in order to avert the negative consequences of the wrong. The punishment rehabilitates not only the individual but also the community and the environment. The ultimate purpose is to restore the original power of life.

But, as sometimes happens, the presumed wrongdoer may deny culpability or afflictions may occur without a known cause. What, then, must be done to restore balance in the world? African religious perception demands that everything possible must be done to ascertain the nature and causes of the wrongdoing that resulted in misfortune and disorder. Only then can proper procedures be undertaken to restore the disturbed power

---

[38]For examples of remedies prescribed for different illnesses, see M. Gelfand, *Witch Doctor: Traditional Medicine Man of Rhodesia* (New York: Frederick Praeger, 1964), pp. 169-77 and Evans-Pritchard, *Witchcraft, Oracles, and Magic,* pp. 387-510. The treatment of mumps among the Shona illustrates what is being said here. It involves a mixture of rat flesh, the bark of a specific tree, and the cast-off skin of a snake. Some of the mixture is applied to the swelling and some is wrapped into a charm and worn around the sick person's neck as protection. See M. Gelfand, *Witch Doctor,* p. 173. Another example refers to aphrodisiacs given to the bridegroom by the Ndembu of Zambia. The herbs collected, mixed, and boiled for this purpose, and introduced into the body, mean to underline the connection between nature and potency, that is to say, nature and human life. See V. W. Turner, *The Drums of Affliction: A Study of Religious Processes Among the Ndembu of Zambia* (Oxford: Clarendon Press, 1968), p. 259.

of life. It is understandable, then, that diagnosing the causes of affliction is a central preoccupation of African Religion.

There are people who have the power to "sniff out" hidden sources of disorder, who can advise on procedures to correct the situation. They are generally known as "diviners." More recent studies refer to them by their indigenous names, which clarify the subtle and overlapping distinctions in specialization. Here, though, I shall refer to them primarily as diviners and distinguish them (as does African Religion) by the methods they use to determine sources of affliction, on the one hand, and how they deal with them, on the other. For example, mediums are distinguished from other categories of diviners by their use of seances and dreams to determine the cause of suffering, while medicine-doctors dispense protective and curative medicines. However, as noted above, diviners/mediums can also be medicine-doctors or herbalists and vice-versa. As Gelfand indicates, there are two types of divination, distinguishable by their functions: one is diagnostic and the other therapeutic. The diviner, properly so called, is a diagnostician who is concerned with the spiritual causes of the affliction, and the medicine-doctor or herbalist a therapeutist who is more concerned with treating the physical effects of the affliction. But the herbalist also depends on his spirit to find the appropriate cure, and the spirit may convey, usually in dreams, which herbs to look for, and where and how to apply them. There are diviners who are both diagnosticians and therapeutists.[39]

Despite these distinctions, it is important to realize that whatever is done to promote healing—the process of restoring the force of life—is in itself a force. It is therefore understandable that African Religion categorizes a range of forces as "medicine," in addition to herbs and other physical curative material. As S. F. Nadel realized among the Nupe of Nigeria, medicine goes beyond physical substances or the treatment of diseases of the body. Medicine also means, and perhaps principally so, any power that has (greater) influence over other powers. In Nadel's words, it is any "substance or object which exercises remote and

---

[39]Gelfand, *Witch Doctor*, p. 63.

miraculous effects upon the efficacy of other objects, for example, tools or weapons, upon the outcome of human efforts of all kinds, and upon human fate in general."[40] For this reason, Nadel suggests that it is correct to understand medicine in the sense of "efficacious substance" or "force-in-substance." Whatever strengthens the power of life is good medicine and all power contrary to life (such as witchcraft) is bad medicine. Thus, specialists who help to diagnose the reasons for the weakness of life are an essential part of society; each one of them has medicinal powers in this broad sense. Because the power and procedures of diviners, mediums, and medicine-doctors often overlap, they are not always clearly distinguishable.

Diviners, therefore, are persons who use "medicinal" powers, particularly supranormal powers, in favor of life.[41] Throughout Africa, their profession consists "in finding out whether a witch or a spirit has caused the illness, in advising . . . [their] patients on the procedure necessary to propitiate whichever is the cause, and [often, though not always] in prescribing the right herbal remedy to cure the physical damage already sustained by the patient."[42] Accordingly, a diviner in Zanaki (Tanzania), describes his task in almost those exact terms. "People come to me," he explained to Michael Kirwen, "to find out what is causing their problems. It is my work to divine the cause of the evil, to figure out the source of the immorality that is provoking the problem. Once the immorality is identified, then the person can take steps to neutralize it." The diviner goes on to give examples of sources of affliction (or immorality), some of which were discussed in the last chapter, and to indicate how to deal with them in order to reestablish universal moral order. "For example, in the case of witchcraft," he confided, "evil can be warded off by a powerful charm, or in the case of offended ancestors by offering a sacrifice

[40]S. F. Nadel, *Nupe Religion: Traditional Beliefs and the Influence of Islam in a West African Chiefdom* (New York: Schocken Books, 1970), p. 132.
[41]See R. E. S. Tanner, *Transition in African Beliefs: Traditional Religion and Christian Change— A Study in Sukumaland, Tanzania, East Africa* (Maryknoll, New York: Maryknoll Publications, 1967), p. 42.
[42]Gelfand, *Witch Doctor*, pp. 24-5. See also P. M. Peek, ed., *African Divination Systems*.

of atonement. Often it appears that the breaking of the clan rules, such as the improper burial of an elder or marriage between forbidden clans, provokes the ancestors into sending suffering—and even death—until the immorality is corrected."[43]

Divination systems, then, are "ways of knowing."[44] "An understanding pervades African societies that the true reasons for all events can be known, but sufficient knowledge is seldom available through mundane means of inquiry; therefore, divination is employed to ensure that all relevant information is brought forward before action is undertaken."[45] This means that the scope of competence of diviners is extremely wide. Their "spiritual" gifts render them capable of diagnosing what kind of spirit or "force substance" is causing what kind of affliction to the individual, the family, or the society, and they also advise on what steps must be taken to obtain healing or "coolness."

Gunter Wagner has drawn up a comprehensive list of situations in which people might seek the help of a diviner. They span every aspect of life and the central concern is to make sure that the forces of life prevail over the powers that attempt to destroy it. They include sudden and violent illness; persistent disease of any kind; gradual physical deterioration despite treatment; visits by ghosts or spirits; encounter with creatures associated with witches (such as owls or hyenas); suspicion of having been bewitched; sterility or undue delay of pregnancy; complications during pregnancy or birth; impotence; sudden insanity; death by lightning; accidents; death suspected of witchcraft; disease or a lack of productivity in cattle; repeated poor harvest while others reap well; poor human relations; bad omens; and epidemics and other suspicious events on a large scale.[46]

---

[43]M. C. Kirwen, *The Missionary and the Diviner: Contending Theologies of Christian and African Religions* (Maryknoll, New York: Orbis Books, 1987), p. 29.

[44]P. M. Peek, "Introduction: The Study of Divination, Present and Past," in Peek, *African Divination Systems*, p. 1.

[45]Peek, "The Search for Knowledge," p. 37.

[46]See G. Wagner, *The Bantu of Western Kenya: With Special Reference to the Vugusu and Logoli, Vol. I* (London: Oxford University Press, 1949), pp. 221-2. Evans-Pritchard, in *Witchcraft, Oracles, and Magic* (pp. 261-2), lists

Since diviners constitute a category of people endowed with the power to fathom spiritual secrets—power not granted indiscriminately to everyone—they are referred to among the Yoruba of Nigeria as *babalawo* that is, literally, "father has secrets." "Father," in this nomenclature, refers to one or another of the four-hundred-odd pantheon of gods[47] in Yorubaland of whom the diviners are devotees and from whom they ultimately derive their powers. One of the most venerated by diviners is the god Ifa or Orunmila, described in divination verses as "Wisdom." Irving observed of him in 1853: "*Ifa*, the god of palm nuts, or the god of divination, is said to be superior to all the rest. He is consulted on every undertaking—on going on a journey, entering into a speculation, going to war, or on a kidnapping expedition, in sickness, and, in short, whenever there is a doubt of the future. To him are dedicated palm-nuts, as by these the oracle is con-

---

the following similar circumstances that would lead a person to consult a diviner: "To discover why a wife has not conceived. During pregnancy of wife, about place of delivery, about her safety in childbirth, and about the safety of her child. Before circumcision of son. Before marriage of daughter. Before sending son to act a page at court. In sickness of any member of family. Will he die? Who is the witch responsible? &c. To discover the agent responsible for any misfortune. At death of kinsman . . . Who killed him? Who will execute the witch? &c. Before exacting vengeance by magic. Who will keep the taboos? Who will make the magic? &c. In cases of sorcery. In cases of adultery. Before gathering oracle poison. Before making blood-brotherhood. Before long journeys. A man before marrying a wife. Before presenting a prince with beer. Before large-scale hunting. A commoner in choosing a new homestead site . . . Before becoming a witch-doctor. Before joining a closed association. A man before he and his adult sons go to war. In cases of disloyalty to a prince. A prince before making war. To determine disposition of warriors, place and time of attack, and all other matters pertaining to warfare. A prince before appointing governors, deputies, or any other officials. A prince before moving his court. A prince to discover whether communal ceremony will terminate drought . . . A prince before accepting presents and tribute."

[47]The number of gods (spirits) is uncertain. Some authors estimate up to 3,200. See W. Bascom, *Sixteen Cowries: Yoruba Divination from Africa to the New World* (Bloomington and London: Indiana University Press, 1980), pp. 32-52.

sulted."[48] The wisdom of Ifa/Orunmila flows from the fact that he was present when the Creator (*Olodumare*) made the universe and established the destinies of human beings. Since Ifa is privy to this knowledge, he can impart it to his priests (*babalawo*) in divination.[49]

In this sense, diviners are "instruments" of higher powers. It is from the latter, and often on their behalf, that they function. A Shona (Zimbabwe) diviner (*nganga*), for example, would assert "that it is not he, the corporeal *nganga,* who diagnoses the cause of illness or prescribes the right treatment, but the healing spirit of his relative who enters him (literally taking possession of him) when he divines and often too when he is asleep, revealing to him in dreams the remedy he should prescribe and where he should look for a particular herb." Consequently, "if for some reason his healing spirit were to forsake him, he would lose his powers of vision and clairvoyance and he would be unable to function as a *nganga* until he had propitiated the spirit and persuaded it to return to him."[50]

The process of becoming a diviner sheds light on the significance of the calling and the serious role a diviner plays in society. The particular ways a person is called are varied and complex. Among the Zulu, according to Henry Callaway, the prospective diviner (*inyanga*) begins to waste away. "At first he is apparently robust; but in process of time he begins to be delicate, not having any real disease, but being very delicate." He becomes very particular about food, avoiding many types of food he used to eat previously. With time he feels constant pain and "dreams of many things." He is brought to the diviners, who at first may misdiagnose his condition. After a long period of time, perhaps as long as two years, the signs that he is possessed by the spirits of divination become evident. He yawns frequently; "he has slight

---

[48]See W. Bascom, *Ifa Divination: Communication Between Gods and Men in West Africa* (Bloomington and Indianapolis: Indiana University Press, 1969), p. 13.

[49]See S. Gbadegesin, *African Philosophy: Traditional Yoruba Philosophy and Contemporary African Realities* (New York: Peter Lang, 1991), pp. 134-6.

[50]Gelfand, *Witch Doctor,* pp. 27-8.

convulsions, and has water poured on him, and they cease for a time. He habitually sheds tears, at first sight, and at last he weeps aloud, and in the middle of the night, when people are asleep, he is heard making a noise, and wakes people by singing; he has composed a song, and men and women awake and go to sing in concert with him."[51] This is the diviner's initiation. At this stage all the people of the village are involved, for whenever the neophyte sings and dances, the village must accompany him and encourage him to become a diviner. At last he is completely possessed by the spirits and begins to divine through dreams. If, as sometimes happens, the relatives of an individual do not want him to become a diviner, they make him undertake treatment from "a great doctor." If the treatment is successful, he will not divine but will remain a very wise person, "like a diviner" in that regard.[52]

Apprenticeship to become an Ifa diviner in Yorubaland takes a long time and can be very expensive. Instruction begins early, at five, six, or seven years of age, and can last up to nine or ten years. It is more accurate, however, to say that learning Ifa divination continues throughout much of the diviner's lifetime, "either by associating with their colleagues while they are divining, or by paying other diviners to teach them specific [divining] verses or medicines."[53] Bascom notes that not many boys "adopt divination as a career . . . because the initiations are too expensive and the work of learning the figures and memorizing the verses, sacrifices, medicines, and other rituals associated with the worship of Ifa are too tedious. No one becomes a *babalawo* to make money, they say. It is usually through misfortune that one becomes a diviner: through illness, losses in trade, the lack of children, or the death of one's wives or children."[54] As with the Zulu, an Ifa diviner may go through initiation by way of illness or personal misfortune that convinces both him and the community of his "destiny" as a diviner.

---

[51]H. Calloway, "The Initiation of a Zulu Diviner," in Peek, *African Divination Systems*, p. 28.
[52]Ibid., pp. 28-9.
[53]Bascom, *Ifa Divination*, p. 86.
[54]Ibid., p. 88.

The pattern of training into divination is essentially the same among the Sukuma. Apprentices may be young or old, but symptoms of the call often include inexplicable and persistent illnesses or other strange behavior. This can be seen in the account recorded by C. R. Hatfield of a person (Masudi) possessed by ancestral spirits (*masamva*) to become a diviner (*nfumu*):

> When I was contacted by the *masamva*, I started speaking Kinaturu or Kishashi [neighboring languages]. I never heard these languages before, yet I understood them. One night I woke up, ran to the water hole and remained there until well after sunrise. I hadn't eaten the night before but I was feeling happy. I slept by the water hole and during my sleep I was seeing pictures of the dead, the future and the past coming one by one speaking to me. Also at this time I could see the *balogi* (witches) here in the village and abroad. I saw them dancing, going to kill somebody, and I was always telling them to stop. Once I stayed in the cattle kraal for eight hours in the hot sun. I didn't feel the heat at all, but I was cold... As the *masamva* attack increased I was getting thinner and thinner. Let's put it that I didn't eat, drink, or laugh, but I was happy in my heart.[55]

---

[55]C. R. Hatfield, *The Nfumu in Tradition and Change: A Study of the Position of Religious Practitioners Among the Sukuma of Tanzania, East Africa*, Ph. D. Dissertation (Washington, D.C., Catholic University of America, 1968), p. 161.

Another call involving a fifty-year-old woman, by the name of Ng'wana Kasonda, took the following course: "I started out as a *saji* (mad woman). I must have been about twenty. When they took me to an *nfumu* he said that I was on my way to becoming a *nfumu*. When they brought me back home my family offered sacrifices, but shortly afterwards I was attacked again. So I returned to the *nfumu*. This time he said I was being troubled by my maternal ancestors who wanted me to be a *nfumu* also but to follow their kind of work. My family made another sacrifice. This cooled me down, so I started using the *ng'hambo* [twig divination] and *nzege* [rattle divination] and only advising people to see the root doctor for treatments. Then people started complaining. They said I wasn't completely *nfumu* because I didn't know medicines. I told them I had no idea at all about medicines. I was not a medicine *nfumu*, but they continued their complaints. I guess my *masamva*

A Sukuma diviner's apprenticeship usually lasts a long time and the apprentice often works for his or her mentor at the latter's home. This place is a veritable school where many apprentices learn various kinds of medicines and have to endure many kinds of trials together. Not surprisingly, many give up and leave. Those who endure and complete the training are "reborn" into the profession of divination and receive public recognition. Even diviners who claim to have been directly initiated by the ancestral spirits often have to undergo an apprenticeship to acquire their "accreditation," so to speak, in the eyes of the people. As Hatfield puts it, this kind of "Training in *bufumu* [divination] serves a variety of purposes for the trainee. In addition to providing . . . skills in certain kinds of medicines, divination, and diagnoses, it also instills . . . a necessary personal quality for practice—confidence."[56]

With the Sukuma, all apprentices training under one expert refer to themselves as members, or indeed *children,* of the expert's household. They will refer to themselves for example, as *"wa Manzaga,"* that is to say, "of the house or family of Manzaga." The apprentices are Manzaga's sons and he their father, with all the reciprocal rights and responsibilities of that relationship. This fictive relationship has important religious implications that are similar to those of the natural family, but at times perhaps even stronger. The apprentices supplicate the specialist's ancestors as their own and any successes the apprentices may have are attributed to the depth of this relationship.[57]

Many examples can be cited[58] that demonstrate the degree to

---

[ancestors] heard them because they started troubling me again. Now, one night I was taken out by my paternal ancestors into a forest where they showed me all sorts of trees and the diseases which they treat. Then my maternal ancestors came and said they couldn't tolerate my not knowing their medicine, so they taught me as well. It was, I tell you, like a competition, but so far as I can see, neither outdoes the other. I was dealing with nzege, but they weren't pleased with that either. They showed me another method which works very well" (ibid., p. 146).

[56]Ibid., p. 178.

[57]Ibid., pp. 178-87.

[58]For example, see Evans-Pritchard, Witchcraft, Oracles, and Magic, pp. 202-57 and V. Turner, *Revelation and Divination in Ndembu Ritual* (Ithaca and London: Cornell University Press, 1975), pp. 289-90, 243-68.

which divination is a highly specialized religious calling and activity in Africa. It demands in both men and women the proper disposition, training, and discipline. As we have noted, in Yorubaland it may require as much as ten years of instruction and training while the Yaka of Zaire require one year of rigorous instruction. In many other places, novices are publicly tested before being presented to the community as diviners. Frequently, learning the intricacies of the vocation is a life-long process.[59]

Just as disease and suffering are a necessary part of life, divination as a way of dealing with them forms part and parcel of the African way of life. Divination is intricately intertwined with notions of health and disease, success and failure, goodness and badness. It is thus central to the understanding of morality in African Religion because of the role it plays in ensuring the continuation of right relationships and order. Divination is the most important way of determining how to ensure the society's collective ethical ideals.

METHODS OF DIVINATION

For the sake of convenience, we will consider the methods of divination in African Religion under three broad and inclusive categories, following John Beattie's references to the Nyoro of Uganda.[60] The first category, the manipulation of certain specific mechanical objects and the interpretation of the results, is by far the most widespread. Second is the observation and interpretation "in specially prepared conditions," as Beattie points out, of the behavior of a live animal or some aspect of a dead one. Third, there is divination by what can generally be referred to as possession by spiritual powers. These categories can in turn be

---

[59]See Peek, "Becoming a Diviner," in Peek, *African Divination Systems*, p. 25.

[60]J. Beattie, "Divination in Bunyoro, Uganda," in J. Middleton, ed., *Magic Witchcraft, and Curing* (Garden City, New York: The Natural History Press, 1967), pp. 211-31. For an exhaustive account of divination and healing processes among the Douala of Cameroon, see E. de Rosny, *Healers in the Night*. Trans. by R. R. Barr (Maryknoll, New York: Orbis Books, 1985).

grouped into two systems of divination: instrumental, mechanical, or augurial divination constitutes the oracular system of divination; and divination by possession constitutes the mediumistic system.

Instrumental or mechanical divination has many forms throughout Africa. However, perhaps one of the most sophisticated and most famous is the Ifa divination of the Yoruba, referred to above, in which sixteen palm nuts are manipulated or a divining chain is cast. This latter form of divination has a simpler form called divination by "sixteen cowries." Both methods involve a specialized knowledge of divining verses that are both difficult and time-consuming to learn. While the technical mechanics of the procedure go beyond the scope of this study,[61] we can note that both involve an intricate reading and interpretation of palm nuts or cowries that have been tossed to the ground by the diviner. The simpler form of sixteen cowries allows only seventeen possible positions, whereas the classic Ifa divination involves 256 possibilities. Bascom describes the latter's basic procedure in this way:

> Three principal steps are involved in Ifa divination. The first is the selection of the correct figure, associated with which is the message that Ifa wishes to have conveyed to the client. This is achieved by the manipulation of the palm nuts or by a cast of the divining chain, and can be interpreted in terms of the laws of probability, with each of the figures having one chance in 256 of appearing. As viewed by the Yoruba diviners and clients, the choice is not left to chance; rather it is controlled by Ifa himself... The initial figure cast determines the group of verses that will be recited.
>
> Secondly, the correct verse bearing on the client's problems must be selected from those which the diviner has memorized for this figure. The verses deal with a variety of

---

[61]These two forms of divination, and the verses involved, have been studied and recorded in great detail by W. Bascom in his two books, *Sixteen Cowries* and *Ifa Divination*.

problems that may confront the client, including illness and death, poverty and debt, getting married and having children, taking new land and building a new house, choosing a chief and acquiring a title, undertaking a business venture, taking a trip, and recovering lost property. The verses prescribe the sacrifice to be offered, although this may be somewhat modified, and they predict the outcome of the client's problem. The verses are the key to the entire system of divination; and the selection of the correct verse, containing the message that Ifa wishes to have conveyed to the client, is the crucial point in the procedure. Finally, it is necessary for the client to offer the sacrifice in the prescribed manner in order to assure the blessings or to avert the evil consequences that have been foretold.[62]

In both Ifa divination and in divination with sixteen cowries, the central objective is to determine what kind of sacrifice the client must make to get rid of an affliction or to obtain a favor. This information is contained in the divination verses. According to the arrangements of the nuts, shells, or chain, the diviner recites the appropriate verses containing the predictions and the type of sacrifices required. It is up to the client to determine the specific verse that applies to his/her case and to stop the diviner at that point. If the client needs more specific information about the issue in question, additional casts can be made. Then the indicated sacrifice must be offered. As Bascom notes, "the failure to sacrifice when blessings are prophesied may result not only in their forfeiture, but in evil consequences."[63]

---

[62]Bascom, *Ifa Divination*, p. 68.
[63]Bascom, *Ifa Divination*, p. 60. See also Bascom, *Sixteen Cowries*, p. 5. Verses 170-1, for example (see *Ifa Divination*, pp. 105 and 107), run: "'When we have seen a conspiracy we run,' 'Naked like the chief of parrots,' and 'Young palm fruit grow large and becomes ripe palm fruit; if young palm fruit does not die it will be ripe palm fruit tomorrow' were the ones who cast Ifa for Frog Kokeyo, who was the child of Onishinko. They said two blessings were coming to him, and that he should sacrifice so that both would be able to reach him. Frog refused to sacrifice; he said that when he saw the blessings, he would make the sacrifice. He did not appease Eshu at

In Bunyoro, in addition to cowry shells, diviners also use strips of leather, wooden charms, grain, or a rubbing stick. The Ndembu of Zambia also use several methods: divination by basket (*ng'ombu yakusekula*); by pounding pole (*ng'ombu yamwishi*); by rattle (*ng'ombu yanzenzi* or *dawulang'ang'a*); by calabash (*katuwa kang'ombu*); by bushbuck horn (*ng'ombu yamuseng'u wambala*); by stick bundle (*ng'ombu yanzeli*); by tortoise-shell (*ng'ombu yambachi*), among others.[64] The Lugbara, like the Nyoro, employ a rubbing stick. Nupe divination mechanisms, on the other hand, resemble the Yoruba palm nut and cowry shell procedure. But the Nupe also employ the tortoise-shell-on-a-taut-string process.[65] Nadel has referred to the latter as "a crude oracle, permitting only three answers—'yes' (if the tortoise glides down quickly), 'no' (if it does not glide down at all), and 'doubtful' (if it glides down slowly)."[66] But whether "crude" or "sophisticated" is clearly a matter of comparison.

---

all. They said he should sacrifice one he-goat, one red cloth with light stripes, and one shilling seven pence eight *oninis*.

Frog was the child of the King of Oyo. He had one wife who had lived with him for some time but who was not pregnant and who had not yet borne a child. At the very time that they said he should make this sacrifice, the wife of Frog became pregnant, and Frog was very happy. When the day came that this woman gave birth, Frog was at his farm, and there they came to tell him that his wife had borne a child. When Frog heard this, he was very happy; he said that before he went home he would tap some palm wine. As Frog left the farm storehouse, a messenger came from home to tell him that they were calling Frog at home, because the king had died and they wanted to make Frog king. Because he was not at the store house, they went and found Frog in the middle of the farm, where he was tapping palm wine at the top of a palm tree. When they told Frog, he was so happy that he forgot that he was up in a palm tree and he fell down and broke his legs. When they saw he had broken his legs, they carried him home, but both his arms and legs were broken. When they tried to cure him and failed, they gave the title to another person, and left Frog alone. From that day on, people have been saying, "Too much happiness broke Frog's legs."

[64] See Turner, *Revelation and Divination*, pp. 207-338.

[65] See G. Parrinder, *West African Religion: A Study of the Beliefs and Practices of Akam, Ewe, Yoruba, Ibo, and Kindred Peoples* (London: The Epworth Press, 1961), pp. 147-50.

[66] S. F. Nadel, *Nupe Religion* (New York: Schocken Books, 1970), p. 38.

What is central in Africa is the belief that divination is a tool "bestowed by God upon man so that he may be better fitted to cope with the practical problems of life on earth; but these include also the problem of handling successfully all the other transcendental tools. And just because divination is such a twofold 'prerequisite' and so basically indispensable, its presence is simply taken for granted."[67]

The second form of the oracular system of divination involves augury. By observing the behavior of a living animal or some feature of an animal killed specifically for that purpose, the diviner foretells (augurs) what is in store for the client. There are numerous forms of augury[68] just as there are many forms of mechanical divination. Two representative types of augurial divination are the poison oracle and what we may call the "bad signs" oracle.

The poison oracle is straightforward. Essentially, it involves the introduction of a poison into a live animal, usually a fowl. Among the Azande, the poison comes from a creeping plant called *benge*. The seance includes three people: the owner, who brings the fowl and whose problems are the subject of the divination procedure (several "owners" may participate in one seance); the operator, who holds the fowl and introduces the poison; and the questioner, who addresses the pertinent inquiries to the oracle. The questions are casuistic and go more or less like this: "If such is the case, poison oracle kill the fowl," or "If such is the case, poison oracle spare the fowl."[69] The verdict depends on whether the fowl lives or dies. But the questioning requires a certain level of sophistication. As Evans-Pritchard notes in relation to the whole process of the poison oracle among the Azande,

> Great experience is necessary to conduct a seance in the correct manner and to know how to interpret the findings of the oracle. One must know how many doses of poison to administer, whether the oracle is working properly, in what order to take the questions, whether to put them in a posi-

---

[67]Ibid., p. 65.
[68]See, for example, Evans-Pritchard, *Witchcraft, Oracles, and Magic*, pp. 258-386; Beattie, "Divination in Bunyoro," pp. 220-2.
[69]Evans-Pritchard, *Witchcraft, Oracles, and Magic*, p. 295.

tive or negative form, how long a fowl is to be held between the toes or in the hand while a question is being put to the oracle, when it ought to be jerked to stir up the poison, and when it is time to throw it on the ground for final inspection. One must know how to observe not only whether the fowl lives or dies, but also the exact manner in which the poison affects it, for while it is under the influence of the oracle its every movement is significant to the experienced eye. Also one must know the phraseology of address in order to put questions clearly to the oracle without error or ambiguity, and this is no easy task when a single question may be asked in a harangue lasting as long as five or ten minutes.[70]

In Zande poison divination, a judgment of the accuracy or validity of the oracle depends on the testimony of two tests. "If a fowl dies in the first test then another fowl must survive the second test, and if a fowl survives the first test another fowl must die in the second test for the judgment to be accepted as valid."[71] The framing of the questions assures the outcome of either of these alternatives.[72]

Oracles that employ the reading of "bad signs" involve autop-

---

[70]Ibid., p. 285.

[71]Ibid., p. 299.

[72]This is fascinating. Let me cite Evans-Pritchard's illustration of how this comes about (see ibid., p. 300):

A.

First Test. If X has committed adultery poison oracle kill the fowl. If X is innocent poison oracle spare the fowl. The fowl dies.

Second test. The poison oracle has declared X guilty of adultery by slaying the fowl. If its declaration is true let it spare this second fowl. The fowl survives.

Result. A valid verdict. X is guilty.

B.

First Test. If X has committed adultery poison oracle kill the fowl. If X is innocent poison oracle spare the fowl. The fowl lives.

Second test. The poison oracle has declared X innocent of adultery by sparing the fowl. If its declaration is true let it slay the second fowl. The fowl dies.

Result. A valid verdict. X is innocent.

sies of animals killed for the purpose. Although fowls are often used, larger animals, such as goats, sheep, or even cows may be used for very important issues. The animal is handled by the client, or made to come into contact with some vital part of the client (e.g., saliva), so as to assume his or her being. It is then ritually killed and dissected and a section of it, most often the entrails, is examined. Among the Banyoro, "The diviner begins by examining the cavity where the liver lies . . . ; if there are *nkebe* [small white spots] there it is a sign that his client will die [or suffer some other misfortune]. He also examines the liver itself . . . ; the broad part of the intestine . . . ; its middle part . . . ; and its lower parts; also the part where the gizzard is . . . The way in which these organs are lying is also important. If the anus is swollen . . . this is also a bad sign."[73] The absence of all of these "bad" signs means that the diagnosis is favorable. As with the Azande poison oracle, two attempts at such haruspication are usually made to verify the prognosis.

A special form of mechanical divination is the ordeal, which combines the elements of prognosis and punishment. Unlike other forms of divination, ordeals have a highly jural aspect with the goal of identifying the guilty party who is then judged and punished by the ordeal itself.

One of the simplest forms of ordeal among the Logoli and Vugusu is to invite suspected ill-wishers to a meal. If they are

---

C.

First Test. If X has committed adultery poison oracle kill the fowl. If X is innocent poison oracle spare the fowl. The fowl dies.

Second test. The poison oracle has declared X guilty of adultery by slaying the fowl. If its declaration is true let it spare the second fowl. The fowl dies.

Result. The verdict is contradictory and therefore invalid.

D.

First Test. If X has committed adultery poison oracle kill the fowl. If X is innocent poison oracle spare the fowl. The fowl survives.

Second test. The poison oracle has declared X innocent of adultery by sparing the fowl. If its declaration is true let it slay the second fowl. The fowl survives.

Result. The verdict is contradictory and therefore invalid.

[73]Beattie, "Divination in Bunyoro," pp. 221-2.

guilty but consent to partake in the meal, they will fall sick and even die. "The efficacy of this ordeal," Gunter Wagner explains, "rests on the . . . notion . . . that somebody who is harbouring ill will towards another person cannot accept food or drink or any other hospitality from that person without thereby coming to grief himself . . . " Order and disorder are antithetical and cannot exist together. Thus, even dancing around a suspected witch by the community (a sign of community and communion) can eventually harm an ill-disposed person because, in the communion of the dance, he/she embodies the disorder of disunity and hatred. For such a person, the dance itself is a form of ordeal.[74]

Another kind of ordeal described by Wagner takes the form of an acted-out oath. A suspected witch is given a dagger. The accused then plunges it as hard as possible into the trunk of a specific anti-witchcraft tree. As the accused withdraws the dagger the following words are addressed to him: "If you have killed so-and-so may you die, but if you have not killed him, may you live." If the accused is guilty he will suffer illness and death. If innocent, nothing will happen to him.[75]

There are more complex forms of ordeals as well. Eugene Mendonsa, for example, gives an account of "the scorpion ordeal" among the Sisala of northern Ghana:

One day, upon his return from the farm, Dasuki noticed some millet grains near the lineage granary (*virebalin*). It is forbidden for anyone to remove millet from this granary without the headman's permission, so he, as headman, called all the women of the lineage together and asked who had stolen the grain. None spoke, so he ordered a scorpion ordeal. Dasuki instructed the children of the lineage to look for a scorpion. When one was found, Dasuki again assembled the women and asked if anyone had anything to say. Since none did, he placed the scorpion on the arm of the first woman. It did not sting her, so he placed it on the arm

---

[74]Wagner, *The Bantu of Western Kenya*, pp. 272-7.
[75]Ibid., p. 274. From Wagner's description, it seems that this kind of ordeal is reserved to men in western Kenya.

of the second, with the same result. When he approached the third woman in line, she began to cry. He asked her why, and she confessed to the crime. It is thought that such theft is punishable by death through ancestral anger, so her husband, Babgadere, was required to sacrifice a goat, two hens, a guinea fowl, and a fine of 100 cowries. There was no need to consult a diviner in this case because the rule is unambiguous, as is the result."[76]

Ingestion of a special medicine (usually poisonous) by the accused, or by an animal representing the suspect, is a form of ordeal widely used in many parts of Africa. It reminds one of the poison oracle that the Azande administer to fowls during divination. Among the Shona of Zimbabwe, vomiting by the accused is a sign of innocence. But the accusers have to pay a hefty fine for having made a false accusation. A failure of the accused to vomit, on the other hand, indicates guilt and the suspect may suffer death or any other punishment at the discretion of the accusers.[77] Similarly, among the Ndembu, poison (called *mwaji*) can be given to the accused, but it is usually introduced into the mouth of a chicken substituting for the accused. If the chicken dies, the accused is guilty. But if it survives, a second dose of poison is administered to a different chicken. If this chicken survives, the ordeal is repeated on a third chicken. If it does not die, the accused is not guilty."[78] For this type of divination, the Nupe use snake-bite medicine, which is ingested by the accused. If guilty, the suspect will eventually die.[79]

As can be seen from these examples, some ordeals take time while others are instantaneous. Hot iron and boiling water ordeals, which provide instantaneous verdicts, are preferred by many peoples throughout the continent. A red-hot iron is applied

---

[76]E. L. Mendonsa, *The Politics of Divination: A Processual View of Reactions to Illness and Deviance Among the Sisala of Northern Ghana* (Berkeley and Los Angeles, California: University of California Press, 1982), pp. 184-5.

[77]M. Gelfand, *The Spiritual Beliefs of the Shona: A Study Based on Fieldwork among the East Central Shona* (Gwelo: Mambo Press, 1977), p. 191.

[78]Turner, *Revelation and Divination*, p. 321.

[79]Nadel, *Nupe Religion*, p. 188.

to a part of the body of the accused, or both the accused and the accuser. The one with the worst burn is guilty of wrongdoing or of having made a false accusation. A variation requires both the accused and the accuser to handle a sharp knife. Again, the person who suffers the worst cuts is either a wrongdoer or a false accuser. Among the Ndembu, "a suspected sorcerer or witch must plunge his or her arm into a pot of boiling water and medicines. If the arm is not scalded the person is innocent."[80]

An important aspect of divination by ordeal is its public nature. The physical presence of the conflicting parties, or their representatives, is usually necessary. Sometimes the accuser is the community itself, in which case representatives of the community may be required to prove the truth of the accusation by undergoing the ordeal themselves.

DIVINATION BY MEDIUMS

In the case of mediumistic divination, the diviner is the object through whom the oracle is given. The spiritual power speaks through the diviner, who becomes the medium. The form of spirit possession that the diviner undergoes is characterized by a subtle but important nuance. As Peter Fry explains (citing R. Firth), possession as "a form of trance in which the behavior patterns of a person *are interpreted as* evidence of a control of his behavior by a spirit external to him," is not proper to mediumistic divination. What is proper to this kind of divination is "a form of possession in which the person *is conceived* as serving as an intermediary between spirits and men. The accent here is on communication; the actions and words of mediums must be translatable, which differentiates them from [otherwise] mere spirit possession or madness."[81] The former indicates an increase in one's vital power, and is therefore a blessing. The latter indi-

---

[80]Turner, *Revelation and Divination*, p. 320.

[81]See P. Fry, *Spirits of Protest: Spirit-mediums and the Articulation of Consensus Among the Zezuru of Southern Rhodesia (Zimbabwe)* (Cambridge: Cambridge University Press, 1976), p. 30.

cates a diminishment of life, and is therefore an affliction to be removed.

Another mediumistic system of divination employs a sacred divining instrument, such as *mahembe* or *mayembe* (horns) in Bunyoro and Buganda, Uganda,[82] which become the elements through which the powers speak. This should not be confused with mechanical divination. In mediumistic "horn" divination, the horn is neither manipulated nor observed for the oracle. The horn itself, or the horn through the mouth of a person, audibly articulates the oracle, providing direct verbal communication. Though generically known as *mayembe* (horns), the instruments used as mediums in this kind of divination are different kinds of objects. The king of Buganda (Kabaka) usually has many for different needs. One, called *Mjabwe,* acts as a judge with no appeal possible. John Roscoe observes that in the past the king used to send prisoners to *Mjabwe* to explain their cases. Invariably, all prisoners sent to *Mjabwe* were condemned to death. Perhaps this was to exonerate the king from being accountable for the blood of his subjects; it is important to note, however, that it is the *mayembe* that delivers a verdict requiring capital punishment.[83]

As mentioned above, in mediumistic divination the diviner always goes into a state of possession and becomes an instrument of speech for the possessing spirit. Yet, at the same time the diviner becomes, in a sense, possessor of the spirit because he or she can induce it to speak when need be. Wim van Binsbergen has distinguished four major states of possession:

1. Possession as an extremely momentary and very intensive state (usually accompanied by drumming, singing, sometimes smoking) . . . ; 2. Possession as a permanent condition with diffuse, non-intensive manifestations, but which is at intervals re-activated as under 1; 3. Possession as a permanent condition with diffuse, non-intensive man-

---

[82]See Beattie, "Divination in Bunyoro," pp. 225-30, and J. O'Donahue, *Magic and Witchcraft in Southern Uganda* (Kampala: Gaba Publications, Pastoral Paper no. 36, n.d.), pp. 23-6.
[83]See O'Donohue, *Magic and Witchcraft,* pp. 24-5.

ifestations, a condition reached after a short, unique period of more acute and intensive manifestations; [and] 4. Possession as a permanent condition throughout life, with only diffuse, non-intensive manifestations.[84]

The two symptoms described in the first type of possession above are by far the most common. Among the Yaka of Zaire, for example, at the most intensive moment of possession, the diviner goes into a trance, jumps great heights without assistance, twitches his body, and foams at the mouth. He makes strange sounds "in the esoteric language of the diviners," as Rene Devisch noted. "After the oracle, the diviner often shows clear signs of fatigue and great irritability."[85] Among the Shona, divination-possession takes more or less the same form. At the sound of music played for the purpose, and while people sing and dance, the medium becomes possessed. "As the music continues the medium's head begins to shake, his limbs move up and down, almost vibrating with the music, and the muscles become taut. Many emit sighs and grunts as if inspiring deeply. The movements of the limbs become more violent, the medium may sing, move around . . . " At this time, questions are put to the spirit, who may respond. The spirit may also enumerate specific moral irregularities in the community which must be rectified.[86]

Of significance here is obviously not the symptoms, but what the symptoms reveal to the medium. Turner describes the mediumistic diviner's task as "bringing into the open what is hidden or unknown," so that people can deal with relevant situations in an appropriate way. If, for example, it is revealed that an ancestral spirit is causing disease or other kinds of disorders, the diviner will identify the procedure to achieve health and luck.

---

[84]W. M. J. van Binsbergen, *Religious Change in Zambia: Exploratory Studies* (London: Kegan Paul International, 1981), pp. 90-1.

[85]R. Devisch, "Mediumistic Divination Among the Northern Yaka of Zaire: Etiology and Ways of Knowing," in Peek, *African Divination Systems,* p. 113.

[86]Gelfand, "The *Mhondoro* Cult of the Shona-speaking People of Southern Rhodesia," in M. Fortes and G. Dieterlen, eds., *African Systems of Thought* (London: Oxford University Press, 1965), p. 346.

This may involve a sacrifice or simply a mention of the name of the ancestor in question. As Turner explains, "The belief is that the spirit is aggrieved because it has been forgotten, not only by the victim, but also by many of its other kin. It afflicts its living kinsman sometimes in his personal capacity, but more often in his capacity as representative of a kinsgroup. If, however, it is mentioned, and hence remembered, by many people, it will cease to afflict and will henceforward benefit its victim, who becomes a sort of living memorial to it."[87]

It should be emphasized once more that such revelation is rarely juridical. Even when open conflict between individuals and groups is concerned, the medium's primary task is merely to seek to discover and make known the cause of the problem. The medium will address these negative social-ethical attitudes and behavior, but, as a rule, not point out the guilty or prescribe retribution.

Like many other African peoples, the Yaka ascribe extraordinary powers of smell, hearing, and sight to mediumistic diviners. By smelling articles that have been in close contact with the body of the afflicted client, a diviner is often able to detect the cause of the affliction. Such articles are particularly important if they have come into contact with those parts of the body where vital powers are concentrated. It is much better still if they are part of the body itself, such as blood, hair, nails, spittle, and so on. The diviner's power of smell is identified with the power of smell of a hunting dog. That is why, in order to preserve the distinction between the two, a Yaka diviner will scrupulously avoid indis-

---

[87]Turner, *The Drums of Affliction,* 1968, p. 29. "Another way [of appeasement] is through representing the shade in some kind of material form, either as a figurine named after it, or as a contraption of branches covered with a blanket whitened with cassava meal. These representations are made at the end of protracted rituals, in sacred sites which only cult-adepts may enter, called *masoli* (from the verb *ku-solola,* 'to make visible' or 'reveal'). It is said that when the spirit is afflicting its victim, it is concealed in his or her body. This is thought especially to be the case where women suffer from some reproductive disorder. But when the spirit has been adequately represented in symbolic form, and frequently named, it is believed to emerge, reconciled with the victim and his whole kin-group" (ibid., p. 29).

criminate contact with dogs. As noted above, those similar in creation must not be confused.

Since the spirits often deliver revelatory messages at night during dreams, a diviner will sometimes place the intermediary article in or near the ear so as to hear what they say. During sleep or a sleep-like trance, a diviner obtains the power of perception.[88] The connection between dreams and divination is important because dreams play an important part in both disease and health. While for the diviner dreams are a way of seeing, for everyone else they are actual experiences. One lives what one dreams about and vice versa. If, for example, one dreams that one is or has been bewitched, there is no question that this is also fact. The only question is who the witch may be. In fact, the Azande

---

[88]Among the Yaka, Devisch, "Mediumistic Divination," in Peek, *African Divination Systems*, pp. 118-9, notes: "The clairvoyance draws on dreamlike images. During the oracle, the diviner always uses such expressions as 'see' or 'dream.' Questioned about this, the diviners say that the oracle consists in expressing what they have seen or were seeing at that moment in a dream, or what appeared suddenly to them from outside. They describe scenes crossing their vision. The people in these scenes appear vaguely, in a way the diviners describe as 'people seen through an open door. You can see how tall they are, whether they are man or woman, what they carry with them, what they do, but you cannot recognize their faces.' The diviner translates the 'internal voices' that on such occasions may speak to him in a way that is hardly comprehensible. By contemplating these images and messages in his heart and by transposing them to the afflicted individual's problem the diviner establishes a metaphoric link between the problem situation and the initial divinatory interpretation. Many of these dreamlike images are concerned with avuncular gestures (e.g., 'I see the uncle who is approaching the bed, who is offering kaolin, . . .'); other images concern allies, sorcery, ritual care for the patient, initiation, illness, and so on. This connotation makes clear the importance and efficiency of the images, by the fact that they inscribe the given problem into the self-generative articulation of meaning in the oracle.

The diviner's extraordinary powers are also metonymically spoken of as 'dreams,' i.e., as a dreamlike form of understanding the hidden. The Yaka diviner defines himself in a song as 'the one who crosses all divisions, limits, barriers, the one who can see into the deepest darknesses of the forest.' That the oracle is founded on an extended consciousness which brings to light hidden forgotten meanings is also metonymically symbolized. Before the oracle, the diviner eats a piece of kola nut (a stimulant) mixed with wood that has been sucked into a whirlpool and has resurfaced."

compare dreams to the poison oracle. "The speech of the poison oracle," they ask rhetorically, "is it not like a dream? It tells you of a matter confusedly as when a man wakes from sleep to tell his dream and it seems to be like a jest, whereas in fact what a man sees in a dream is real." Accordingly, bad dreams and nightmares portend bad consequences, and pleasant dreams good consequences. In the opinion of the Azande, "That which is going to happen to a man in the future is that which dreams reveal to you."[89]

REESTABLISHING TIES: RECONCILIATION RITES

The sacrifices, offerings, and attitudinal and behavioral changes mandated by divination are intended to reestablish harmony and equilibrium in life. Tacit in every divination procedure is the need to reestablish ties in the community and/or between the living and the spirits, the ancestors, and God. Many oracles specifically insist on this by demanding the performance of reconciliation rites. One of the clearest examples is found among the Taita of Kenya. In fact, reconciliation (*kutasa*) penetrates practically the entire religious system (*ßutasi*) of the Taita. Elements of nature, such as cane juice, beer, or water, are used in this ritual, but its central point is to acknowledge divisive anger and resentment in one's heart and cast them away. It is also intended to deflect the anger of the mystical powers and reestablish harmony and beneficence. The central purpose of Taita religion, Grace

---

[89]Evans-Pritchard, *Witchcraft, Oracles, and Magic,* p. 379. On pp. 378-86 of this book, Evans-Pritchard provides numerous examples of dreams and their interpretations among the Azande. But let us refer to another example, recorded by Aylward Shorter, which had very sad consequences. Shorter relates that one day in the early 1970s he had a dream in which he noticed that the toes on his library assistant's right foot were snakes. He told his dream to his assistant. The latter was horrified. He began to feel sick immediately, and pointed to the dream as the source of his illness. His condition continued to worsen so that he had to be admitted to a psychiatric hospital. Such is the power of dreams experienced as realities in Africa. See Shorter, *Jesus and the Witchdoctor: An Approach to Healing and Wholeness* (Maryknoll, New York: Orbis Books, 1985), p. 149.

Harris explains, is the restoration of *"sere*: peace, health and general well-being. In realizing its primary aims, getting rid of anger, *ßutasi* used special versions of the ordinary Taita means of maintaining and re-establishing amicable relations between those in long-term relationship: the giving of gifts, especially gifts of food, and commensalism."[90]

According to Taita religious thought, anger is the emotion generated in human hearts, and even in the hearts of domestic animals, as well as among spiritual powers, through infringement of their proper rights. In the preceding chapters, we have seen how elders, ancestors, God, and human and non-human spirits must be treated by the living if misfortune is not to be visited on the community. The elders must be respected; the ancestors, God, and the spirits must frequently be offered sacrifices and other offerings of appeasement. Failure to do any of these things causes anger in the "hearts" of these elements of the universe. The only way to restore the desired relationships is to "cast out" that anger through ritual. As the performer of the ritual of integration and equilibrium, the human agent must make sure, first of all, that his or her own heart is free from anger. As Harris notes,

> In *kutasa* [reconciliation], utterances directed towards turning away the anger of a *personal* or *personified* mystical agent were at some point matched by declarations signifying and effecting the end of anger in the performer. But the Taita held that for the entire ritual to be efficacious, it was necessary for the celebrant to be "sincere": he must not have inner reservations. Although the performance of *kutasa* was correctly achieved in gesture and word, these had to be matched by the person's inner state.[91]

The Nyakyusa in Tanzania stress the same thing. Their reconciliation rituals apply to the whole range of social relationships: "between rulers; between chief and people; and above all

---

[90]G. G. Harris, *Casting Out Anger: Religion Among the Taita of Kenya* (Cambridge, Cambridge University Press, 1978), p. 28.
[91]Ibid., p. 46.

between kinsmen," as Monica Wilson points out. But their hearts must be calm and cool in performing these rituals. For "If there is anger in their hearts the rituals may be ineffective. So, repeatedly, in the rituals there is confession of anger, symbolized . . . by blowing out water," the end of which, as with the Taita, is the establishment of a new situation, void of anger, sealed with the sharing of food and drink (commensality or communion).[92]

For African Religion, therefore, misfortune or affliction point to the presence of anger somewhere in the visible or invisible world. The purpose of divination is to establish and identify the source of the anger and why it has come about. After these are known, reconciliation or anger-removal rites provide the means to unambiguously acknowledge this reality and then to deal with it by eliminating or "finishing" it. The forms of the rites vary in their details, of course. The subject of the anger must be clearly known so as to avoid the risk of compounding insult and injury by delaying or not performing the rite in the proper way. One concrete instance of a reconciliation among the Taita should illustrate this point.

In 1952 a man of central Dabida had a goat killed so that a reading of its entrails might reveal why, after three of his children had already died, a fourth was seriously ill. *ßula* [the entrails] showed that the wife's anger at the husband had killed the other three children and was now threatening the fourth. Since the couple had not been getting along well for some years, the wife had no difficulty in bringing up many grievances against her husband. She said that he neglected her and that she did not think he loved her. She said that she had felt that "there was no use in bearing all these children" if all she was to get was ill treatment or indifference.

At the direction of the presiding elder, a senior agnate of the husband, the couple squatted just outside their doorway, facing each other. The husband, using beer which the

---

[92]M. Wilson, *Religion and the Transformation of Society: A Study in Social Change in Africa* (Cambridge: Cambridge University Press, 1971), p. 65.

wife had brewed for him, did *kutasa* first, saying that "The curse of her anger upon the children should be finished." His wife, he said, had been making a lot of fuss. She ought to realize that it was *he* who married *her*—he had given bridewealth for her. He was therefore master of the house and she should realize that she had no right to make so many complaints. The wife then did *kutasa* with cane juice. She said that it was true that her heart had been injured and she was sure that her anger had caused the death of the three children and the illness of the fourth. Now she was casting away her anger forever, so that the remaining children would be well. The curse of her anger would be "completely cut."[93]

This illustration also emphasizes the perspective of African Religion that all human beings are potentially wrongdoers or witches. Every human person is capable not only of harboring wrong and destructive thoughts, but of acting them out as well. Although a person may not be conscious of one's destructive power against life, this does not obstruct its potency. Divination reveals one starkly to oneself, so to speak, as well as to other people. It forces the individual or the community to manage its destructive forces ritually in the interests of enhancing life.

In this sense, rituals are symbolic re-enactments of the primordial relationship between human life and the mystical sources of life. They mark crisis moments in the life of the individual or the community. To use Nadel's phrase, they indicate "ends and new beginnings."[94] They express transition, dependence, solidarity, social order, and reconciliation. Even at the final crisis of death, the end must be balanced, or even counteracted, with attestations of new beginnings. When death occurs among the Nyakyusa, Monica Wilson relates, the mourners symbolically and ritually go through both death and rebirth:

They must realize death and accept it, not washing, shav-

---

[93]Harris, *Casting Out Anger,* p. 96.
[94]Nadel, *Nupe Religion,* p. 103.

ing, or anointing themselves, for the dead are "brooding over" them and they must not drive them off. Then they turn again to life, washing and shaving and separating themselves from the dead. The Nyakyusa widow, having wept, is pressed to put her grief behind her and turn again to life. The dirges change to dance rhythms and the same friends who urged her to weep, now urge her to drive away dreams of the dead, and look to her children and her husband's heir who will father them.[95]

We should note certain types of reconciliation rituals that may seem confusing to the uninitiated in their outward symbolic manifestations. What may appear at first sight to be "rituals of rebellion,"[96] are in fact rituals of reconciliation and integration. Examples are ritual transvestism and asexuality (such as happens in funeral rites and divination rituals);[97] ritual "killing" of the new chief (as is done in installation rites); ritual hostility between social groups (such as happens between the escorting bands of bride and groom or between joking groups); and the ritual use of obscene language (as in joking relationships). As we have indicated, all of these constitute liminal situations whose final purpose is equilibrium in society and nature. In normal circumstances, what is different must not be needlessly confused. The male and female sex or the intensity and weakness of the life

---

[95]Wilson, *Religion and the Transformation of Society*, p. 64.

[96]As in actual fact they have been mistakenly characterized by M. Gluckman, among others. See his *Rituals of Rebellion in South-east Africa* (Manchester, Manchester University Press, 1954).

[97]For example, J. Middleton writes that with reference to Lugbara diviners, "The men are said occasionally to be impotent or homosexual, and those that are not, the elders and rainmakers, act [as such] when under the observance of sexual taboos which make them temporarily 'like women' (*okule*). The women are either barren or pre-pubertal, or post-menopausal, or temporarily not having intercourse with their husbands or other men; they are regarded as 'like men' (*agule*). Among the Lugbara this permanent or temporary asexuality is an essential characteristic of their being able to act as a medium between the social and the Spirit spheres. It is a symbolic attribute, and has nothing to do with their other, normal, social roles." Quoted in Peek, *African Divination Systems*, p. 196.

force in a ruler, for example, must be clearly distinguished in daily life for the sake of order. However, sometimes the difference needs to be temporarily blurred through ritual to underline its importance when the ritual is over.[98]

Finally, a word is needed about dance, an extremely important element of ritual in divination and reconciliation. Dancing accompanies almost every event that affirms life—birth, initiation, marriage, induction into an age set, and so on. There is also dancing to ward off destructive forces during illness and death, in which context dance has a therapeutic power. The destructive forces of disease are "shooed away," so to speak, by the dance. The presence of the dancing community integrates the sick person into the health of the society, as the whole society shares its accumulated health with the sick person. Dancing gives added strength in a mystical way to whatever medicines are being employed to attain health and wholeness. Coupled as it often is with some form of commensality, dancing is an expression of rejecting anger and embracing communion.

Dance is itself a form of power quite often employed to

---

[98]See E. Norbeck, "African Rituals of Conflict," in Middleton, ed., *Gods and Rituals*, pp. 197-226. Also M. Zuesse, *Ritual Cosmos*, passim.

Liminality, which is intended to evoke harmony or synthesis between the various elements of the universe, and so effect communication and communion between them, is also symbolized by the carefully chosen locations "of the divination event in space and time," as well as (frequently among some societies) the deliberate use of the left hand in divination activities. As Peek notes, "The use of the left/right duality in divination has as its goal a resolution in complementarity; both sides are necessary for completeness." Further, loss of consciousness in divination possession, heightened auricular or olfactory powers to "hear" or "smell" messages, and the power to "see" events in prophetic divination, all converge in the goal of synthesis or harmony through liminality. The association of "natural" elements in divination—such as tortoise shells, dogs, vultures, and so on—with the desired mystical effects on humanity, will also call to mind what we have said about the harmony desired in African Religion between humanity and nature. Finally, the various forms of ongoing conversation between the diviner and client, point to the need to create a bond between the two for the same purpose of holistic understanding and integration. See Peek, "African Divination Systems," pp. 196-206.

enhance the intensity of life.[99] Bosman, an early Dutch observer of Africa who is cited by Rattray, describes (albeit in the supercilious tones characteristic of his time) the manner of the ritual dance for the health of the king among the Ashanti:

> A Feast of eight days, accompanied with all manner of Singing, Skipping, Dancing, Mirth, and Jollity: in which time a perfect lampooning liberty is allowed, and Scandal so highly exalted, that they may freely sing of all the Faults, Villainies, and Frauds of their Superiours, as well as Inferiours without Punishment, or so much as the least interruption; and the only way to stop their mouths is to ply them lustily with Drink, which alters their tone immediately, and turns their Satyrical Ballads into Commendation Songs on the good Qualities of him who hath so nobly treated them.[100]

FINAL ETHICAL CONSIDERATIONS

Given the abundance of descriptions and illustrations of divination, it may be somewhat difficult to see clearly the ethical implications of divination. First of all, it is important to note that

---

[99] Among the Sukuma, C. R. Hatfield reports in this connection that "To learn *bulingi* [the art of singing], a man apprentices himself to a renowned singer, *ningi*, just as another man would apprentice himself to a master nfumu. As a student he is taught the techniques of song making and dancing. But in addition he also learns a series of medicines which are of paramount importance to the success and maintenance of the society: protective medicines, which one obtains by merely residing at the singer's homestead; assertive medicines, important in song competitions; and aggressive medicines, which when used in the contact of dance competitions serve to blast away the power of the rival society and its leaders." See his *The Nfumu*, p. 135.

It should be noted that even witches employ the power of dance to sustain them and increase their destructive energy without which it would dissipate. Dance is therefore not only an expression of holism and equilibrium, it brings them about. For example, see T. G. Christensen, *An African Tree of Life* (Maryknoll, New York: Orbis Books, 1990), pp. 45-8, 71-83.

[100] Quoted by Norbeck, "African Rituals of Conflict," p. 213.

even though the oracle constrains both belief and action on the part of the client, clients do not usually accept blindly the verdicts of divination. Neither are clients "simply 'flipping a coin' to avoid personal responsibility for making difficult decisions," as Philip Peek points out. "Divination is approached seriously and cautiously because the quality of the divination process determines the quality of the results and thereby the action taken."[101] There are several ways to test the authenticity of the oracle and to make sure that diviners are not mere charlatans. For example, sometimes the Yoruba *Ifa* may not be consulted unless an inferior oracle, called *Awpele* or *Awpepere* has been consulted first. But even when *Ifa* is consulted, the procedure can be as thorough as the client wants it to be. As William Bascom has shown, a casting of the cowries requires exhaustive steps:

> The first cast is made to determine the figure for which the verses are recited. (2) Two casts are made to determine whether the prognostication is for good or for evil. (3) Five casts are made to find out what kind of good or evil is indicated. (4) A succession of double casts may be made to find out in more detail about the evil. (5) Two casts are made to find whether a sacrifice (*ebo*) is sufficient, or whether *adimu* [offering] is required in addition. (6) If *adimu* is indicated, five casts are made to learn to whom it should be offered. (7) If *adimu* is to be made to a "white deity," it is identified by a succession of double casts. (8) Five casts are made to determine what is required as *adimu*. (9) If a live animal is required, a succession of double casts may be made to find out what kind. (10) The verses of the figure of the initial cast are recited, and the appropriate verse is selected. (11) The correct sacrifice is determined by a succession of double casts. If at point 5 *ebo* is indicated, steps 6 through 9 are omitted; and if the client wishes, steps 2 through 9 may be skipped; and if palm nuts are used, the process may be reduced to steps 1 and 10 only.[102]

[101]Peek, "African Divination Systems," p. 195.
[102]See Bascom, *Ifa Divination*, p. 59.

Clients, therefore, have a considerable amount of say in the whole divination process. Almost universally throughout Africa, the oracle is expected to know the nature of the problems it is being consulted about, and clients are generally not required to divulge them explicitly *a priori*. If a client is not satisfied with one diviner, he or she may consult another to test the veracity of the previous oracle. This is common practice among the Azande. Thus, the good reputation of the diviner is not automatic; rather, it much depends on his or her success in making correct diagnoses. Peter Fry noticed among the Zezuru of Zimbabwe that, based on poor performance, a medium may be discredited "either totally, partially or situationally." Fry relates the case of a famous medium who was totally discredited because he used the prestige of his position to commit incest and to induce a client to do the same. Another medium was partially discredited because he claimed to be possessed by a spirit which "belonged" to some other diviner. Situational discreditation, Fry notes, is very common among the Zezuru. It occurs when clients suspect that the diviner is feigning a trance. In such cases, clients will refuse to accept the oracle. The point is that all of these possibilities are means of ensuring that the practice of divination remains honest and ethical.[103]

Africans know that there are fraudulent, dishonest, and unscrupulous diviners who engage in divination not as a service but primarily as a means of making a living. Thus, there is a code of professional ethics binding on the work of diviners. With regard to the amount of sacrifices and divination (service) charges, the general rule is reasonableness. It is expected that there will be a marked difference between what the oracle demands of a rich person as sacrifice or offering and what it requires of a poor person. Thus, it is generally professionally unethical "to take advantage of a sick person or to charge strangers more than relatives."[104]

In many African societies, diviners are publicly known but are not generally distinguished from the rest of society except during

---

[103]See Fry, *Spirits of Protest*, pp. 42-44.
[104]Bascom, *Ifa Divination*, p. 76.

actual divination. In others, however, they are clearly marked by their mode of dress or some other abnormal behavior. In either case, what fundamentally characterizes them is their liminal state. As agents of communication between the everyday and mystical worlds, they do not, at least temporarily at the height of the divination process, belong to either.

In the final analysis, divination is a recognition that there are deeper realities in life than meet the eye. Divination provides a way of knowing these deeper realities, that is, the whys and wherefores of suffering, illness, anger, discord, floods, drought, poverty, barrenness, impotence, all kinds of loss, and death. To know the causes and reasons of these calamities is to name them; it is to give one power to eliminate or neutralize them. This is the power that enables one to achieve the purpose of being human: long life, good relations with other people, with the ancestral and other spirits, and with God.

Chapter 7

"POLITICAL" ETHICS

Given the communal nature of human existence in Africa, it is not surprising that heads of households and sodalities and various religious specialists count among the moral guardians of the vital force of their families, groups, clients, and, inevitably, of society at large. They are also seen as guardians of the moral order of the universe through their observance and transmission of both life and tradition. The mystical powers of God, the ancestors, and the spirits—whom they represent by their life and in their speech and actions—have charged them with this responsibility. Similarly responsible, although on a much higher level, are kings, chiefs, and other types of authority figures whose power extends beyond the family or the small community. Even though each paterfamilias does share mystically in the wider authority of his group through his religious, social, and economic functions, authority figures at social levels beyond the family are "political" leaders, if we wish to use that term.

The phrase, "if we wish to use that term," that is, "political" leaders, is used with good reason. As with the concept of "law," which we shall consider below, the concept of "politics," "political," and so on, is ambiguous when applied to African organization, because it cannot be easily abstracted from the religious, moral/ethical system. In other words, in traditional Africa there is generally no specific "political" structure that is distinct from the social and religious structures of society. The same persons usually occupy both positions. At any rate, as Victor Turner has pointed out, "if a person occupies political and religious positions of some importance, his *political* power is reinforced at

245

those points in the seasonal cycle or group's developmental cycle where his *ritual* office gives him enhanced authority."[1]

Leaders at the higher social levels of the lineage, clan, sodality, or ethnic group represent and personify the life-force of the entire people more intensively than the family heads. They also personify the order of the world and the harmony that enables its life to continue for the benefit of humanity. This implies that the vital force of these leaders—or the lack of it—signifies the actual condition and environment of the entire society. In practical terms, the most significant purpose of existence of these leaders is to guard the power of life of the community.

FUNDAMENTAL OBSERVATIONS

The study of the political organization of African societies has identified at least three major systems.

> Firstly, there are those very small societies . . . in which even the large political unit embraces a group of people all of whom are united to one another by ties of kinship, so that political relations are coterminous with kinship relations and the political structure and kinship organization are completely fused. Secondly, there are societies in which a lineage structure is the framework of the political system, there being a precise co-ordination between the two, so that they are consistent with each other, though each remains distinct and autonomous in its own sphere. Thirdly, there are societies in which an administrative organization is the framework of the political structures.[2]

---

[1]V. W. Turner, "Ritual Aspects of Conflict Control in African Micropolitics," in M. J. Swartz et al., eds., *Political Anthropology* (Chicago: Aldine Publishing Company, 1966), p. 246. See also G. K. Park, "Kinga Priests: The Politics of Pestilence," in ibid., pp. 229-37.

[2]M. Fortes and E. E. Evans-Pritchard, eds., "Introduction," in M. Fortes and E. E. Evans-Pritchard, *African Political Systems* (London: Oxford University Press, 1940), pp. 6-7.

While a discussion of these three types of political organization is not the primary purpose of this study,[3] it is important to highlight the moral or ethical intent which these structures share and which is the reason for their existence. Thus, it is helpful to summarize how each system is constructed in order to appreciate how and why they are fundamentally related. A brief outline of the organizational structure of a representative group of each type of organization will illustrate how this works in practice.

Political Organization Based on Kinship

The !Kung people of the Kalahari Desert Basin of Botswana and Namibia exemplify the first type of political organization, that based on kinship.[4] The !Kung are hunters and gatherers with an exclusive division of labor between the sexes: the men hunt wild game and the women gather vegetables, roots, and nuts (called *veldkos* in Afrikaans) for food. They live around waterholes in autonomous consanguineous and affinal kinship bands. John Marshall estimates that in 1958 there were about 1,000 !Kung grouped in 28 bands in separate camps (*werfs*) in an area

---

[3]For example, neither Fortes and Evans-Pritchard nor this chapter discuss the unique and (in the light of recent tragic events) very important political system of the Tutsi and Hutu peoples of Rwanda and Burundi. Taking his cue from Max Weber, R. Lemarchand describes it as being a combination of "caste structure" and "ethnic coexistence." Nevertheless, the ethical motivation behind this organization does not differ greatly, in my opinion, from the systems listed by the above authors. For the political structure in Rwanda see J. J. Maquet, "The Problem of Tutsi Domination," in S. and P. Ottenberg, eds., *Cultures and Societies of Africa* (New York: Random House, 1960), pp. 312-7, J. Maquet, *Power and Society in Africa*. Trans. by J. Kupfermann (New York: McGraw-Hill Book Company, 1971), pp. 197-216, and R. Lemarchand, "Power and Stratification in Rwanda: A Reconsideration," in E. P. Skinner, ed., *Peoples and Cultures of Africa: An Anthropological Reader* (Garden City, New York: The Doubleday/Natural History Press, 1973), pp. 416-36.

[4]"!" symbolizes the alveolar palatal click in the !Kung language. The other symbols are / dental; =/= alveolar; and // lateral.

of about 10,000 square miles.[5] The !Kung do not own land either individually or collectively. While they consider the ground, the soil, as "worthless," each band does lay claim on the game and *veldkos* on its side of the waterhole. This is determined by long-term mutual understanding among all the neighboring bands and no trespassing is tolerated. A person has access to hunting and gathering rights on the particular side of the waterhole according to his or her band affiliation.[6] This band, which is based almost exclusively on kinship ties, is the basic political entity for the !Kung. The headman's position is hereditary, according to the patrilineal line. He is obliged to stay with this band at the water-hole or risk losing his position as headman.[7] It is the nature of the headman's authority—his political authority—that is of interest here.

Besides being a symbol around which the band coheres and identifies itself, and the custodian of the territory's *veldkos* and waterhole, the headman is distinguished by no special authority or power ascribed to him by !Kung social structures. For this, he must be a leader as well, and these two positions are not necessarily identical. It is the leader, rather than the headman *per se,* who wields administrative authority in the !Kung band. As John Marshall notes, leadership among the !Kung "depends heavily on a man's character, his hunting prowess, and especially his ability to focus people's opinions."[8] He has no coercive or administrative power, but only the authority of persuasion. He functions as "an arbiter, in quarrels, as focal point in discussion of plans, a comfort to the bereaved and a strength for those in doubt."[9] If

---

[5]J. Marshall, "Hunting Among the Kalahari Bushmen," in Skinner, *Peoples and Cultures of Africa*, p. 112. In 1959 Lorna Marshall counted 36 or 38 communities. See her "!Kung Bushman Bands," in R. Cohen and J. Middleton, *Comparative Political Systems: Studies in the Politics of Pre-Industrial Societies* (Garden City, New York: The Natural History Press, 1967), p. 17.

[6]C. D. Forde, *Habitat, Economy and Society: A Geographical Introduction to Ethnology* (New York: E. P. Dutton, 1963), pp. 26-7.

[7]Marshall, "Hunting Among the Kalahari Bushmen," p. 119.

[8]Ibid., p. 118.

[9]Ibid., pp. 118-9.

he succeeds in influencing the band to disown and banish a member, he will have exercised his authority by meting out the most serious form of punishment available to the !Kung.

Neither headmanship nor leadership is greatly desired in !Kung society, and neither position is particularly advantageous for an individual. Lorna Marshall reports that "No regalia, special honors, or attributes mark them out."[10] An extremely egalitarian people, the !Kung do not attribute social rank to their "leaders." The latter's responsibility can be characterized rather as ontological and moral authority that establishes the unity of the group symbolically (headman) and maintains order by force of persuasion and exemplary goodness (leader).

Political Organization Based on Lineage and Clan

The second form of political organization is found among peoples who base their systems on lineage and clan, such as the Tallensi, Logoli, and Nuer. Since I have referred several times to the Logoli and Nuer, I will describe briefly the system of the Tallensi of Ghana. Among the Tallensi, as in most societies organized by lineage, political structures, authority, and power are much more pronounced than in societies organized on a kinship basis. The primary political unit of the Tallensi is the settlement, which is conceived of in a social sense rather than in a territorial sense. A settlement is seen first of all as a clan, or a composite of clans of several relatively autonomous lineages, each tracing its ancestry agnatically (or through male descent) back to a common remembered ancestor. According to Meyer Fortes, this goes about "eight to eleven generations back."[11] Members of a clan consider themselves to be "of one blood," and the rules of local custom forbidding war and those relating to exogamy and levirate custom apply. However, adjacent clans, though different by lineage, may also be "asymmetrically linked by ties of clanship

---

[10]Marshall, "!Kung Bushman Bands," p. 38.

[11]M. Fortes, "The Political System of the Tallensi of the Northern Territories of the Gold Coast," in Fortes and Evans-Pritchard, *African Political Systems*, p. 243. n. 1.

identical with those that unite constituent maximal lineages of the same clan, and cut across the latter ties.[12] The rules we have just mentioned also apply here, for members of these clans are also considered to be of "the same blood."

The primary leadership structure of the Tallensi is constituted by the head of the lineage. Invariably male, the head is determined either by seniority of generation within the lineage or, where this is not possible to determine, by seniority of age. The head of the lineage, called the *kpeem,* claims only moral and ritual authority over the lineage. Any coercive power he might have is very limited. The moral authority of his position focuses the unity and identity of the lineage. He effects political power through moral or ritual prestige, respect, and honor.

This is also true of the two leadership offices that transcend the *kpeem* in Taleland, the offices of chiefship and guardianship of the Earth. Theoretically, each of these offices is held by different sets of clans, but in reality they cut across lineages and clans. They are the highest political offices in the land, but like lineage headship, they have little actual coercive power that is usually associated with political authority. Their moral and ritual authority, however, is considerable and is more apparent than among the !Kung. It provides cohesion and identity and balances natural social allegiances to kin and lineage.

Tallensi chiefs are selected from the male agnatic descendants

---

[12]Fortes, "The Political System of the Tallensi," p. 244. Fortes explains this intricate network as follows: "Thus, for instance, three adjacent clans, A, B, and C, are interlinked as follows: A has three maximal lineages, A1, A2, A3; B has four, B1, B2, B3, B4; C has two, C1, C2. Lineage A1 has ties of clanship with lineages B1 and C1, but *not* with the other B or C lineages, nor have B1 and C1 ties of clanship with A2 and A3. Members of A1, B1 and C1 may not intermarry; they may inherit one another's widows and have the reciprocal ceremonial obligations of clansmen. Members of A1 marry into the other B or C lineages, and B1 and C1 intermarry with A2 and A3. Similarly A2 has ties of clanship with B4, but not with the other B or C lineages, and A3 ties of clanship with B3. Maximal lineages linked in this way have the same relationship towards one another as the constituent units of a single clan have, but rights and duties pertaining to it are less rigorously effective than within the clan. Clan C has similar criss-crossing linkages with clan D, D with E, and so on."

of the founder of the chiefship for ritual reasons: only they can relate satisfactorily with the chiefly ancestors. Chiefs should be people of good moral reputation, prestige, and material means. These are the qualities the ancestors favor, and to select someone without such qualities as chief is to bring down their wrath, because the chief serves as the head of the clan or group of clans for ritual purposes.

The influence of the chief is balanced in Tale political structure by the custodians of the Earth who confirm, so to speak, the mystical powers of the chiefs by presenting them to their shrines and by seeking blessings for them. Without this blessing, a chief's powers are believed to be void. As Fortes reports, the chief "is powerless to ensure the welfare of the community without . . . [the] ritual collaboration [of the custodians of the Earth]."[13] Every significant action of the chief must have the blessing of the Earth. The custodians of the Earth, on the other hand, cannot enhance the prosperity of the community without the collaboration of the chiefs. Only the chiefs have mystical power over rain, for example, so that in times of drought or flood, the custodians of the Earth must implore the chiefs to deal with the situation. Thus, the offices of chief and custodian of the Earth balance each other, culminating in their "joint responsibility for the common good."[14]

It is important to note that both the Tallensi and !Kung loathe war and the shedding of human blood. This is not only because of the kinship lineage and clan ties binding them into people of "the same blood," but also because of the respect they have for the mystical power of the Earth. "The Earth is impersonal, but 'alive'—that is, a controlling agency in the lives of men," Fortes explains. "Incalculable, like all mystical agencies, the source of prosperity, fertility and health as well as of drastic retribution for sin or sacrilege, witting or unwitting, it is regarded with great awe."[15] In this sense, the Earth is the mother of all, and shedding blood on it through strife is a great offense. If and when murder

---

[13]Fortes, "The Political Systems of the Tallensi," p. 260.

[14]Ibid., p. 260.

[15]Ibid., p. 255.

takes place, it is the task of the custodians of the Earth to offer cleansing sacrifices.

The political power of Tale leaders, therefore, is gained through the power of ritual, particularly in the area of ancestor veneration. The Tallensi, like other African religionists in general, "both fear and venerate their ancestors, seeking to placate and coerce them with sacrifices, so that health, fruitfulness, and prosperity may prevail."[16] Thus, the ancestor cult serves as "the supreme sanction of kinship ties"[17] as well as political authority. The *kpeem*, chiefs, and custodians of the Earth are the guardians of the ancestral shrines and the visible representatives (and representations) of the ancestors on earth. This is how their honor, authority and power is derived. Their power is mystical but also real, because the society cannot exist without frequent recourse to ancestral benevolence and these leaders hold the keys.

Political Organization Based on Administrative Authority

While the foregoing types of societies do not have a central administrative authority, strictly speaking, many others in Africa do.[18] This last type of socio-political organization in Africa is used in the kingdom of the Banyoro in Uganda, as studied by John Beattie.[19] The structure and underlying philosophy of the

---

[16]Ibid., p. 253.

[17]Ibid.

[18]In the book *African Political Systems*, Fortes and Evans-Pritchard have included discussion on the kingdom of the Zulu (by Max Gluckman), the Ngwato (by I. Schapera), the Bemba (by Audrey I. Richards), the Banyankole (by K. Oberg), and the Kede (by S. F. Nadel). In J. Middleton and D. Tait, eds., *Tribes Without Rulers: Studies in African Segmentary Systems* (London: Routledge & Kegan Paul, 1958), are discussed the political organizations of the Tiv (by L. Bohannan), the Mandari (by J. Buxton), the Dinka (by G. Lienhardt), the Bwamba (by E. Winter), the Konkomba (by D. Tait), and the Lugbara (by J. Middleton). And L. Mair, in *African Kingdoms* (Oxford: Clarendon Press, 1977), provides a brief survey of the African worldview on which the more centralized governmental systems are based.

[19]J. Beattie, *Bunyoro: An African Kingdom* (New York: Holt, Rinehart and Winston, 1960). See also, Cohen and Middleton, *Comparative Political*

Bunyoro kingdom demonstrate clearly the differences and the similarities in organizational approach between this centralized system and the other more segmentary political systems of the continent.

In the Bunyoro kingdom, as Beattie explains, "all political authority stemmed from the king. Advised by his formal and informal counsellors, he appointed his territorial chiefs to office, and their authority, down to the lowest level, had to be confirmed by him personally."[20] The Nyoro system is therefore "hierarchical" in the strictest sense of the word, in that the king is at the pinnacle of power and all authority flows from him. Thus, even though chiefships are as a rule hereditary, the king can in principle take away any chiefship and do with it as he likes; that is, he can give it away to someone else, even to an individual outside of the incumbent chief's lineage. In this system, the most important qualification for chiefship is loyalty to the king. It is not surprising, then, that a very significant amount of any chief's time and energy in Bunyoro is spent courting the favor of the king. Independent action is extremely limited because of the danger that such an action might be interpreted as disloyalty to the king and dealt with as such.

What the king expects of the chief, the chief expects of the sub-chief, and so on, down to the lowest village and house elder. This is the nature of a hierarchical organization. In Nyoro society, it influences even the family structure and the behavior of its members toward one another. Between parents and children, but particularly between fathers and children, the relationship is one of superiority and subordination. It is one of "marked inequality: fathers 'rule' their children and children 'fear' their fathers"[21]

Systems, passim; Skinner, *Peoples and Cultures of Africa: An Anthropological Reader,* pp. 393-502; Forde, *African Worlds;* A. Atmore and G. Stacey, *Black Kingdoms, Black Peoples: The West African Heritage* (London: Orbis, 1979); H. Kuper, *The Swazi: A South African Kingdom* (New York: Holt, Rinehart and Winston, 1963); and K. S. Carlston, *Social Theory and African Tribal Organization: The Development of Socio-Legal Theory* (Urbana, Chicago: University of Illinois Press, 1968).
[20]Ibid., p. 36.
[21]Ibid., p. 53.

and whoever else is considered "father" in the kinship system sometimes referred to as the "extended family" structure.[22] The paterfamilias, or his male representative, is the "king" of the household and owns virtually everything in it. These relationships and attitudes at the family level, described by Beattie, have undoubtedly inspired and shaped the wider Nyoro political ethos.

> Though there may be genuine affection between them, Nyoro culture stresses the authority of the father and the dependence and subordination of the son. A son should always be polite and deferential, and he should address his father as "sir" or "my master"—the very same terms that he would use to a chief. A man should not sit on a chair or stool in his father's presence; he should sit or squat on the floor. He should not marry a girl whom his father has not selected for him, or at least approved. He should never wear any of his father's clothes or use his spear. And he may not begin to shave or smoke until he has made a small token

---

[22]As M. D. Sahlins explains in his *Tribesmen* (Englewood Cliffs, New Jersey: Prentice Hall, 1968), p. 11: "In classificatory schemes, certain people related to oneself in a direct line of descent are in a class with collateral relatives. Thus in a common classificatory usage, the brother of my father is related to me in the same way as my father: I call them both by the same term—translated, 'father'—and behave more or less the same way toward both. Said differently, relatives of the same broad social status are classed together. My father and his brothers may be in critical social attributes the same: males of my lineage of the same senior generation The social similarity is embodied in a common kinship designation. Now, the important thing is that once kinship categories are thus widely defined they are widely extendable. If my father is socially equivalent to his brother, the latter's son is logically equivalent to my brother; hence FaBrSo=Br. By the same principles, my father's father and his brother are equivalent, my father's father's brother's son is 'father,' his son is 'brother,' and so on . . . Classificatory kinship has a logic of expandability. However remote genealogically, kinsmen need not be lost track of, nor in fact conceived remote in kinship class. Of course the people can and do make distinctions between a mother's husband ('own' father) and other 'fathers,' and between 'near' and 'distant' kinsmen of a given class. But the expandability of kinship classes, and their manifest designation as familial categories, is an obvious help to peacemaking."

payment to his father. Thus the relationship is essentially an unequal one, and it may even be said to express a latent hostility between fathers and sons. Such hostility is to be expected in a strongly patrilineal society, where the father's very considerable authority and status pass on his death to his son. It is as though the son's growing up were a kind of challenge to the father, whose authority the son will soon take over; and the father seems accordingly almost to resent his son's developing adulthood as a threat to his own pre-eminence.

The pattern of Nyoro inheritance is consistent with the existence of such attitudes as these. The heir (who [unlike in many other societies] should not be the oldest son) is ceremonially installed in the presence of his agnates. The ceremony stresses the transfer of authority rather than the transfer of property, and the heir is even said to "become" his father. Indeed after he has been installed his sisters' husbands should address him as "father-in-law" not as "brother-in-law" as they formerly did, and they should treat him with great respect. It is also of significance that in Bunyoro there can be only one heir; the household and the patrimonial land are never divided up (though movables may be), for they are indivisible, like the parental authority which they symbolize.

The relations between fathers and daughters express the same theme of superordination and subordination; a father "rules" his daughters just as he rules everyone else in his household. Indeed a daughter is doubly subordinate, for as well as being a child she is also a woman, and women should always be subservient and respectful to men. She will marry elsewhere, and the bride-wealth which is obtained for her may be used to obtain a wife for her brother, perhaps even another wife for her father himself. Her children will not increase her father's posterity; they will belong to another clan, her husband's.[23]

---

[23]Ibid., p. 52.

Because the power and authority of the father is reproduced at all levels of societal organization, the difference between the Nyoro system and the !Kung and Tallensi systems, for example, may seem unbridgeable. It may appear that African societies that are highly fragmentary have nothing in common with the centralized ones, at least as far as government is concerned. On the level of observable structures this may be so. But structures hide a deeper meaning, an intentionality, which is intended to serve people, regardless of the structures in place. In Bunyoro, just as in Nyae Nyae (!Kung-land), Taleland, and all over Africa, political structures have a religious meaning, and are meant to serve the fullness of life of the entire community.

For the Nyoro, the system of kingship is the means to fullness of life for the community. The king implements his authority through the rituals associated with his office. Beattie identifies three categories of ritual: rites associated with the kingship itself; rites related to its acquisition and investiture and to the transference of power in case of serious illness or at death; and rites having to do with delegation of his authority.[24] Because the king incorporates in his person the entire country and its welfare, his physical, psychological, and moral condition literally mirrors the condition of the country and the Nyoro people. The king's personal shortcomings and his strengths are not only his own but those of the whole population. Because they affect both the population and the land, the king has to ensure that he is always in good physical, ritual, and spiritual condition. The sacrifices and offerings he makes at certain times through his mediums and other elders (for he himself is not directly required to be such a functionary) are made "for the good of the country."[25]

---

[24]Ibid., p. 26.

[25]Ibid., p. 27. Keeping physically, mentally, and morally healthy and strong is a universal requirement for African leaders. We have already exemplified it among the Dinka. Of the Swazi of Swaziland, H. Kuper makes the same point: "Once the king is selected he must be kept strong and virile because the prosperity of the nation is associated with his health. Every new year he

At accession to kingship of the Bunyoro, after the mandatory arduous and violent campaign in which a prince has to subdue or banish his other brothers who are also aspirants to the throne, the victorious prince is invested with the instruments of office, which include weapons of war. But his investiture ritual also includes significant instructions: the new king "is formally admonished . . . to rule wisely, to kill his enemies, and to protect his people."[26] This duty to protect the people cannot always be effected by the king himself, so Nyoro structures provide for the king to delegate some of his power and authority to some of his chiefs. Once the chiefs have received this authority, they obtain *ipso facto* some of the spiritual force of the life of the king, which they have to use for the good of their various chiefships. These chiefs, as well as certain clans, the king's "official sister," and his mother, act as advisors to him and also play a big role in limiting and balancing some of his power. At any rate, any failure of the king to protect the people, either through negligence (bad government), moral shortcoming (breaking taboos), or physical disability, invalidates his authority. In cases of serious illness or feebleness due to age, he is expected to commit suicide or is killed in order to allow a healthier, more energetic king to preserve the health of the country.

---

is treated with medicines to 'renew' him, and he is always protected for contacts that might weaken him.

"A Swazi king must avoid all contact with death. He must neither see nor touch a corpse nor approach a grave. Until he has been purified, he may not travel over a road along which the corpse of an important person has been carried, nor may he come near kinsmen of the deceased. No one may die at a royal village, and as soon as any of the inhabitants fall dangerously ill they are removed to homesteads that he will not visit. He may not mourn a death for more than a few days, since mourning is a period of dangerous affiliation with the dead: 'When the king is in blackness, [the Swazi say], the whole nation is without strength.' " See her *An African Aristocracy: Rank Among the Swazi* (London: Oxford University Press, 1947), pp. 85-6.

(There have been examples of this even among the new, westernized, political dispensations in Africa. It was considered a crime in Kenya and Malawi respectively to as much as entertain the thought of President Kenyatta's or Banda's eventual death. And when Kenyatta died, his death was kept secret for a long time before being announced.)

[26]Ibid., p. 28.

UNIFYING FACTORS

As there are great dissimilarities in the political structure among the three peoples we have discussed above, the !Kung, the Tallensi, and the Banyoro, so differences also exist among peoples who employ the same system of organization, such as the Tallensi and the Nuer, for example, both of whom employ the segmentary lineage system of organization. Similarly, there are differences between the Banyoro and the Ashanti, both of whose political systems enjoy vast central authority. Whereas political authority is highly patriarchal in Bunyoro, among the Ashanti it is the other way round. Among the Ashanti, who are a matrilineal people, descent is determined by matriliny, and it is the uterine affiliation that gives a man his legal and political standing. Also, the Ashanti system is much more federal in nature, and the kingdom is constituted by a federation of chiefships. The *Asantehene* (the Ashanti paramount chief) is admittedly the central ruler, but the limiting influence of his various chiefs is much more pronounced than of his counterparts in Bunyoro.

While these structural variations in organizing political life in Africa may often be readily observable, they do not always reveal the unifying factors within and among these apparently disparate systems across the continent. As is true of many other aspects of African life, these unifying factors tend to be consistently religious, being primarily moral or ethical in nature. The underlying and unifying factors in these disparate types of political organization become more apparent when we look at how the main agents in the political structure of these societies acquire authority and power, and how and why they exercise that power. It is not until we examine the ethical orientation and the ethical principles upon which these political systems are based, in other words, the worldview underlying the political structures, that a fuller understanding comes to light.

In discussing the age-grade villages of the Nyakyusa people of Tanzania, Monica Wilson describes the values desired and "most constantly stressed" by the people. She lists these as "good company," "dignity," "display," "decency," and "wisdom."[27] But, these are not simply social values: they constitute the moral pillars on which African political organization is based, and they define the meaning and legitimacy of both the political order and political leadership throughout Africa.

Good Company

Good company implies community, that is, the establishment and maintenance of harmonious relationships among people. For the Nyakyusa, Wilson notes that good company includes the exchange of "aid and sympathy which spring from personal friendship. It implies urbane manners and a friendliness which expresses itself in eating and drinking together; not only merry conversation, but also discussion between equals, which the Nyakyusa regard as the principle form of education [and means to acquire wisdom]."[28] All of these—practical sharing, communion, and communication—are essential factors of any African political system. They are concretized very intensely in the institutions of blood friendship, secret or open societies, age-grade structures, joking relationships, and other kinds of sodalities. Any leadership that does not actively promote them has doubtful legitimacy in the eyes of the people. In African chiefships and kingdoms, for instance, one of the primary functions of the chief or king is to entertain his nobles, converse with them, and thus learn wisdom and justice by consulting them on matters of state. But his responsibilities do not stop there. The leader also has tribute regularly paid to him, so that in case of need he can provide for his subjects. Thus, the king or chief is able to keep dire need at bay and maintain the strength of the life force of the whole society. As mentioned earlier, an ill, elderly, or otherwise incapacitated leader may ask to be "eliminated" for this very reason—because so much depends on the leader. Similarly, if there are persistent calamities in the country, such as lack of food

---

[27]M. Wilson, *Good Company: A Study of Nyakyusa Age-Villages* (London: Oxford University Press, 1951), pp. 66-90.
[28]Ibid., p. 66.

because of drought, floods, locusts, and so on, the leader may make way for someone stronger.

The consideration of "good company" in the sense just described, then, is one of the foundations of the practice of government in Africa. Fortes and Evans-Pritchard perceive it to consist "in a balance between power and authority on the one side and obligation and responsibility on the other. Every one who holds political office has responsibilities for the public weal corresponding to his rights and privileges. The distribution of political authority provides a machinery by which the various agents of government can be held to their responsibilities." These authors explain that, in practical terms,

> A chief or a king has the right to exact tax, tribute and labor service from his subjects; he has the corresponding obligation to dispense justice to them, to ensure their protection from enemies and to safeguard their general welfare by ritual acts and observances. The structure of an African state implies that kings and chiefs rule by consent. A ruler's subjects are as fully aware of the duties he owes to them as they are of the duties they owe to him, and are able to exert pressure to make him discharge these duties.[29]

In all types of political organization, government and leader-

[29]Fortes and Evans-Pritchard, "Introduction," p. 12. Also, Hilda Kuper discusses the institutions that guard against abuse of authority among the Swazi. "The first check on the abuse of power and privilege by rulers," she explains, "is contained in the dual monarchy itself. The king owes his position to a woman whose rank—more than his own personal qualities—determined his selection for kingship, and between the two rulers there is a delicate balance of power. He presides over the highest court, and, formerly, he alone could sanction the death-sentence meted out for witchcraft and treason, but she is in charge of the second highest court and the shrine hut in her homestead is a sanctuary for people appealing for protection. He controls the age regiments, but the commander in chief presides at the capital. He has power to distribute land . . . but together they work the rain magic that fructifies it. Sacred national objects are in her charge, but are not effec-

ship are validated, therefore, by "everything . . . which gives life and happiness to people."[30] Even where non-centralized leadership is concerned, an elder gains respect by promoting good company in the band, lineage, or clan. A !Kung elder, for example, would not accept a gift of meat if it might arouse jealousy in the band. He would prefer it be offered to someone else in the interests of good company.[31] And if a headman "is too young or too old, or lacks personal qualities of leadership the [!Kung] people may turn quite informally to some other man for leadership—go to him for advice, ask his help and fall in with his plans."[32]

A considerable part of the various rituals of accession to chiefship or kingship consists of rites that make this requirement paramount. Rattray reports that at the induction of the *Asantehene* [the paramount ruler of the Ashanti], the people send a public message to him through a messenger to this effect:

> Tell him [that] . . . we do not wish that he should disclose the origin of any person [since some are descended from slaves]. We do not wish that he should curse us. We do not wish greediness. We do not wish that his ears should be hard of hearing. We do not wish that he should call people fools. We do not wish that he should act out of his own head [without consultation]. We do not wish things to be done as in Kumase. We do not wish that it should ever be

---

tive without his cooperation. He is associated with 'hardness,' expressed in thunder, she with the 'softness' of water. He represents the line of past kings and speaks to the dead in the shrine hut of the capital; she provides the beer for the libations. He is revitalized in the annual ritual of kingship, which is held at her home. He is entitled to use cattle from the royal herds, but she may rebuke him publicly if he wastes national wealth. In short, they are expected to assist and advise each other in all activities and to complement each other." H. Kuper, *The Swazi: A South African Kingdom* (New York: Holt, Rinehart and Winston, 1963), p. 30.

[30]Ibid., p. 18.

[31]Marshall, "!Kung Bushman Bands," p. 38.

[32]Ibid., p. 41.

that he should say "I have no time." We do not wish personal violence.[33]

The text simply stresses the harmony that is required of the ruler with his subjects, for essentially they are one and the same, even equal. Thus, for the same reasons, the Yoruba king-elect is ritually "beaten and dressed in rags before being inducted into the position into which his person would be sacred." The message is that his position depends on the good will of the elders and people generally.[34]

The major values of good government are incorporated in, and actually are seen to flow from, the value of good company. It is the requirement of good company that links the political sys-

---

[33]See Mair, *African Kingdoms*, p. 46. E. A. Hoebel, *The Law of Primitive Man: A Study in Comparative Legal Dynamics* (Cambridge, Massachusetts: Harvard University Press, 1961), p. 223, says that these words are addressed to the *Asantehene*-elect directly, "in the presence of the elders and the members of the royal lineage," by the *Akimbo* or "Talking Chief." After his investiture, the *Asantehene* is required to swear the most sacred oath of the land, that of the Goddess of the Earth whose day is Thursday, that he would abide by the admonition pronounced by the *Akimbo*, in these words: "I ask you permission . . . to speak the forbidden oath of Thursday . . . Today you have elected me: . . . if I do not listen to the advice of my elders; if I make war upon them; if I run away from battle; then have I violated the oath." Hoeble notes that violation of this oath means destoolment (impeachment).
[34]Ibid., p. 43. See also Turner, *The Ritual Process: Structure and Anti-Structure* (Ithaca, New York: Cornell University Press, 1969), pp. 97-102 and 170-2 for Ndembu (Zambia) and Njogoni (Gabon) installation rites respectively, with similar symbolism and the same implications as the Ashanti and Yoruba rituals.

We may consider the Baganda as another illustration. K. S. Carlston (*Social Theory and African Tribal Organization: The Development of Socio-Legal Theory,* Urbana, University of Illinois Press, 1968, pp. 248-9), notes with reference to the installation of the Buganda king (the *Kabaka*) that "In the coronation ceremonies, his role as guardian of the welfare of his people was emphasized in the abjuration: 'Look with kindness upon all your people, from the highest to the lowest; be mindful of your land, deal justice among your people.' His role as supreme authority and the source of military power was indicated by giving him spears and a shield accompanied by the explanation: 'With these spears you will fight those who scorn you, who trouble you, your enemies. The king is not despised, he is not thwarted nor

tem to the religious vision and makes moral demands on it. The political system, therefore, becomes a religious system as it intertwines the "vertical" and the "horizontal" dimensions of life. The demands of the religious order of fealty to God and the ancestors for the sake of the health of the universe are the demands of the political order as well. Thus, rituals of accession are rich in symbols that seek to relate and connect the chief "metonymically to the first institution of the power he claims; recitations of tradition and genealogy; earth from ancestral graves; objects handed down; white clay from streambeds; and possession by spirits," and so on.[35]

Dignity

Besides impressiveness of manners, cheerfulness, wit, and geniality, which the Nyakyusa greatly admire, the quality of dignity takes on added importance in matters of governance. As far as the entire society is concerned, dignity means, of course, absence of want. It means wealth in crops, animals, and children.

---

contradicted. You are to overcome rebels with these spears and this shield.' His role as the dispenser of justice was symbolized by the *Katikiro* [Prime Minister] handing him a rod and saying: 'With this rod you shall judge Buganda; it shall be given to your *Katikiro* to judge Buganda, you shall both judge Buganda.' The rod was thereafter returned to the *Katikiro*. The king was also given a two-edge knife to symbolize his duty to 'cut cases' or decide disputes impartially. He was held to be above bribery."

"As he was led to the throne," Carlston continues to explain, "he was proclaimed to the people with the statement: 'This is your king, hear him, honour him, obey him, fight for him.' Mair draws the conclusion that: 'From this ceremonial emerges the idea of a monarch having not only rights but obligations. His subjects' duties were given in the expectation of a return from him; their obedience was the counterpart of his leadership, both being necessary to make the people victorious over his enemies. Absolute as was his power he was expected to respect established rights, to uphold justice, and to behave with 'kindness' or generosity in rewarding the deserving. This reciprocal relationship was explicitly affirmed before the active obligations of chiefs and people, in abeyance since the death of the late king, were resumed.' "

[35]W. MacGaffey, *Religion and Society in Central Africa: The Bakongo of Lower Zaire* (Chicago and London: The University of Chicago Press, 1986), p. 169.

It means the absence of disease and other social afflictions. It means there is practical evidence of abundant life. In terms of political leadership, dignity includes all of these qualities and more. For while certain lapses of dignity may be tolerated in an ordinary individual, they cannot be in a leader, because a leader puts the whole society at risk. If, for example, a chief does not entertain frequently and lavishly, he breaks the code of dignity. A stingy leader fails to promote communion among his subjects. If he does not judge justly, he may be suspected of anger or favoritism. A chief must not harbor bad feelings or bitterness toward any one of his subjects. Above all, he must be above corruption. Soliciting or accepting bribes is beneath him; as chief, as the representative of the people, everything in the realm in essence belongs to him. He must always be beyond reproach.

The social controls of shame and guilt are important factors in the political organization, particularly if a leader betrays the dignity expected of him. Eugene Mendonsa notes that the primary "weapons of the elders in their struggle with subordinates are public opinion and shame... When a deviant is ritually accused, he is drawn into a sequence of events that demand public confession and retribution through sacrifice to the community, both the living and the dead. The right to disgrace someone publicly is a common means of social control which rests with an office holder, but he is also constrained in his abuse of that right by public opinion."[36] Social control through shame, the fear of transgressing taboos, or the upholding of dignity, is also the reason behind the formation and maintenance of the various sodalities previously discussed; blood friendships, secret societies, age grades, and joking relationships play a conspicuous political role, each one at its own level, in African societies.

Display, Decency, and Wisdom

In the social context and within the political organization, dignity includes and implies display, decency, and wisdom. Socially,

---

[36]E. L. Mendonsa, *The Politics of Divination: A Processual View of Reactions to Illness and Deviance Among the Sisala of Northern Ghana* (Berkeley: University of California, 1982), pp. 189-90.

decency means, first of all, living and acting according to one's gender and position on the social ladder. Separation and division of labor by gender usually holds across the continent. This is clearly delineated by custom throughout the continent, even if customs differ somewhat among different societies. At certain stages in life, usually signified by rituals, a person is expected to change behavior: for example, a married man or woman is not to behave like an unmarried boy or girl; and similarly, an elder is expected to behave differently from an adult person. These expectations preserve the order of the universe by clearly distinguishing what creation intended to be different.

There is nothing wrong in displaying one's material possessions or physical and mental prowess within acceptable limits and within the context of an individual's social status at that moment. Thus, it is proper for young men to demonstrate their physical strength and courage. This is one of the lessons inculcated by the initiation process. It is expected, likewise, that pubescent girls will flaunt their physical beauty and their facility with household tasks, particularly cooking and, in some societies, brewing beer. Qualities like these are sought in a prospective bride.[37] A married man, especially a paterfamilias, must prove that he can take care of his home. In fact, he must demonstrate this capability before he enters into any sort of plural marriage. Finally, an elder must demonstrate wisdom and good judgment if he is not to be rejected or abandoned by the people for another leader.

In political terms, display, decency, and wisdom translate into a system of government we might call "relative gerontocracy," whether we speak of a band, a lineage, or a monarchical system.[38] Africans are almost universally governed by people of more or less advanced age. In some monarchies, the queen or

---

[37]For example, see M. Read, *Children of Their Fathers: Growing Up Among the Ngoni of Nyasaland* (New Haven: Yale University Press, 1960), pp.122-48.

[38]Among the most significant studies that show this, see J. Middleton and D. Tait, eds., *Tribes Without Rulers: Studies in African Segmentary Systems* (London: Routledge & Kegan Paul, 1958), and Fortes and Evans-Pritchard, *African Political Systems*.

queen mother may stand as the "head of state," but, in most cases, actual government will be in the hands of elderly men. Again, there is a religious foundation for this practice in the belief that greater strength of vital power resides in men of advanced age. Thus, even in matrilineal societies, government stays mostly in men's hands. Yet, this is relative because of the institutional restraints in place, some of which were noted above, against the abuse of power.[39]

Elochukwu Uzukwu has used the image of "large ears" to characterize this underlying motif of African systems of governing. He borrows this image from the Manja of the Central African Republic:

> Among the Manja . . . the totem for the chief is the rabbit because this unobtrusive animal has "large ears." As is common all over Africa, the chief is considered to be very close to God, to the ancestors and to the protective spirits of the community. He does not replace the ancestors. But, along with other elders, he makes them present (represents them) in his person and behaviour. The Manja underline "listening" as the most dominant characteristic of the chief. His "large ears" bring him close to God, ancestors and divinities, and close to the conversations taking place in the community. He has the "last word" because he speaks after having assimilated and digested the Word in the community. He is the guardian of the dynamic, life-giving Word which creates and recreates the community. "Word" means Truthfulness, Fairness, Honesty, Communication.
>
> One may legitimately compare this custodianship of the Word, imaged in the "large ears" of the chief, with the Bam-

---

[39]J. Beattie, "Checks on the Abuse of Political Power in Some African States: A Preliminary Framework for Analysis," in Cohen and Middleton, *Comparative Political Systems,* pp. 355-73. Besides the ritual admonition of the ruler upon accession, we might point out that even when kingship is considered to be a divine right, such as in the Oyo Kingdom of the Yoruba of Nigeria, the manner of leadership of the *Alafin* (Oyo king) is discussed twice a day by a number of leading powerful chiefs. The king must listen to their advice.

bara (Malian) philosophy of the *immensity of the Word*. "Word" "embraces" the whole of humanity. When uttered it heals and provides humane living. Such a sacred Word is "too large" for the mouth. This "Word" is an almost personalized phenomenon. No speaker ever totally masters or appropriates it; rather it belongs to the human community. Each sacred speech (of the community leader or of the representative of the community) approximates to this Word.

For the chief to be fair, he must be a patient listener. And this listening takes plenty of time. This is what is generally referred to as "African palaver": the liberation of speech at all levels of community in order to come close to that Word which is too large for an individual mouth; the Word which saves and heals.[40]

Throughout Africa generally, the moral legitimation of government and leadership depends to a large extent on the capacity of the leader(s) to listen. The enforcement of law and social order is basically an exercise in listening and must be seen within this context.

LAW, SOCIAL ORDER, AND CONFLICT RESOLUTION

At times, however, leadership fails and what Kenneth Carlston describes as "constitutive conflict" arises, which is "a product of the incongruence of an ideal, valued social order and the actual social order, as perceived by the members of such order." Carlston argues that "Unless those who are the leaders or the occupants of posts or offices of authority in such social order are able to arrest the trend towards disintegration by controlling the conditions leading towards its occurrence, disintegration and the constitution of a new social order or new social orders will take place."[41] The cause of such disintegration is usually interpersonal

---

[40]E. E. Uzukwu, *A Listening Church: Autonomy and Communion in African Churches* (Maryknoll, New York: Orbis Books, 1996), pp. 127-8.
[41]K. S. Carlston, *Social Theory and African Tribal Organization: The Development of Socio-Legal Theory* (Urbana, University of Illinois Press, 1968), p. 77.

conflict arising from personal dissatisfaction with the *status quo* that manifests itself empirically in hostility and in the failure to observe the values of the group or society as a whole. The procedure of "law" is designed to offset such social disintegration in African societies. When successful, law provides a motive for greater social identification and cohesion. But it does not always succeed, and there is always the possibility that the conflict will expand.

Conflict on a scale larger than interpersonal or "constitutive" conflict is war. Carlston divides the causes of war into two categories: acquisitive and retributive. "First," he explains, "it [war] was the use of force upon another group for the purpose of acquiring land, booty, or slaves. Second, it was retributive action visited by one group upon another for offenses committed upon its members, such as murder, rape, abduction, seduction, and theft." The conduct of war also falls into two categories, according to Carlston. "When uncontrolled in its violence, as a result of the perception that the opposing groups shared no common identity in a larger social order, it was war in the pure sense of the term. When it took the form of *lex talionis* and was subject to social controls which regulated the expression of violence, it became a sanctioning process and an emerging form of legal behavior."[42] At any rate, war is part and parcel of the political organization of any society, and in African Religion, it is perceived and sanctioned in terms of the preservation of the life of the society.

Whether it takes the form of a feud, a raid for cattle, the acquisition of land and other property, or repulsion of an attack—in other words, whether it is acquisitive or retributive—its ethical validity is established within that context. Among societies that harbor an extreme abhorrence of war (such as the !Kung) and those which are more warlike (as, for example, the pastoral peoples of East Africa or the Zulu of Southern Africa[43]), the shed-

---

[42]Ibid., p. 40.

[43]For the organization of the Zulu army under Shaka, see E. J. Krige, "The Military Organization of the Zulus," in Skinner, *Peoples and Cultures of Africa*, pp. 483-502.

ding of blood—even of enemy blood—is always inauspicious and is invariably followed by elaborate rituals of purification. Paradoxically, however, a war gives those segments of society that are physically able to engage in fighting considerable recognition in the political structures of both societies. Thus, even though it is the elders who determine the times and places for war, the warriors have a voice in the political structures of Africa because of their status as warriors.

Law and the resolution of conflict in African societies are closely related to the whole system of morality/ethics of African Religion. It is hard to separate "law" in African tradition[44] from custom, taboos, divination, mediumship, ordeals, and the expectations of sharing, harmony, play, and good company in general.[45] It is also difficult to separate it from the structures of family, lineage, clan, and the various sodalities. While distinctions can be made with regard to levels of significance, all are considered, nonetheless, within the realm of tradition.[46] Tradition is handed down through the normal socialization of the individual, and particularly through the rites of passage. I. Schapera explains, "Every man participates fully in the life of his tribe, and learns by actual experience what he may or should

---

[44]On the ambivalence of the terminology of the concept of law, see M. Gluckman, *Politics, Law and Ritual in Tribal Society* (Chicago: Aldine Publishing Company, 1965), pp. 178-83. See also note 1 above on the ambiguity of the concept of "politics."

[45]For the role of divination, ordeal, and play, for example, in the political procedures of Africa, see respectively, E. Colson, "The Alien Diviner and Local Politics Among the Tonga of Zambia," in Swartz, *Political Anthropology*, pp. 221-8; E. Warner, "A Liberian Ordeal," in P. Bohannan, ed., *Law and Warfare: Studies in the Anthropology of Conflict* (Garden City, New York: The Natural History Press, 1967), pp. 271-5; and Bohannan, "Drumming the Scandal Among the Tiv," in ibid., pp. 263-5.

[46]See note 1 above. In his article, "The Attributes of Law," in Bohannan, *Law and Warfare*, p. 25, L. Pospisil argues that "If law is conceived as 'rules or modes of conduct made obligatory by some sanction which is imposed and enforced for their violation by a controlling authority,' then the analysis of such legal phenomena reveals common patterns of attributes ... [which], if considered in turn as criteria of law, separate it objectively from all other social phenomena." But, as should by now be clear in our discussion, no such "objective separation" exists in the African social world.

lawfully do and what is forbidden or resented." One's position in life determines the seriousness of one's moral behavior. "As husband, father, kinsman, subject, fellow tribesman, worker, and owner of property . . . [a person] soon becomes aware, through his dealings with his family, neighbours, and political superiors, of the rights to which he is entitled and the duties he must fulfill."[47]

Writing about the Bena of Tanzania, M. J. Swartz has described the main characteristics that determine and orient their legal conception and practice negatively as "distrust," "dependence," and "hostility."[48] In fact, if one considers the entire African perception of life, Swartz's labels are incorrect. As psychological and moral characteristics, they are more correctly interpreted as the desire for openness, sharing, and community. If, as Swartz himself indicates, "Everything of consequence in social life must be done in such a way that it can be proved," with the consequence that gifts should be given and accepted publicly, or debts advanced and paid in the same way, the controlling motive is not distrust. Rather, it is based on the moral requirement of openness. Secretiveness, except when permitted, may be used to hide wrongdoing. The basis of Bena tradition is the central principle of community and relationships, which each person must try to build and uphold at all costs. For this reason, social behavior is characterized by the expression of "elaborate politeness, amiability, and ingratiating behavior," as well as reluctance to express "even the mildest hostility."[49] The higher goal is to

---

What is operative in many African societies in terms of "legal" order are the norms and customs of the people. If, to become law, these must be "restated in such a way that they can be 'applied' by an institution designed (or, at the very least, utilized) specifically for that purpose," as P. Bohannan, in his contribution entitled "The Differing Realms of the Law," in Bohannan, *Law and Welfare*, pp. 47 and 48, points out, they are not so restated, and so remain norms and customs. But, for the sake of simplicity of expression, we shall use the terminology "law" here to describe this African reality.

[47]I. Schapera, *A Handbook of Tswana Law and Custom* (London: Oxford University Press, 1955), p. 36.

[48]M. J. Swartz, "Bases for Political Compliance in Bena Villages," in Swartz, *Political Anthropology*, pp. 89-96.

[49]Ibid., pp. 94-5.

maintain the life force of the community in its various forms.

The primary "court" is the community in which an individual lives and has immediate responsibilities and rights, whether this community is the family, the village, or the age-set. All other levels of judgment, where these exist (such as in chiefship or kingdom political or legal structures), may be termed "courts of appeal." This understanding of the legal process is achieved, in the words of Schapera, by the modes of socialization.

> Throughout a man's life, . . . his behaviour is being either deliberately or unconsciously moulded into conformity with the social norms for law and order. At every stage, moreover, pressure is brought to bear upon him in the form of sanctions, definite forms of social control restraining him from violating established rules of conduct. Diligent adherence to tribal usage earns for him the approval and respect of his fellows. Failure to comply with it is, on the other hand, penalized in various ways, according to the nature of his offence.
>
> Punishment or coercion generally takes the form of moral pressure. The person in question may suffer loss of self-esteem, or be treated with ridicule and contempt, as when a girl is notoriously promiscuous, or a man recklessly squanders his wealth or drinks too much. He may, as when he neglects his kinship obligations, be denied services akin to those he has failed to render. Or, if he breaks any of the numerous taboos pervading Tswana life, he will, it is maintained, be afflicted with sickness or some other misfortune by the offended ancestor spirits or some other supernatural agency.[50]

In brief, the African legal system and the moral system are inseparable. Both are founded on kinship, lineage, joking, and clan relationships. Their purpose is the same: to protect and enhance the power of life in the universe. Similarly, resolution of conflict is connected to the religious system and inseparable from

---

[50]Schapira, *A Handbook of Tswana Law and Custom*, p. 36.

it. To speak of law and reconciliation in Africa is to speak of morality and ritual at the same time.

REDRESSING WRONGS

Relationships between individuals and communities form the basis of the African conception and practice of law. Just as in the moral order, wrongdoing from a "legal" point of view concerns the disturbance of these relationships. A breach of law, in this sense, is more likely to constitute a tort or delict rather than a crime, if the term crime refers to the violation of a formal legislation of the state. Torts and delicts, on the other hand, are wrongs against norms and customs, and the punishment of these wrongdoers involves compensation, to be determined by those structures in society that may, in this sense, be called "courts." The process, as Robert Redfield has explained it, operates as follows: "*A* has done some injury to *B*; *B* is disposed to retaliate; the customs of the group say how he is to do it; and we have a very simple anticipation of law. If not curbed by convention a retaliation is likely to lead to counter-retaliation, and so to public disorder."[51]

Gluckman is correct, therefore, in calling this "a process of adjudication, rather than law." As he explains, "This is the process by which . . . judges take and assess the evidence, examine what they regard as the facts, and come to a decision in favour of one party rather than another."[52] But the meaning and point of "judgment" is usually to obtain concurrence on the judgment by both parties, rather than to force a decision on one of the parties. This, in fact, is the first and foremost task of the judge. A

---

[51]R. Redfield, "Primitive Law," in Bohannan, *Law and Warfare*, p. 8. Conflict is primarily kept in check in African societies by being discouraged by custom. But when it erupts, as it often does, law comes into play. So, the process of law is constituted, to use Redfield's way of putting it, "in procedures and standards by which custom regulates disputes between bodies of kin and assures the composition of these disputes in the interest of public peace" (ibid., p. 12).

[52]Gluckman, *Politics, Law and Ritual*, p. 183.

successful judgment is one that brings about concurrence and reconciliation between the litigants. Sometimes judges make the decision "to postpone a ruling in the hope that the parties will reach accord on their own."[53]

What is central to the judicial process is the act of listening by those whose task is to make the judgment between litigant and plaintiff. Among the Barotse of Zimbabwe, for example, as Gluckman noticed, each side is allowed to present its side of the story "without interruption." This is usually done at great length, sometimes with details seemingly irrelevant to the case. Then the principal actors and their witnesses are cross-examined by the councilors "in ascending order of seniority," with the last councilor to speak giving the final judgment.[54]

Evidence is weighed and valued on the basis of sensation or perception—or a combination of both—which constitute knowledge and truth. As Ocholla-Ayayo has illustrated among the Luo, seeing and hearing constitute the most credible sources of witness.

In the answer given by four witnesses, A says, I saw it with my eyes, B says, I heard it with my ears, and C says that I heard it with my ears and saw it with my eyes, but D says I was told about it. The Luo judge will always take C as the first witness with sufficient knowledge of the truth, and A as the second witness, while B will be taken as the third witness, but often refuses D as a witness. The Luo judges assume that the statements made by C, A and B are likely

---

[53]Ibid., p. 185.

[54]M. Gluckman, *The Judicial Process Among the Barotse of Northern Rhodesia* (Manchester: Manchester University Press, 1955), p. 15. See also E. A. Hoebel, *The Law of Primitive Man*, pp. 246-51. As M. J. Swartz notes in "Bases for Political Compliance," p. 104, the higher the adjudicating person or body, the easier the acceptance of a settlement becomes by the parties concerned. "As ascension of the hierarchy progresses, the prestige of adjudicators increases, and with this increase comes an intensification of social pressure on the disputants." The principle of respect is what plays a role here. For this, see J. Middleton, "The Resolution of Conflict Among the Lugbara of Uganda," in Swartz, *Political Anthropology*, esp. p. 144.

to be the truth of the historical state of affairs to which it was correlated by the demonstrative conventions.[55]

The cross-examination, therefore, focuses "exclusively on the external facts of the matter, and questions of motive and past history are scrupulously avoided . . . [For] Once the agreement on facts is achieved, there is usually little difficulty in gaining agreement on a solution, since the solution is the obvious one in terms of what has been agreed upon as having happened."[56]

A good example is described by Swartz. Two women, wives of the same man, came before the village court, one accusing the other of having stolen her fowl.

> The accused agreed that her co-wife's chickens were disappearing, but said that a cat was taking them. The village executive officer and his elders began to take the accused through an account of the food she had eaten during the period of the chicken's disappearance, and asked her what she was feeding her adult son, who was visiting while on leave from his job on a distant sisal plantation. They scorned her claim of having provided the son with nothing better than the usual diet of cornmeal, greens, and beans, and finally brought her to admit that she had given him meat. A few questions indicating the impossibility of her getting meat either through gift or purchase left her with no other recourse than to admit she had taken the chickens.

With no threat of force, the court got the accused to replace the chickens and the accuser to accept them, as she was demanding.[57]

As can be seen, the judgment, whose central element is always reconciliation, was accepted by both sides; only very rarely is this not so. The parties in a litigation, including the judges and the

---

[55]A. B. C. Ocholla-Ayayo, *Traditional Ideology and Ethics Among the Southern Luo* (Uppsala, Sweden: Scandinavian Institute of African Studies, 1976), pp. 93-4.

[56]Swartz, "Bases for Political Compliance in Bena Villages," p. 102.

[57]Ibid., pp. 102-3.

onlookers, are directed by this motivation from the very beginning. "The Lozi," says Gluckman, "disapprove of any irremediable breaking of relationships. For them it is a supreme value that villages should remain united, kinsfolk and families and kinship groups should not separate, lord and underling should remain associated. Throughout a court hearing . . . the judges try to prevent the breaking of relationships, and to make it possible for the parties to live together amicably in the future."[58] Thus, "judgements are sermons on filial, parental, and brotherly love," geared toward educating not only the litigants but the whole community on how to behave.[59]

Judgments are intended to be both conciliatory and therapeutic. As James Gibbs writes of the judgments of the Kpelle of Liberia, "they re-educate the parties [and the entire community] through a type of social learning brought about in a specially structured interpersonal setting."[60] This does not differ significantly from the Bena or from any other African society. Gluckman explains how such legal proceedings function: "The standards of right behaviour against which the behaviour of the parties is assessed to see if they have acted rightly or wrongly, are those of 'the reasonable and customary man.' " But, again, there are several levels of "reason" requiring different levels of behavior.

There is both a generally reasonable man, acting sensibly and conforming to custom, and a particular reasonable and customary incumbent of any social position—father, son, husband, wife, son-in-law, lord, underling. The chief standards of good behaviour and the customary usages of these various social positions are widely known to all Lozi. It is expected that everyone should conform to these standards and usages. Hence wherever it emerges in evidence that a person has departed from them, his actions and motives become suspect, and the judges attack him in cross-examination, demanding that he explain his deviation. This devi-

---

[58]Gluckman, *The Judicial Process Among the Barotse of Northern Rhodesia,* pp. 20-1.
[59]Ibid., pp. 64-5.
[60]J. L. Gibbs, "The Kpelle Moot," in Bohannan, *Law and Warfare,* p. 284.

ation may convict him. Therefore the standard of the reasonable man may be said to provide the main check on evidence and to be the main weapon in judicial cross-examination. The judges thus use custom as a yardstick for controlling the variety of social life. Custom has a social certainty akin to the physical, ecological and physiological certainties of diurnal and seasonal time, vegetation growth, gestation, etc., which are also checks on evidence.[61]

The centrality of reconciliation does not mean that the punishment of the guilty party is completely ignored. Reprimand is one of the forms that punishment takes, and acceptance of wrongdoing is a form of apology. In the Kpelle moot court, for example, "one of the most important rewards is the group approval which goes to the wronged person who accepts an apology and to the person who is magnanimous enough to make one."[62] But there is also material compensation, as we have shown, not only to the party harmed, but often in the form of an offering to the court as well. The latter may be an animal, beer, or food to be consumed by the court and the litigants together as a sign of restored harmony.

The most ominous forms of punishment, however, are mystical. A dying person's last words are usually equivalent to an ancestral law, and failure to honor the express wishes of a departed person is to court disaster. K. A. Busia quotes a case among the Ashanti where a dying man willed part of his property to his son. After his death, according to custom, his brother succeeded to the property and refused to honor the will. A short while later, the latter fell from a roof and subsequently died. "The general belief was that his death was due to his failure to carry out his deceased brother's instructions. The next successor to the property duly gave the cocoa-farm to the son to whom it had been left."[63]

---

[61]Gluckman, *The Judicial Process*, pp. 358-9.
[62]Gibbs, "The Kpelle Moot," p. 287.
[63]Quoted in Hoebel, *The Law of Primitive Man*, p. 229.

THE COMMUNITY OF GOODS

In Africa, organizations, whether social or political, presuppose the existence of material resources to sustain them. Decisions about the use of material resources usually depends on the moral values of the community, its expectations for cooperation and sharing, and its understandings of law and order. Also involved is the manner in which the material resources were acquired and are to be distributed or used.

Property refers to natural or created wealth or sources of wealth. Ownership refers to the acquisition and distribution of, or claim to, property. Such and such a thing is mine or ours, and not yours. I or we have the right to use, deny use, or dispose of it as I or we choose. When this right is granted to an individual or to a specific group of individuals within a given society, it is called private property. On the other hand, if ownership of property belongs, in principle, to the whole society, it is called communal property. Often, communal property may be used by individuals or groups within the society as long as they follow certain rules. At any rate, ownership of property, whether private or communal, works on the principle of division or exclusion, or in some cases, even antagonism.

African Religion emphasizes the communal nature of property within a given community, and, at least to that extent, follows the principle of inclusion. Yet, it does not completely dismiss private or personal ownership. For African Religion, the ethical task is to establish a balance between exclusion and inclusion with regard to the acquisition and use of material resources; in other words, to establish a balance between the rights to private ownership of property and the human meaning of the resources of the universe. Thus, tradition usually indicates the parameters within which personal ownership may be exercised without harming the common good, which, in the end, is always primary. In African religious thought, the right of personal ownership is situated within the context of joint or public right of access to the basic resources necessary for life. Generally, the interplay between an individual's right to own property and his or her expectations with regard to access to communal property assures the least economic inequality in the community. This is not by accident. It is intended to prevent attitudes destructive of relationships, such as arrogance and envy. In the moral perspective of African Religion, disharmony must be constantly guarded against, whether it comes from social or economic inequalities.

When tribute, in the form of cattle, grain or labor, is paid to the chief or any other leader of the community, it is given to them in trust for the entire community. Tribute thus functions as a system of redistribution of the community's resources. In time of need, every community member has a claim to them.[64] This prin-

---

[64]As I. Schapera noticed in South Africa, and as I have pointed out in another connection above, the "accumulation of wealth by the chief was really made on behalf of the tribe. One quality which was always required of the chief was that he should be generous. He had to provide for the members of his tribe in times of necessity. If a man's crops failed he would look to the chief for assistance; the chief gave out his cattle to the poorer members of his tribe to herd for him, and allowed them to use the milk; he rewarded the services of his warriors by gifts of cattle; his subjects frequently visited him in his kraal and during their stay he fed and entertained them." Quoted by G. Dalton, "Traditional Production in Primitive African Economies," in G. Dalton, ed., *Tribal and Peasant Economies: Readings in Economic Anthropology* (Garden City, New York: The Natural History Press, 1967), p. 74.

As the Azande see it, for instance, "*Ru ae*, gifts to a prince, should . . . be balanced by *fu ae*, gifts to his subjects." E. E. Evans-Pritchard observed among them that "If raw beans went into the royal residence they ought to return to court as cooked beans; if termite oil went into the royal residence it ought to return to court as a relish to flavor porridge; if malted eleusine went into the royal residence it ought to return to the inner court as brewed beer; and if the subjects cultivated their masters' eleusine, the harvest ought to be pounded, ground, and cooked as porridge for those same subjects to eat at court." See L. Mair, *African Kingdoms* (Oxford: Oxford University Press, 1977), p. 95.

When royal revenues cannot be immediately physically spread throughout the whole land, to all subjects, it is still necessary to do so by way of proxy, through representatives. Moreover, this is how physical and spiritual benefits are sometimes believed to descend to the subject from mystical powers present in the ruler or leader. Mair explains that in the rather larger court of the Asante, compared to that of the Azande, some amount of money is sent every day to buy palm wine to be shared at the court for the purpose of obtaining such blessings. See ibid., p. 95.

ciple also operates in social relationships. Relatives and friends expect to share in one another's property. In every case, therefore, property is principally communal, even though one may have personal or private use of it. Julius Nyerere explains it this way: In Africa,

> Personal property does . . . exist and is accepted. But it takes second place in the order of things. Certainly no member of the family goes short of food or shelter in order that personal property may be acquired by another member. It is family property that matters, both to the family as such and to the individuals in the family. And because it is family property, all members have an equal right to a share in its use, and all have a right to participate in the process of sharing—in so far as time has not created its own acceptable divisions. Indeed, so strong is this concept of "sharing" that even in relation to private property there develops an expectation of use in case of need; the distinction, however, remains. In the case of family property each individual has a right; in the case of private property there may be an expectation but there is no automatic right.[65]

Thus, a scale of priorities is established based on the relationship of the individual to the community. Since in African Religion the individual can exist as a person only in community, his or her well-being can be assured only in the context of the well-being of the community. It is in the interest of each member of the community that the corporate body be strong and healthy; at the same time, the health and strength of the corporate body has as its primary purpose the assurance of the welfare of each of its members. The ethic of the community, which forms part of the lifestyle of all the members, assures that sharing takes place when necessary. If we may paraphrase Karl Marx, the disposition of production in Africa follows the principle, "From each accord-

---

[65]J. K. Nyerere, *Freedom and Unity (Uhuru na Umoja): A Selection from Writings and Speeches 1952-65* (London: Oxford University Press, 1967), pp. 9-10.

ing to his status obligations in the social system, to each according to his rights in that system."[66]

According to African religious thought, there are some resources that may simply not be privately owned. They are seen as a gift of God to all human beings, without distinction or discrimination. Land, for example, which most Africans regard as an absolute source of sustenance, may only be held in trust for the present and the future. Society entrusts pieces of it to individuals or groups for their own use and for society's well-being and growth. While what is grown on a given piece of land may be personal, in principle the land cannot be. To cite Nyerere again, "It is not God's intention that we should use his free gifts to us—land and air and water—by permission of our fellow human beings."[67]

To Africans, land, like the human community itself, is fundamentally mystical. In fact, land is seen as a spatial extension of the kinship group or the community. So even if land may be divided "by using terrestrial landmarks," such as among the Gikuyu of Kenya and the Bahaya of Tanzania, as Paul Bohannan has pointed out, we cannot speak of "land tenure" in the sense that land or any other part of the environment becomes an article of possession. We can speak only of "land use" or usufructory rights over land. In the same way, because the community and the land are two aspects of the same concept in African thought, it is incorrect to speak even of "communal ownership" of land. Bohannan rightly derides this notion, which Western scholarship has widely and inaccurately applied to African conceptions of land, as "silly" and "farcical." Bohannan explains the difference between the African and Western approaches to land:

> instead of seeing their [land] maps primarily in terms of man-thing units such as property, many Africans at least saw something like a map in terms of social relationships in space. They thus axiomized, so to speak, the spatial aspect

---

[66]Raymond Firth, as quoted by Dalton, "Traditional Production in Primitive African Economies," p. 71.
[67]Nyerere, *Freedom and Unity*, p. 56.

of their social groups and provided themselves with a social map, so that they were left free to question the ways in which they attached either social groups or individuals to exploitational rights in the earth. Usually they were imprecise, group membership being the valued quality.[68]

In the West, Bohannan argues, the inverse is the case. "Westerners... axiomize their map in terms of their property norms and values, and see the social system which results as fundamentally a series of contracts and hence open to question. As a result, Westerners question the social system that lies behind land usage, while Africans question the property ideas associated with it."[69]

In the "economic" organization of Africa, community and not association is the underlying principle.[70] Indeed, if we have to speak about African economic organization, we must do so with care, as we noted above in reference to politics and law. For, if it is true that *"It is only when production activities become divorced from activities expressing social obligation that production becomes marked off as a peculiarly economic activity, apart from other activities...,"*[71] we cannot separate the economic sphere from other spheres of life for the African person. In African tradition, "production processes, and the disposition of goods and services—in short, production and distribution—are expressions of underlying kinship obligation, tribal affiliation,

---

[68]Bohannan, "Africa's Land," in Dalton, *Tribal and Peasant Economies*, pp. 56-7.

[69]Ibid. See also, P. H. Gulliver, *Land Tenure and Social Change Among the Nyakyusa* (Kampala, Uganda: East African Institute of Social Research, 1958), pp. 5-10.

[70]R. M. MacIver makes an important distinction between association and community. He describes an association as "a group specifically organized for the purpose of an interest or group of interests which its members have in common... Community [on the other hand], is a circle of people who live together, who belong together, so that they share not this or that particular interest, but a whole set of interests wide enough and comprehensive enough to include their lives." The two are not, however, exclusive of each other, but are two ends of a spectrum of emphasis. See Dalton, "Traditional Production," p. 63.

[71]Dalton, "Traditional Production," p. 72. Italics in original.

and religious and moral duty. There is no separate economic system to be analysed independently of social organization. Labor, land, services and produced goods are allocated, exchanged, or appropriated through transactional modes of reciprocity and redistribution . . ."[72]

The arrangement of the African community's goods indicates an interest in the common humanity of all human beings and in solidarity and reciprocity. Each person has essential needs for living life. Any individual variations—physical, mental or any others—do not and are not allowed to affect this belief, even if they are recognized and appreciated by others for the way in which they contribute to the solidarity of the community. Thus, any inequalities of human qualities are compensated for by such "mutual supplementation." This is one of the hinges for the existence of society.

Any person in authority is invested *ipso facto* with the power and the responsibility to guard and allocate justly the community of goods. This is true of parents and heads of families in caring for their children and also of various officials and chiefs caring for the entire ethnic group. Justice is the deciding factor in their deployment and distribution of resources. This primary belief in African Religion arises out of the conviction that the earth's resources belong to all before they belong to any one individual. So, as previously noted, in African eyes, both the ability to lead and the validity of any leadership depend greatly on whether or not the leader is fair and just. A man with two or more wives who does not treat his wives justly or equally, we have pointed out, loses the respect of the community and lacks the moral qualities of a husband and a human being. Favoritism is a vice frowned upon by God and the ancestors. Justice is also required in raising children. Stepmothers who favor their own children more than their stepchildren are often seen as immoral or even as witches by African religionists; but when a stepmother manages to act fairly and justly, she is extremely honored and respected. By being fair

---

[72]Dalton, "The Development of Subsistence and Peasant Economies in Africa," in Dalton, *Tribal and Peasant Economies*, p. 157. See also, Sahlins, *Tribesmen*, pp. 74-95.

and just, she exhibits exceptional moral qualities in a difficult situation.

Lazy parents and greedy clan leaders and chiefs sometimes must forfeit their leadership roles. In times of need, those clan leaders and chiefs who do not or cannot bring succor to their people risk being deposed for failing in their responsibilities. This is seen not only as a social failure, but ultimately a moral failure. Failing to provide food to one's people in times of famine diminishes the life of the community, a very serious wrong indeed.[73] However, even neglecting to properly entertain one's age mates from time to time with food and beer can indicate moral culpability in that it also diminishes life. Entertaining people, particularly for a person who can afford it, is both a social and moral duty that affirms and enhances life. It is accepted that resources are to be used to effect communion through complementarity and mutuality. Leaders must see to the wise use of all resources to avoid an affront or offense against the ancestors and God.

African Religion recognizes that human wrong-doing against the ancestors and God will sometimes bring times of adversity and suffering to the family, clan, or community. Individuals at the various levels of the community are expected to foresee these occasions and to manage the community's goods and resources so that people are not caught unawares. One of the tasks of leadership is to consult experts in various fields and to advise people what to do to avoid such calamities as floods, droughts, hail, or locusts, and their consequences. In other words, leaders are also "economic planners," and leadership is an important factor in the production, preservation, and distribution of the community of goods. It is the function of both the religious structure and the consciousness of the community to curb any negative elements that might put individual or community well-being at risk and to maximize those positive elements that enhance it.

---

[73]See note 64 above.

CONCLUSION

The fundamental element, or foundational "principle," so to speak, of African religious life and thought centers on the fact of creation. Created reality, including humanity, exists on account of the will of God. To continue to live peacefully, therefore, created reality must organize itself according to that will which God established for it from the very beginning. God's will for creation is preserved in the traditions of the people and is transmitted from generation to generation through the instructions of the elders and the mystical actions of the ancestors. Hence, to speak of and understand African Religion means to analyze Africans' perspectives on created order or, in a word, the African world view. What essential elements, according to African Religion, constitute the universe? How do they operate? What perception of the Divine and divine activity do they call attention to? Answers to questions such as these provide us with insight into the nature of African Religion, a religion which is not dogmatic in the sense of proffering doctrines for belief. Instead, African Religion is moral or ethical in the sense that it mandates a certain way of living and relating.

What the African religious world view emphasizes, therefore, are relationships. Through the act of creation, God is related in an unbreakable way to the entire universe. At the center of the universe is humanity, but it too is intrinsically and inseparably connected to all living and non-living creation by means of each creature's life-force. Although God, spiritual beings, ancestors, humanity, living things and non-living things enjoy life-forces with greater and lesser powers, all the forces are intertwined. Their purpose is ultimately humanity; they can act either to increase or suppress the vital force of an individual person or of a community. The relationships of the vital forces in the universe constitute the complex of African Religion; the "management" of these forces so that they promote the abundance of human life and not diminish it constitutes the sum of Africa's religious activity.

With regard to relationships of the vital forces in the universe, community stands as the determinant factor. This means that such relationships occur, and can only occur, because the elements involved *know* one another and have a certain interest in one another. This interest is usually positive, that is, life-enhancing; but it can also be negative or life-destroying. In this sense, the preoccupation that African Religion shows with the ancestors, elders, and the various spirits is understandable. The vital forces of the ancestors and elders must constantly be courted to enhance the vital forces of the individual, the family, and the entire community because they are linked to each of them and have a direct and lasting interest in their healthy development. Since they have the capacity to cause good or harm, the spirits must not be ignored: it is necessary to curry their favor so their powers will increase the human vital force and prevent or limit the damage to human life they might otherwise cause. The vital forces of individual persons are seen and treated in African Religion in the same way.

How does the individual, the family, or the community manage the various vital forces in the universe so that they foster fullness of life, the purpose and goal of African religious activity? It is, first of all, by conducting one's life and that of the entire community in a manner consistent with the order of the universe as preserved in that community's tradition. However, when this order is violated, as it often is through human wrongdoing, it must be restored for life to continue and grow. The way to do this is through reconciliation, and reconciliation is achieved through prayer, offerings, and sacrifices. These are called for particularly when affliction—that is, famine, drought, flood, illness and so on—strikes. The source of an affliction can generally be determined through such religious expertise as divination. It is essential to determine the source of an affliction in order to know how to proceed to restore the disturbed order or balance of existence.

As African Religion sees it, there is one very sinister reality among human beings that distorts most seriously the universal balance: namely, witchcraft. It is, in one word, the very "incarnation of evil" in the world. As it is an ever-present reality in all human relationships, it is incumbent on every person to protect herelf or himself against it or to counteract it when need be.

So, from beginning to end, from birth to death, African Religion stresses and orients its adherents, directly or symbolically, toward the "abundance of life" motif. Thus, birth, all the rites of passage marking different stages in the development of the vital force, and indeed earth itself as the culmination of life, receive special attention in African religious activity. So do other "social" elements closely related or linked to life; these include economic activity of any kind, and social and political arrangements. By their relation to life, they become *ipso facto* religious activities.

As a view of life, but especially as a way of life, African Religion must therefore be counted among the great world religions whose perceptions of God and created order direct the lives of millions of people, not only in Africa but also in various other places throughout the world. Its ridicule and attempted wholesale suppression, especially by the "missionary religions"—that is, Islam and Christianity—are characteristic of these religions' tendencies toward extreme exclusivism. These are the tendencies that refuse or fail to see value in any other perception of God and the world but their own thought and symbol system. Such attitudes are often reinforced by conscious or unconscious prejudice.

What situation has this attitude created in Africa? With regard to Christianity, it has created what Robert J. Schreiter has called a "dual religious system." "In dual religious systems," he explains, "a people follows the religious practices of two distinct systems. The two systems are kept discrete; they can operate side by side. Sometimes one system is followed more faithfully than the other . . . ; in other instances the two systems may be followed almost equally . . . "[1] Yet, the ambiguity and psychological suffering this has caused in the life of many Africans is considerable. In addition, dual religious systems hardly serve the cause of pro-

---

[1] R. J. Schreiter, *Constructing Local Theologies* (Maryknoll, New York: Orbis Books, 1985), p. 145.

moting dialogue between and among religions or the development of the wholeness of life among Africans.

Further, Schreiter has written in reference to Christianity that "The Christian tradition is too precious a heritage to be squandered carelessly or treated lightly. But without its continued incarnation in local communities it becomes like that treasure buried in the ground, producing no profit."[2] The same must be said of African Religion, and indeed, of any major religion. The African tradition is "too precious a heritage to be squandered carelessly or treated lightly," as has been done in the past. It must not be buried underground but must be helped to emerge from centuries of ridicule so that it can interact with other religious orientations for its own benefit and theirs as well.

---

[2]Ibid., p. 103.

INDEX

Abrahams, R. G., 105
Administrative authority, 252-257
Adultery, 84-85, 145
Afflictions: cures for, 193-195, 211 n 38; diagnosing, 211-220; medicines, 174, 209-211. *See also* Illness
African Christianity, 7, 9-12; African religion, influence on, 9; and baptism, 7; converts to, 20-21
African philosophy, 15
African Religion: African Christianity, influence on, 9; analysis, difficulty of, 58; anthropological study of, 29-32; attitudes toward, 287-288; and baptism, 7; characteristics of, 70-71; and Christianity, 4-12; and colonialism, 19-20; and creation, 74, 285-286; and death, 86, 87, 129, 154-159; and destiny, 72; dialogue with other religions, 4-12; elders of, 67-71; English language and, 32-33; on freedom, 74; on greed, 62-64, 169; hospitality and sharing in, 63-66, 137-138; and illness, 52, 81, 172, 174, 177-179, 209-211; initiation ceremonies of, 94-104; leaders of, 68-71, 245-246; life, sacrality of, 52-53; as a lived religion, 57-58; morality and ethics of, 5, 6, 31-32, 35-36, 57-71; multi-plicity of, 14-18; and myth and language, 36-39; and naming, 82, 89-94; oral tradition of, 22, 29; and personal identity, 51-52, 82-83; popularity of, 28; proselytizing, lack of, 23-24; religious symbols in, 3-4; revelations of, 22-23; sacrifices and offerings, 201-240; scriptures, lack of, 22; survival of, 6; teaching of, 13-14; and totem, 75-76; and the universe, 37, 39-40, 62-64, 71-74; varieties of, 17; as a world religion, 18-28. *See also* Ancestors; God; Marriage; Nature; Prayer; Spirits; Taboos; Witchcraft
African Religions and Philosophy (Mbiti), 15
African society: administrative authority of, 252-257; archeological discoveries about, 26-27; common policy in, 29-30; and community, 51-53, 57-58, 70, 259-263; coercion in, 271; conflict resolution in, 267-272; and dignity, 262-263; display, decency and wisdom, 264-267; and good company, 259-263; kinship organization of, 247-249; and the law in, 30, 267-272; leadership in, 256 n 25; lineage and clan organizations in, 249-252; manners in, 29; morality and ethics in, 5-6, 29-30; organiza-